The Weaving of Glory

Books by George H. Morrison

Highways of the Heart

The Weaving of Glory

Wind on the Heath

The Wings of the Morning

The Morrison Classic Sermon Series

The Weaving of Glory

George H. Morrison

Grand Rapids, MI 49501

The Weaving of Glory by George H. Morrison.

Published in 1994 by Kregel Publications, a division of Kregel, Inc., P.O. Box 2607, Grand Rapids, MI 49501. Kregel Publications provides trusted, biblical publications for Christian growth and service. Your comments and suggestions are valued.

Cover Photograph: POSITIVE IMAGES, Patricia Sgrignoli
Cover and Book Design: Alan G. Hartman

Library of Congress Cataloging-in-Publication Data
Morrison, George H. (George Herbert), 1866–1928.
The weaving of glory / George H. Morrison.
p. cm. (The Morrison Classic Sermon Series)
Originally published: London: Hodder and Stoughton.
1. Sermons, English—Scotland. 2. United Free Church of Scotland—Sermons. 3. Presbyterian Church—Scotland—Sermons. I. Title. II. Series: Morrison, George H. (George Herbert). The Morrison Classic Sermon Series.
BX9178.M6W43 1994 252'.052—dc20 94-25570
CIP

ISBN 0-8254-3291-x (paperback)

1 2 3 4 5 Printing / Year 98 97 96 95 94

Printed in the United States of America

Contents

Publisher's Foreword 7
Dedication 10
Introduction 11

1. The God of the Patriarchs (Acts 7:32) 13
2. Sleep and Death (Mark 5:39; Luke 15:32) 20
3. The Category of Genius (Mark 8:27) 27
4. The Prevenient God (Deut. 31:8) 33
5. The Singer in the Street (2 Tim. 1:10) 39
6. The Sacramental Idea (Matt. 28:19; 1 Cor. 11:24) 45
7. The Net Mender (Matt. 4:21; 1 Peter 5:10) 51
8. The Eternal Son (Isa. 9:6; John 8:58) 58
9. The Old Orchard (Song 2:5) 64
10. The Road to Emmaus (Luke 24:13–35) 72
11. The Anguish of the Light (Heb. 10:32) 79
12. The Cross and the World (Matt. 15:24; John 12:32) 84
13. The Quality of Courage (Ps. 27:14) 90
14. The God of Nature (Isa. 40:28) 96
15. The Reawakening of Mysticism 103
16. The Gentleness of God (Ps. 18:35) 111
17. The Conflict of Duties (Luke 9:59) 117
18. Inspiration Not Private Interpretation (2 Peter 1:20) 123
19. The Medicine of the Merry Heart (Prov. 17:22) 131

20. The Hopefulness of Christ (1 Cor. 13:7) 138
21. The Veiled Faces of the Seraphim (Isa. 6:2) 145
22. The Tidings of the Breeze (John 3:8) 151
23. The Sinlessness of Christ (Heb. 4:15) 157
24. The Dissolution of Doubt (Dan. 5:16) 165
25. Society and Solitude (Gen. 2:18; Dan. 10:8) 172
26. He Knocks (Rev. 3:20) 179
27. Rending and Sewing (Eccl. 3:7) 184
28. Christ's Teaching on Man (Matt. 12:12) 190
29. Secret Faults (Ps. 19:12) 198
30. The Decisiveness of Christ (Matt. 11:22) 203

Publisher's Foreword

One wonders if the old wit's comment on sermons applies to sermon books as well when he said that a sermon was something a preacher would travel across the country to give but most people wouldn't walk across the street to hear. The initial response to a book of sermons by a turn-of-the-century Scotsman may be somewhat skeptical—in an era dominated by sophisticated media, savvy marketing analysis, and seeker-sensitive communication models, the pressured pastor might wonder about the benefits of reading "relic" sermons.

It was C. S. Lewis who referred to the historical fallacy of regarding works of the past, particularly the classics and the Bible, as irrelevant and untrustworthy based on the criterion of age alone. His comment—"This mistaken preference for the modern books and this shyness of the old ones is nowhere more rampant than in theology"—applies equally as well to pastoral theology.[1]

Issues of truth ought not to be subject to a statute of limitations, but to paraphrase Thomas Oden, we blithely assume that in preaching—"just as in corn poppers, electric toothbrushes, and automobile

1. C. S. Lewis, "On the Reading of Old Books" in *God in the Dock*, ed. Walter Hooper (Grand Rapids: Eerdmans, 1970), 200.

exhaust systems—new is good, newer is better, and newest is best."[2] Morrison's sermons represent, without question, not only a different culture (early twentieth-century Scotland which had more in common with the nineteenth century than with our own era) but also a different pastoral model. If pastors are physicians of the soul, then Morrison's ministry had more in common with the hometown doctor who made housecalls (Morrison was legendary for his visitation ministry, sometimes averaging a thousand calls a year) than the modern medical specialist (and pastor) with his sophisticated array of technology.

Morrison's value, therefore, for the modern pastor-preacher does not lie in his insights into church management, church growth, or contemporary worship. Morrison most likely would have eschewed the whole notion of a "contemporary gospel." What he would have championed today—passionately and patiently—was the relevant and compelling presentation of biblical truth that touches both the intellects and the emotions of contemporary listeners. His value for the modern reader lies in appreciating and learning from a style and sermonic approach that was contemporary in its time and whose principles have enduring value.

What can we learn, then, from Morrison? For one thing, he respected the intelligence of his listeners. His sermons are filled with allusions and quotations from a wide range of literature common to the experience of his people—Burns, Milton, Dickens, and Shakespeare—but without any hint of intellectualism or pedantry. Morrison perfectly prefigures Charles Swindoll's comment that preachers should get a good education and then get over it!

Modern preachers would do well to analyze Morrison's style of literary reference and determine the common cultural mediums of our own day. Lacking a similarly cohesive cultural identity, we may have to search harder for the insightful reference or provide a window for the congregation through which to view another world (consider, for example, the difference between quoting Shakespeare and any current TV commercial). Morrison not only spoke of beautiful truths, but he sought to speak the truth beautifully and for help turned to the great English writers and poets.

Morrison also placed the sermon in a strategic context—the awful carnage of World War I (in which Morrison's own son was

---

2. Thomas Oden, "On Not Whoring After the Spirit of the Age," in *No God But God*, ed. Os Guinness and John Seel (Chicago: Moody Press, 1992), 195.

killed), the emerging discoveries of modern science, or the urbanization of the once predominately rural Scottish society and the corresponding problems of secularization, alienation, and loneliness. Morrison addressed the developing cultural, social, and political dynamics of the day with both challenging and comforting truths from the Word. If we look closely at the changing demographics and family structures in our own society, we will find ample opportunities for strategically-formulated points of reference.

One other obvious characteristic of Morrison's sermons is their personal appeal. Morrison spoke directly to the needs and concerns of real people: the grieving, the lonely, the guilt-ridden, the worried, and the spiritually hungry. He described his approach thus: "It has been my habit . . . at the evening service to allow myself a wider scope . . . to win the attention, in honorable ways, of some at least of that vast class of people who today sit so lightly to the church." Judging from the full pews at the Wellington United Free Church, the success of his sermons can be measured by the phrase used in Mark 12:37—"The common people heard him gladly."

In this new edition of Morrison's sermons, Kregel Publications has attempted to "open a window" into the culture of Morrison's ministry and times. Uncommon terms (in today's usage) have been noted, and the frequent quotes, allusions, and personalities identified. In a few places grammatical constructions that might have rolled off the Scottish tongue have been modified with the modern reader in mind. It is our hope that by appreciating the richness of Morrison's style, readers will be encouraged to creatively speak to both the intellect and emotion of today's congregations. Lewis's comments are a fitting encouragement: "Every age has its own outlook. It is especially good at seeing certain truths and specially liable to make certain mistakes. We all, therefore, need the books that will correct the characteristic mistakes of our own period. And that means old books."[3]

DENNIS R. HILLMAN, Senior Editor

---

3. Lewis, 202.

To my session

who in my weakness

as now in my strength

have never failed me.

Introduction

Dr. George Herbert Morrison had a gift of saying things that we all would have said, had it occurred to us to say them; and he said those inevitable things as we could not, in English prose that had the effect of "poetry on the heart." This quotation of James Denney aptly sums up the "secret"—if there was such a thing—of Dr. Morrison's classic sermons delivered from his pulpit in Wellington Church, Glasgow, Scotland, from 1902 to 1928.

Throughout his ministry he was known for his concentrated study, his regular pastoral visitation, and his constant writing for publication. His appeal lay not in any physical stature, for he lacked that; not in any tricks or oratory, for he never preached for effect; but in the quiet winsome way in which he spoke to the heart from a heart suffused with the love and grace of Christ. He never lost sight of the fact that as a minister of Christ his first concern must be how best to bring his hearers closer to the heart of the Lord.

Although written early in this century, his sermons are modern in touch and spirit; the tone and temper are admirably effective for use today. Their simplicity of phrase came out of arduous toil as the writer worked in his preparation. The style is the man—quiet and genial—and his preaching was like this. Morrison was always the pastor-preacher, ever seeking to meet life's needs with some word from God.

Whatever he did had the hallmark of preparation and finality. Some sermons came easily like the bird on the wing; others came after much hard work and sweat of mind and heart. The fact that he brooded over his texts with something of an artist's unconsciousness and superb leisure is one of the elements in his power as a preacher. He brooded over the Word of God until it became translucent. His loyalty to Christ and his devotion in the secret place are wedded to his daily practice of study and writing.

His counsel to the young preacher is most revealing as the secret of his own success: "I can think of nothing, except that young preachers will do well to guard against the tendency to rush which is the bane of modern life. The habit of unprofitable bustle and rush, the present-day preoccupation with small affairs and engagements, is withholding many good things from us. For myself it is essential that I have leisure to brood and meditate."

To read and study these selections from the author's many volumes of messages will be to open new vistas of truth and to learn how old and familiar truths can be clothed in fresh and living words which will glow with unsuspected meaning.

RALPH G. TURNBULL

The God of Abraham, and the God of Isaac, and the God of Jacob (Acts 7:32).

1

The God of the Patriarchs

There is no knowledge attainable by man so vital as the knowledge of his God. To know Him with whom we have to do is the most important thing in human life. When we remember that without His hand not a blade of grass would have been green—when we remember that we depend on Him for every heartbeat and for every breath—when we remember that time is but an island engirdled by the ocean of eternity, who does not feel the pressure to know God? If life eternal be life in glorious fullness, then to God must be eternal life. Did we know God in all His height and depth, we should have conquered time and death forevermore. And that is why, in this strange life of ours, with all its struggling interests and ambitions, there is nothing that can for a moment be compared with knowing Him with whom we have to do. Far more important than attaining wealth, though that be the one passion of the market—far more important than achieving fame, that last infirmity of noble mind—far more important than anything on earth, in present influence and in eternal issue, is knowing whose we are and whom we serve. Now that is the value of such texts as this. They illuminate the character of God. They draw aside, if only by a little, the cloudy curtain that conceals the throne. And so tonight I would dwell upon this text, for it has given me a threefold glimpse of God, and what in quiet hours it has given me, it is my duty and my joy to give to you.

The first truth I learn from our text is this, that God is the God of separate individuals.[1]

When we go back in thought to those dim days that lie upon the farthest verge of history, we are oppressed, wherever we may turn, by a strange feeling as of shadowy multitude. We catch the confused sound of human voices, as in a distant murmuring of ocean; we come on traces of unnumbered hordes, moving across the world like tidal waters; we light on relics of pyramid or fort, where thousands must have ingloriously toiled, and of battles where thousands must have fallen, and some, it may be, gloriously died. Always, in that dim and distant past, the feeling of multitude is overwhelming. Always there are confused and shadowy masses, till the sense of the individual is lost. And it is then, over that boundless welter—above that rocking and surging of humanity—that there rings out from the eternal throne, "I am the God of Abraham, of Isaac, and of Jacob." He is not only the God of the innumerable; He is the God of the individual soul. Where you and I hear but a distant murmuring, He hears the separate beat of every heart. Viewed from the standpoint of the twentieth century, there is nothing visible save shadowy multitude; but viewed from the altitude of heaven, the one is as conspicuous as the all. Not only was God guiding those migrations which moved in a wisdom higher than their own. Not only, as on primeval chaos, was there the brooding of the Holy Spirit. Every hand had its distinctive touch, and every lip had its peculiar cry, and every heart had its own separate burden, for the God of Abraham, of Isaac, and of Jacob.

Indeed, that is one great distinction between natural and revealed religion, for the one thing that natural religion cannot do is to assure us of the individual care of God. The god of natural religion, as it seems to me, is like the driver of some eastern caravan, and he drives his caravan, with skill unerring, over the desert to the gleaming city. But he never halts for any bruised mortal, nor waits to minister to any dying woman, nor even for a moment checks his team to ease the agonies of any child. That is the god of natural religion—the mighty tendency that makes for righteousness. Impe-

1. The suggestion of these divisions, as well as of the sermon itself, I owe to my recollection of an altogether memorable discourse by the Rev. W. S. Dickie of Irvine, to which I listened with boundless delight in a little Highland church one beautiful summer day last year.

rially careful of the whole, he is sovereignly careless of the one. And over against that god, so dark and terrible, there stands forever the God of revelation, saying in infinite and individual mercy, "I am the God of Abraham, of Isaac, and of Jacob." He, too, is making for a city which has foundations, and whose streets are golden. But He has an ear for every feeble cry, and a great compassion for every bruised heart, and a watchful pity, like a mother's pity, for lips that are craving for a little water. It was a great thought which Peter uttered when he said to all who read, "He careth for you." But Paul was nearer the heart of the eternal when he said, "He loved me, and gave Himself for me."

This thought of God, as I need hardly tell you, is countersigned in the clearest way by Christ. The God of Christ, in communistic ages, is the asylum of individuality. It is true that there was something in a crowd that stirred our Savior to His depths. He was moved with compassion when He saw the multitude, as a flock of sheep without a shepherd. And when He came over to the city of Jerusalem, where the murmur of life was, and where the streets were thronged, looking, He was intensely moved, and wept. There was a place for the all within that heart of His. He saw life steadily, and saw it whole. There was not a problem of these teeming multitudes but had its last solution in His blood. Yet He who thus encompassed the totality in a love that was majestic to redeem, had a heart that never for an instant faltered in its passionate devotion to the one. Living for humanity, He spoke His deepest when His whole audience was one listener. Dying for humanity, His heart was thrilled with the agonized entreaty of one thief. For one coin the woman swept the house; for one sheep the shepherd faced the midnight; for one son, and him a sorry prodigal, the father in the home was brokenhearted. My brother, my sister, that is complete assurance that our God is the God of individuals. You are as much His care, as if no other person nor angel moved in heaven or earth. He is Almighty, and takes the whole wide universe into the covering hollow of His hand, yet He is the God of Abraham, of Isaac, and of Jacob.

The second truth I learn from our text is this, that God is the God of differing personalities.

As the three figures mentioned in our text move silently across the page of Scripture, one of the first things to impress us in them is the distinctness of their personalities. I have seen sometimes in an old Scottish home a series of pictures of the family ancestors. I have no doubt these ancestors existed in the warm imagination of the artist. But what has often struck me in these pictures is not the differences of face and form, but the extraordinary and unearthly likeness among these elegant tokens of gentility. Now if the picture-gallery of God were such a fiction, I should expect to find a sameness of that kind. I would expect to find these ancestors of Israel painted, as it were, with common lineaments. And to me it is a kind of quiet assurance that I am dealing in the Word with real people, when I discover in the remotest of them a personality that could never be mistaken. You never could confuse one with the other. You never could mistake one for the other. They are as different in tone and temper as is the twilight from the dawn. And yet that God who is the God of one is not less really God of the other two—the God of Abraham, of Isaac, and of Jacob.

Think for a moment of these three personalities, that you may understand the grandeur of our text.

First you have *Abraham, the man of faith*, and of the splendid heroism which faith inspires—the man to whom the call of God is everything, and who is never disobedient to that call—the man who sees with an inspired directness, who dares with the fine audacity of greatness, who, when he rears his tent against the storm, close beside his tent he builds an altar. Here is a man who always must be great, gifted with all capacity for leadership, cleaving his way through a thousand lesser things to grasp and grip the things that really matter, a man as large of heart as he is tender, and of a certain sweet and beautiful simplicity—such is the personality of Abraham.

And then you have Isaac, *meditative Isaac*—Isaac who went out into the fields to meditate at evening—Isaac who was never born to greatness, but only had greatness thrust upon him. A man not fitted for the strenuous life, but rather for the quiet and retired life—a lover of the sanctities of home, and of the sweet serenities of nature—a quiet believer in his father's God, though dowered with nothing of his father's heroism, not ardent, not intense, and never masterful. Love divine meant much to Isaac, but the warmth of human love meant even more; a man domesticated, and in love with peace, and hating strife, and with a tinge of melancholy—such is the personality of Isaac.

And then lastly you have *Jacob, different from Isaac as night is from day, a man of power* in every line of him, who would have been a millionaire but for the grace of God. Shrewd, subtle, infinitely capable, not gifted at his birth with scrupulosity, a man whom the devil could have used magnificently had not God in His preventing mercy been beforehand; a man with that splendid genius for commerce, yet never lacking that awful sense of an Almighty God. In every sense of the word a strong man—a man who knew what he wanted, and would have it—a man who was not to be baffled in his quest, whether his quest was a bargain or a woman—a man who could spring as swiftly as a tiger, and yet like a tiger could lie still and wait—such is the personality of Jacob. The God of Abraham, of Isaac, and of Jacob—do you see the glorious compass of that now? Separate as the east is from the west, each found his rest and his reward in Him. So do I learn that the God of revelation has a heart that is bigger than our widest difference, and has room in His love, and in His service too, for people who stand apart as night from day.

This feature, too, of the divine character is clearly exhibited by Jesus Christ. His God appeals not to one type of man; His God appeals to all. There are certain theologies which so exhibit God as to make Him the possession of a party. The God of Calvinism, for instance, was so stern that one who was not stern was apt to be repelled. But this is the wonder of the God of Jesus, that He has a message for a thousand hearts, and kindles into love and ministry every variety of personality. He is the God of Peter with his fine impetuousness, and of John with his perfect genius for loving; of Thomas with his brooding melancholy, and of Paul with his enthusiastic ardor. He is the God of Martha in her restlessness, and in all her bustling and womanly activity; but not less truly is He the God of Mary, whose eyes are homes of silent prayer. That is why, when God in Christ is preached, you shall have every type within the congregation. That is why the mother in the home may pray with confidence for all her children. She is not praying to the God of Abraham only, though even that would be a glorious privilege. She prays to the God of Abraham, of Isaac, and of Jacob.

Then the third truth I learn from our text is this, that God is the God of succeeding generations.

Abraham and Isaac and Jacob were not only men of differing personality—you must not forget that they were also men of separate and succeeding generations. They were not brothers as Cain and Abel were. They were not contemporaries like John and Peter. They did not live under a common roof, nor share in the fond affection of one mother. One grew to adulthood as the other aged, and took the torch out of a dying hand, and held it aloft that it might guide the pilgrims when the last bearer was sleeping in his grave. Now in history there have been generations that differed but little from those preceding them. The same sun has shone upon the children that fell with beauty upon the fathers' world. But if you have ever studied the book of Genesis (and there is no book more worthy to be studied) you will have found that that does not apply to the generations of the patriarchs. The battles which Isaac had to fight were not the battles which Abraham had to fight. The difficulties which tried the powers of Jacob were not the difficulties which had confronted Isaac. Each of them had his own task that he must do, and his own victory that he must win, and his own trial that he must meet and master if he was ever to hear the triumph song. There was a different environment for each of them; there was a differing outlook on the world. Time moved, and moving brought its changes, and of these changes the children were the heirs. So Jacob woke, and the world that met his eyes was not the world that Isaac had delighted in, nor was the world of Isaac that of Abraham.

My brother, my sister, when you reflect on that, does it not illuminate our text? God is the God of succeeding generations—of Abraham, of Isaac, and of Jacob. No generation can exhaust His name. No single age can know Him in His fullness. Not even Abraham, for all his faith, can learn the largeness of the heart of God. There is something left for Isaac to discover as he meditates in the fields at eventide, and when Isaac has been gathered to his fathers, still is there fresh light to flash on Jacob. No age has a monopoly of God. None must dictate to the coming days. Even an Abraham, for all his faith, only knows in part and sees in part. Abraham shall sleep, and Isaac shall awake, and Isaac dying shall give place to Jacob, and that one God who was the God of Abraham shall be the God of succeeding generations. One might have thought that in a new environment there would have been needed for humanity a new divinity. When knowledge had widened, and all the world was different, would not the heart demand a different God? My friend, this is the strange thing of it, that though everything changes as generations pass, the heart still needs, with an undying need, the God who spoke to men and women so long ago. Isaac hungers for the eternal Being, and finding Him, He is the God of Abraham. Jacob dreams, and dreaming, sees the throne, and on the throne there sits the God of Isaac. He is the God of succeeding generations.

And so tonight, facing our work again, you and I will take comfort in our God. We shall not be cowards when new truth is uttered, for He is the God of succeeding generations. Our fathers trusted in Him and were not ashamed, and now in our new world we need Him still. Still do we hunger, though everything is altered, for Him who was our fathers' God. And when our task is over, and we sleep, and our children are carrying on the warfare, still, though heaven and earth have passed away, the God of Isaac will be the God of Jacob. It is only in that faith we can be hopeful. It is only in that faith we can be true. It is only in that faith we can welcome every discovery which science brings. Let there be light, although the light should penetrate many a secret that seemed big with heaven—He is the God of succeeding generations. We know not what is coming on the world, and we see not the mighty changes yet to be. Dimly we feel that those who are now children will live and battle in an altered universe. But we know that whatever change may come, the human heart will still break through to God, and finding Him who is its deepest need, will find He is the God of long ago. Were He the God of Abraham alone, then all the glory would be in bygone days. Were He the God of Isaac only, then I should have no hope but for tonight. But I look backward with adoring gratitude, and I look forward with a heart at rest, when I remember that the God I trust is the God of Abraham, of Isaac, and of Jacob.

The damsel is not dead, but sleepeth
(Mark 5:39).
This thy brother was dead, and is alive
again (Luke 15:32).

2

Sleep and Death

I wish to speak tonight for a little while on some of our Lord's references to death. I wish to discover in what light He viewed that dark experience of our mortality. You will observe I am not asking your attention to the question of the life beyond the grave. That is a theme on which I have often spoken to you, and on which I hope often to speak again. But tonight we shall look at death just as a fact, as joy and sorrow and love and hate are facts, and ask what our Savior has spoken about that. For those of us who believe in Christ as Lord, it is supremely important to discover that. But I venture to think it is scarcely less important for those of you who take a lower view. For the words of Jesus Christ, whoever Christ was, have influenced the world and altered history in a way as profound as it is unapproached. A little book on death by Mr. Maeterlinck has had some vogue for the past year or two.[1] Now Mr. Maeterlinck has a very beautiful mind, and a deft and subtle literary genius. But to turn to his words on a theme like this, and to ignore the words of

1. Maurice Maeterlinck (1862–1949), Belgium dramatist and Nobel laureate in 1911.

Jesus Christ, is to show that lack of relation and proportion which is always the mark of inferior education. When you think, whoever Jesus was, of the tremendous influence of His words, when you think that they will still be winged, when yours and mine and Maeterlinck's are dead, it becomes the duty of every thoughtful person, who makes any pretense to the balance of true culture, to give the words of Christ his or her first attention. It is important to know what Plato thought of death. It is important to know what Hegel thought of death. It is interesting, though not important, to know what Maeterlinck or Professor Lecky[2] thought of death. But for men and women living in a world that has felt the terrific impact of Christ's words, to know what Christ has said on such a theme is the primary duty of intelligence.

Now when we study Jesus with this end in view, there is one thing which immediately impresses us. It is that Jesus in His ministry spoke comparatively little about death. Familiar with it in the home at Galilee, for Joseph had died when Jesus was still there; lighting oftentimes in boyish wanderings on ghostly sepulchers among the hills, there is no sign that He brooded upon death, nor let it color His imagination, nor that He lived, as people have sometimes lived, with the shadow of death forever by His side. That He spoke much of the life beyond the grave is a fact, of course, which nobody disputes. There is indeed a powerful school today which interprets everything in terms of eschatology. But of the fact of death—that shrouded enemy which lays its icy hand on all humanity—of that He spoke comparatively little. Now that at once separates Jesus from those Stoical teachers who were already beginning to take the ear of Rome.[3] For they, as Bacon[4] has so wisely put it, made death more terrible by dwelling on it so. They thought to conquer death by gazing at it, till familiarity should beget contempt, and instead of contempt there came a haunting terror on the men and women of the Roman empire. A similar thing has happened more than once in the long story of the Christian church. Inspired by the passion of asceticism, people have feasted their eyes upon the grave. And the singular thing is that when we turn to Jesus, with whom the story of the church began, you find wonderfully little of

---

2. William Lecky (1838–1903), British historian.

3. Stoics—philosophical school founded by Zeno (c. 340–c. 265 B.C.) which stressed inner freedom through impassiveness.

4. Francis Bacon (1561–1626), English philosopher and statesman.

all that. Whatever Jesus feasted His eyes upon, He never feasted them upon the grave. You can never imagine Him a medieval saint, clasping a human skull within a charnel house.[5] But you can always imagine Him among the fields, feasting His heart upon the bending corn, and on the innocent merriment of little children, and on the first glimmerings of human love.

This comparative silence grows more notable when you bear in mind two considerations. The first is the old familiar commonplace that death is a universal thing. There have been teachers who have avoided universal themes and loved to handle exceptional experiences. Some of our finest plays, like *Hamlet*, deal with experiences of the rarest kind.[6] But Jesus deliberately chose the universal, and dealt with what is common to humanity, and touched with the finger of a son of humanity the strings that God has put on every harp. The sorrows He soothes are universal sorrows; the joys He shares in are universal joys. The questions He answers are universal questionings; the hopes He kindles are universal hopes. Yet here is death, the universal leveler, stealing with equal foot to every door, and Jesus speaks very little about that.

The other consideration which makes the silence notable is the significance to Christ of His own death. That His own death was profoundly important in His eyes no unbiased reader of the gospels can deny. When He was deeply stirred He spoke of it. It was the one topic of the transfiguration. He watched with eagerness for every sign of readiness that He might unfold its meaning to the Twelve. And yet though He saw the coming of the cross, and knew that His triumph was to include a grave, the theme of the grave was rarely on His lips. Even when death was standing on the threshold, it did not form the theme of His discourse. It is not death that moves with awful mien through the glorious discourse of the upper chamber. It is a message more gladdening than death—it is the music of celestial joy—it is tidings of peace that the world cannot give, and at its darkest cannot take away. On that night on which He was betrayed the shadow of death was on the heart of Jesus. On that night, under the olive trees, He cried, "If it be possible, let this cup pass from Me." Yet on that night, with the finger of death upon Him, the talk of Jesus was no more of death than in the glad days when He had watched the lilies, and taken the little children in His arms.

5. A building in which bodies or bones were deposited.
6. By William Shakespeare (1564–1616).

Now that is very suggestive and significant, and it clearly calls for some interpretation. Let me dismiss in passing one interpretation which might possibly occur to certain minds. It might occur to some that this reserve of Jesus was only the superior silence of indifference. It might seem that Jesus spoke little about death because He scorned the very thought of death. But I venture to say that if you take the gospels and study the story of the Master there, you will dismiss that supposition as untenable. When you and I are silent on a matter, it does not necessarily mean we are indifferent. Sometimes the subject of which the heart is fullest is that on which the lips are strangely still. And as there are thoughts that lie too deep for tears, so are there thoughts that lie too deep for utterance, and people detect them not by any speech, but by a look, or a handclasp, or a tear. Now think of Jesus at the grave of Lazarus, when He was face to face with death. Look at Him—what is that upon His cheek?—it is the dewy glistening of tears. And then a bend of the road reveals the sepulcher, and there is death, in ravage and in victory, and Jesus groans in spirit and is troubled. My friend, whatever else that means, there is one thing that it emphatically means. It means that Jesus, indifferent to so much, was not indifferent to the final tragedy. He wept; He groaned in spirit; He was troubled. He shared in the anguish of the orphaned heart. Whatever His silence, it was not the silence of a serene and philosophic scorn.

Dismissing that, then, we may advance a little if we remember Jesus' favorite name for death. I think there can be little question that the familiar name of Christ for death was *sleep*. I do not insist on the raisings from the dead, though they at once suggest a waking out of sleep. I do not insist on that, though all these raisings at once suggest the thought of sleep to me. But I keep close to Christ's recorded sayings, on two occasions when He confronted death, and on both of them He spoke of death as sleep. Entering the darkened home of Jairus, He said, "The maiden is not dead, but sleepeth." Learning the news that Lazarus was gone, He said at once, "Our friend Lazarus sleepeth." And these expressions, springing from the heart, and of an authenticity that none can question, tell me that Jesus spoke of death as sleep.

But now it will occur to you at once that this is a thought common to all poetry. I know indeed no literature in the world where death is not spoken of in terms of sleep. You will find it in the philosophy of Greece, and you will light on it in the poetry of Rome. The Jews were perfectly familiar with it, for they spoke of their dead as sleeping with their fathers. Dante[7] accepts it as a commonplace; Chaucer[8] speaks of the living and the sleeping; and Shakespeare tells us in words that are immortal how this little life is rounded with a sleep. Now the question I want to ask is this: was our Lord talking as a poet talks? Was He simply using a poetic figure when He said, "The maiden is not dead, but sleepeth"? I have been led to think, for reasons I shall give you, that Christ was not talking as a poet talks, but was using language of intense reality. I certainly hold that Jesus was a poet. I think He was a poet to His fingertips. If poetry be simple, sensuous, and passionate, there never was speech more poetical than His. And yet, granting all that without reserve, I am constrained to think that when Christ spoke of death as sleep, people felt that He spoke, not in poetic figure, but in sober earnestness and truth. Let me suggest to you this one consideration based on the passage that we read tonight.

Suppose I were called, as I am often called, to a home that was under the shadow of bereavement. Suppose that a daughter of twelve years old were dead, and that I went in gently to where the body lay. What words would rise more naturally to my lips, when I had drawn the napkin from the brow, than just the words "How peacefully she sleeps!" They have risen to my lips a score of times, and never once were they misunderstood. I have said them to fathers, to mothers, to brothers, and to sisters, and found I was only uttering what they felt. There is never a trace of misinterpretation—there is always immediate and full response—when in the presence of the quiet dead we whisper that the little life is rounded with a sleep. But now suppose I turned to the sorrowing father, and said with a glowing eye, *She is not dead*! Suppose I turned to him, and with tremendous earnestness said, "I tell you she is not dead, *but sleeping*." First he would look at me with incredulity, then it would flash on him I was beside myself, and then, in the frantic unsettlement of grief, the house would echo with derisive laughter.

My brother, my sister, I want you to remember that that is exactly what happened to our Lord, and that such conduct is utterly incredible if Christ was speaking as a poet speaks. The Jews were far more poetical than we are, and they loved metaphor and all poetic imagery, and they were perfectly familiar from their literature with the figure of death as the last sleep. And yet when Jesus

7. Dante Alighieri (1264–1321), Italian poet.
8. Geoffrey Chaucher (1340?–1400), English poet.

stood beside the dead, and said what all of us have said, "She sleepeth," somehow they utterly misunderstood Him, and heaped on Him the insult of derision. Others had come to Jairus's house that morning, and had said gently, "How peacefully she sleeps." And the father and mother, looking on their loved one, had understood at once that kindly sympathy. And then came Christ, and said, *She is not dead—I tell you she is not dead, but sleeping*—and Him they laughed to scorn. That scorn to me is utterly inexplicable if Christ was speaking in poetic metaphor. There must have been something in His eye and tone that challenged the plainest evidence of sense. They felt instinctively that in the mind of Christ their little daughter was not dead, but living, although her eyes were closed, and all her fingers motionless, and there was not a quiver of breath upon her lips. In other words, this was not *death* to Christ, and every hearer felt He meant it so. Whatever death was in the thought of Jesus, it was not this ceasing of the heart to beat. And that is why these lovers of all imagery, who would have understood us had we said she sleeps, poured upon Him their frenzy of derision.

And so am I gradually led to the conviction that this was not what Jesus meant by death at all. In the habitual thought of that supreme intelligence, death was something darker and more terrible. It was not death to Him when the silver chord was loosed, nor when the pitcher was broken at the fountain. It was not death to Him when the strong men bowed themselves, and when the daughters of music were brought low. All that was life, though it was life asleep, in the mighty arms of the eternal God, and death was something more terrible than that. The maiden is not dead, but sleeps; but—this my son was dead and is alive again. The maiden is not dead, but sleeps; but—let the dead bury their dead. The maiden is not dead, but sleeps; but—he who believes upon Me, though he were dead, yet shall he live. Christ did not find the dead in Jairus's house, nor in any sepulcher among the Galilean hills. He saw the dead where men and women were—in the synagogue and in the market and the home. And so tonight Christ does not find the dead where the flowers are withering on the grave, but here where men are, and where women are, who have a name to live and yet are dead. If half the anguish of the open grave were felt for those who are living useless lives, if half the tears that fall upon the coffin fell upon hearts that are frivolous or obdurate, not only would we be nearer Christ in His deepest thought about humanity, but we should know more than we have ever known of the joy that cometh in the morning. For love and faith and prayer are powerless to bring again the dear one who is lost. No lifting heavenward of anguished hands will give us back again the one we loved. But "this my son was dead and is alive again"—and there is music and dancing in the home tonight, and there is joy in heaven, where the Father dwells, over one sinner who repents.

Whom do men say that I am? (Mark 8:27).

3

The Category of Genius

Among all the recent answers to this question, there is one that has obtained peculiar prominence. It is the answer that describes our Lord in terms of spiritual or religious genius. As one man has a genius for poetry, and another a genius for mathematics, so are we told today in many quarters that Jesus had a genius for religion. What Shakespeare was within the realm of poetry, and Newton[1] or Kepler[2] within that of science, that, though more conspicuously perhaps, was Jesus in the realm of religion. Now of course there is an element of truth in that, for the one passion of Jesus was religion. It filled His heart; it colored all His life; it was the source of all He said and did. Yet if there be one thing that is growing clearer to me, as I study the mind of Christ in Scripture, it is that the category of genius, as we call it, is quite inadequate to the historic Jesus. I beg to remind you that no one is at liberty to construct a Christ out of his inner consciousness. The one valid procedure for the student is to examine every fact the sources give. And I wish tonight to show you, if I can, that if anyone will only do that seriously, it becomes impossible to think of Christ as genius.

1. Isaac Newton (1642–1727), English philosopher and mathematician.
2. Johannes Kepler (1571–1630), German astronomer.

Well, in the first place it is a mark of genius that it is separable from its own achievements. This, I think, is not an accident; it is an essential and universal feature. The history of genius is nothing else than the long struggle to liberate its powers. It is the effort to work into expression the forces that are tumultuous within. It is the passion to body out the soul, in block of marble or in word of beauty, which shall live on and be a joy to others when the creator is sleeping in the grave. You can get all the enrichment of a play like *Hamlet* though you know nothing about William Shakespeare. You can possess the truth of the law of gravitation though you never heard the name of Isaac Newton. You can learn the wonders of modern astronomy, and the interactions of the solar system, though you live in an ignorance as deep as midnight of the life story of Copernicus. That is the characteristic of all genius. It displays its powers in an external medium. Touched from heaven with the creating impulse, it says, "Let there be light," and there is light. And so the Madonna is a joy forever, though Raphael[3] be but the shadow of a name; and *Hamlet* feeds us as with the bread of angels, though Shakespeare be inscrutable and still.

Now the moment you turn to the historic Jesus, you are faced by something absolutely different. There is not the faintest suggestion in the records that Christ was struggling to liberate His powers. The one thing you can never do with Christ is to separate His achievement from Himself. His revelation was His personality, and it is through that that He has blessed the world. You can separate the *Iliad* from Homer,[4] and you can separate *Hamlet* and *Macbeth* from Shakespeare, but you can never separate the Redeemer's triumphs from the personality of the Redeemer. The one impression you do *not* get in Christ is that of forces struggling to express themselves. Christ was not struggling to express Himself; Christ was the expression of the Father. And He was that, not by the way of toil, such as writes anguish on the brow of genius, but naturally and beautifully and constantly, as in the lake is the reflection of the sun. Now I suggest that whatever you call that, it is a misuse of words to call it genius. To talk of Shakespeare and of Raphael and of Christ is to betray an ignorance of data. Think for a moment of what you mean by genius, taking it at its richest and its best, and you will find that it is hopelessly inadequate to cover the fact of the historic Lord.

3. Raphael (1483–1520), Italian painter.
4. Homer (8th century B.C.), Greek epic poet.

In the next place, I ask you to observe that genius is a matter of degrees. In one man it is a flame of splendor, and in another it is a tiny spark. There are poets, for instance, of whom we say that undoubtedly they have a *touch* of genius. Well-nigh every Scottish countryside has had its poet with a touch of genius. There was a touch of genius in Walter Watson,[5] a touch of genius in Hugh Macdonald,[6] a touch of genius in fifty I could name to you, who have sung and sorrowed and suffered at our doors. On some genius lays her hand so lightly that the touch of her fingers is almost imperceptible. Others she grasps into her straining arms, and breathes her very soul upon their lips. And so at the one extreme you have these gentle souls who have lilted beside innumerable waters, and at the other you have a Dante or a Milton.[7] They are more than talented, these differing people; they are united in the gift of genius. Separated by a thousand differences, they are all kindled by a common fire. The humblest maker of a genuine lyric is a true citizen of that immortal kingdom where Chaucer and Spenser[8] and Dryden[9] are the peers, and one who was born by the Avon is the king.[10] Genius, then, has its less and has its more. It is capable of compression and expansion. In one life it is shining as the sun; in another it is gleaming as a star. And all this, mark you, in perfect independence of any theory of what genius is, for we are not discussing that tonight, but taking it in its common acceptation.

Now when you study Jesus Christ in Scripture, one impression becomes overwhelming. It grows upon you that He stands alone, in incommunicable, solitary grandeur. The one thing you can never do with Christ is to regard Him as belonging to a class. The one thing that is utterly incredible is that of Him there should be less or more. You may talk of the goodly fellowship of the martyrs, and of the glorious company of the apostles, but over against us all—confronting us—there stands, alone, the person of our Lord. No man comes to the Father but by Me—no man knows the Father but the Son. I am the way—I am the truth—I am the life—he that believes on Me shall never die. That is not a case of less or more, my friend, that is

5. Walter Watson (1780–1854), Scottish poet.
6. Hugh Macdonald (1817–1860), Scottish poet and literary editor.
7. John Milton (1608–1674), English poet.
8. Edmund Spenser (1522–1599), English poet.
9. John Dryden (1631–1700), English poet and dramatist.
10. Shakespeare was born at Stratford-on-Avon.

absolute truth or it is falsehood, and to say that other people can share in that is to say what is irreverent and ridiculous. You may find shadowings of the virgin birth in many a story of the old mythologies. You may find parallels to every word of Jesus in the literatures of India or of Rome. But the inexplicable thing is this, that, when every religion has been ransacked, the deepest impression made by Christ on humanity is that of an incommunicable grandeur. In the unconditional obedience He demands—in His unparalleled and stupendous claims—in His immediate knowledge of the Father—in the absence of the least consciousness of sin in Him—I say that *there* is a historic fact which is not only different in degree, but is absolutely different in kind from anything that the world has ever seen. Now we are not discussing tonight what we shall call it; we are simply discussing what we shall not call it. And I suggest that if words have any meaning, whatever we call it we shall not call it genius. And we shall not speak of Shakespeare and Christ again as if they stood upon a common platform. Over against us all, including Shakespeare, there stands forever the figure of our Lord.

In the next place, I ask you to observe that genius is notoriously unhappy. It is a dowry that is wet with tears, and wrapped in the sable coverings of anguish. Even in the common relationships of life we know how often genius is unhappy. There is such quivering sensibility in genius that only the grace of God can give serenity. And if you are looking for a happy home, where the wife wakens with a ringing heart, you know, if you are students of biography, that it is rarely in the dwellings of genius that you find it. Yet, after all, that is not the deepest of it; the sorrow of genius is a deeper thing. It is the sorrow of the heart that has seen heaven, and yet cannot climb the ladder to the throne. It is the craving of the soul for the ideal; the haunting of visions that are unrealized; the torture, after years of striving, of an imperfect mastery of one's material. When he has poured himself into his best, the genius feels that there is still a better. When he has wrought out his crowning toil, he is still haunted with a sense of failure. And the singular thing about Jesus Christ is this, that no such sense of failure ever touched Him, though He had a task to do so mighty that beside it that of the artist is but play. You never find Jesus craving for the ideal; you find Him always living in the ideal. You never find Him yearning for a better; you find Him always dwelling with the best. You never find Him, when His day is over, crying "Alas, what a failure I have been"; you find Him crying gloriously "It is finished." My friend, if I know anything of genius, most emphatically that is not genius. It is a fact, and genius is a fact, but the two facts belong to different worlds. And he or she who will have it that Jesus was a genius, has either very hazy thoughts of genius, or else, what is far more deplorable, has very hazy thoughts of Christ.

Another feature of genius is this, that it always makes us conscious of our distance. Indeed to me, who have thought about the matter, that seems one of its essential elements. When I meet with a man of ordinary talent, I am not conscious of any great remoteness. However able my honored brother be, he does not impress me as aloof from me. But whenever I am face to face with genius, even if it only be a spark of genius, then immediately I feel a separation. The life I know best is of course the preacher's life, and that has always been my experience there. When I listen to an average preacher, I am not greatly distressed about my sermons. But when I listen, on some rare occasion, to a preacher of real spiritual genius, then, not as a man but as a minister, I go home miserable and in despair. It is too high for me, I cannot attain it. I want to be silent and never preach again. I want to take these sorry sheets of mine, and burn them, and have done with them forever. Such is the feeling that genius creates, a strange disabling sense as of a distance, leading us to feel that all is useless, and bringing us to the margins of despair. I need hardly tell you that in the presence of Christ people never have been conscious of that feeling. The more they have felt His infinite transcendence, the more they have felt that in Him they had a brother. He is nearer to us a thousand times than Dante. He is nearer to us a thousand times than Shakespeare. In our intensest moments, when the deeps are calling, He is nearer to us than our hands and feet. "Come unto Me and I will give you rest," and people in their multitudes have come to Him. The poor have come, and the prodigals have come, and the waifs and strays and wreckage of humanity. Yet I never read amid all that broken earthenware of one who was overwhelmed with Jesus' distance, but I *have* read of thousands who have cried, "Christ is mine, praise God, and I am His." My friend, whatever you call that, it does not occur to me to call it genius. That is not the impression genius makes, so far as I have any knowledge of the matter. I know how a man feels when faced by Plato.[11] I know how a man feels when faced by Shakespeare. And I know emphatically it is not thus he feels when he is faced by the Lord Jesus Christ.

---

11. Plato (427?–347? B.C.), Greek philosopher.

And so that leads me to my closing thought, that genius evokes wonder and not worship, and all through the ages worship and not wonder has been faith's final attitude to Christ. From first to last, in the New Testament, Christ is the object of adoring worship. Confronted by no august tradition, the apostles found themselves bowing at His feet. And from that day on to this winter evening, every believer in his holiest hours has carried all that he has found in Jesus into the heart of the eternal God. Seeking God's will, he has followed Christ's will; listening for God's voice, he has heard Jesus' voice. The love revealed on the cross is not human love to him; it is the love that harbors in the heart of God. Until, not as a matter of reasoning, but by sheer power of spiritual impression, he has bowed down and worshiped at Christ's feet. The matter was never more beautifully put than in that exquisite story about Charles Lamb.[12] You remember how Lamb and his friends one evening were talking about people they would like to have met. And one said he would like to have met Chaucer, and another brought up the name of Sir Thomas Browne.[13] And at length that sacred name was mentioned—the name which is above every name. And there was a pause, and then Lamb said, in his slow, gentle, and stammering way, "If Shakespeare came into the room we should all stand up, but if *He* came in we should all kneel." Saint Charles!—as Thackeray[14] once called you—you had the right of it with that dear heart of yours. There in a single sentence is the difference, felt always, yet not always uttered. Yes, if Shakespeare came in here tonight, we would all stand up, we students, to acclaim him; but if HE came in, we would all kneel.

---

12. Charles Lamb (1775–1834), English essayist and literary critic.
13. Sir Thomas Browne (1605–1682), English physician and author.
14. William Makepeace Thackery (1811–1863), English novelist and essayist.

The Lord, he it is that doth go before thee
(Deut. 31:8).

4

The Prevenient God

I am not too late, I hope, to wish all my hearers a very happy New Year. I trust it may be a year of spiritual blessing to everyone within this house this evening. It takes a great deal more than a wish to make a happy year: it takes more than a wish, it takes a will. We could all be far happier than we have ever been, if we were quietly determined to be happy. For happiness does not depend so much on the kind of things we shall meet with in the year, as on the way we take them, the light we view them in, the angle from which we look at them. The plant which to the farmer is a weed, may be to the botanist a treasure-trove. The rain that is a disappointment to the child, may be just what the angler has been looking for. And the occurrence which is full of bitterness to one who has no eyes but those of earth, may be but another call to dedication for one who walks in the fellowship of heaven. It is a great thing, if we would be happy, to cultivate strenuously a point of view. Dress makes a wonderful difference in people, and one's thoughts are but the dress of things. In God's light we shall see light: in the deepest valley and in the darkest mile. To learn to look at things in God's perspective is one of the first secrets of repose.

Now I want you to take as your motto for the year the words

which form our text this evening. "The Lord, he it is that doth go before thee" into the unknown land of the New Year. We cannot tell what the year may bring to us, what wealth of joy, what bitterness of sorrow. We cannot tell—why would we want to tell—"What is that to thee? follow thou Me." Right between us and everything that comes, mighty in love and wisdom and in power, there moves in front of us our heavenly Father. You may never have noticed how bent the Bible is on showing that God is everywhere around us. Turn where you will, to any point you please, and the Bible meets us saying, God is there. We hear a great deal about environment today, and about the shaping and molding of environment, but the one environment the Bible preaches is the environment of God. Is it memories out of the past that vex us?—He has beset us behind: He is our reward. Are we tempted by base things that are beneath us? Underneath are the everlasting arms. Are thoughts too high for us beating on our heads? The shadow of His wing is over us. Is it the unknown future that disquiets? "The Lord, he it is that doth go before." I want you, then, to take that as your motto. There is none better in the whole of Scripture. Wishes are kind, but wishes may be vain; resolves are good, but how quickly they are broken. But let a man awaken every morning, and say to himself, "God is ahead today," and it will fill him with such hope and courage that he will be more than conqueror in Him who loves us. If anyone said to you when you were walking that someone you loved was on ahead a little, would you not quicken your pace, set out in earnest, and forget the things that were behind? So God, whose name is love, is on ahead, in this our path to the sunset and the sea, and there is nothing in the world like God before us to quicken and sustain us as we journey.

In a broad and general way we all believe in this anticipative and forestalling providence. It is one of the plainest facts of human life that we are not flung on an unprepared world. When a little child is born into the home, is there no preparation of maternal love? Has not the unseen power been at work changing the heart of womanhood to motherhood? There is not a child, cradled in loving arms, and watched with the passion of a mother's tenderness, but is a loving and perpetual argument for a prevenient and anticipative God. Or think what a misery this life would be if there were no beauty to delight the eye. The eye has been fashioned to feast on what is beautiful, and if there were nothing beautiful our sight were vain. But the God of beauty has gone on before us, decking the world with summer and with winter, and when we waken hungering for the beautiful, morning and sunset and evening star are there. I crave for food, and earth unlocks her treasury, and says to me, Yes, child, there is food. I crave for love, and love has been prepared for me in ties that are as sweet as they are strong. I crave for some assurance of a homeland that shall be fitted for my eternal being, and a voice answers across the mists of time, "I go to prepare a place for you." For anyone who knows what life is, it is not everything to say that God is with us. There are a thousand facts you never can explain unless the love of God be on ahead. And what I want you to do is to take that general truth, and to make it the dynamic of each morning; to say in the joy of trust, come what may, The Lord, He it is who goes before me.

One of the first results of living so is a wonderfully augmented sense of safety. It banishes a hundred fears and glooms, to be quietly sure that God is on ahead. When the king goes a journey on the railway, you know how elaborate are the precautions taken. The line is tested—other trains are blocked—a pilot engine is dispatched in front. So far as human precautions can prevail, the king must be absolutely safe when traveling, and one great pledge of his safety lies in this, that planning and pilotage are on before. It is not enough that officials of the line should travel in the same train as the king. He is guarded in some degree by those beside him; he is guarded also by those who are before. And so with us, who are made kings through Him who loved us and who died for us—our sense of safety is wonderfully augmented by the prevenient wisdom of our Lord. Of all the journeys which a person can take, there is none that is half so perilous as living. We are engirdled to the end by risks, and a hundred hands are snatching at our crowns. And it is when we come to realize all that, as we do through every trial and every fall, that we come to feel the peace and power and blessedness of a prearranging and prevenient God. We need His arm beneath us when we fall, to set us, forgiven, on our feet again. We need His grace behind us when we turn and think of the sorry tangle of our past. But when we think of the unknown tomorrow, with all its surprise and all its possibility, then like a trumpet through the night is this, "The Lord, he it is that doth go before thee."

Another result of realizing this is a deepening sense of daily preparation—a feeling that everything that comes is meant, and that there is a meaning in it I must try to find. When people traveled on the Continent in older days, they used to be preceded by a courier, and how much their comfort depended on the courier may be read in any of our older books of travels. It was the courier who arranged the stages. It was he who had everything ready at the stopping places. Familiar with every road, he went before, and the token of his advance was preparation. Nothing was so important as the courier's character—the comfort of the whole journey lay in that. If he was drunken or careless, there was constant trouble; if he was faithful, everything was well. And God, I may say with reverence, is our courier, familiar with every road and every halting place, perfectly faithful, infinitely wise, loving us with an everlasting love. It is God with us who gives the joy of peace, but God *before* us the joy of preparation. When a man wakens to a prevenient love, he can face anything and everything with fortitude. For not alone is everything prepared, so that he shall have strength to do it and to bear it; but he himself by every turn of providence is being prepared for all that is to come. That was the faith of Christ about the future when He said to His own, "Let not your heart be troubled." It was not only that He was always with them, though that is a mighty and a glorious truth. It was that in every tomorrow there is God, shaping, arranging, ordering, preventing, weighing the burden for tomorrow's strength, smoothing the pathway for tomorrow's feet. For with God there is no future and no past. He dwells above all boundaries of time. With Him a thousand years are as one day, and one day is as a thousand years. And the secret things belong to the Lord, who has His dwelling in the eternal now, and who sees altogether and at once that which unfolds itself to us in time successively.

Once again to realize our text is the secret of a strong and radiant hope. No man can ever be hopeless for the future who lives in the faith of a prevenient God. It is one of the characters of human life that hope is essential to its well-being. Without hope we cannot live, and without hope we cannot serve. And I know not how any one can cling to hope amid the shadow and the chance of time, without the faith that God is in the future, the goal of every effort and all history. There are some hopes which are like those snow bridges which many of you have seen among the higher Alps. They span the crevasses in their fantastic beauty, and they are safe enough for the practiced mountaineer. But they would never bear the weight of thronging feet, nor give any foothold to the unpracticed climber. For common men and common women you want a far more solid bridge than that. If there is one thing in life, then, that is of vital moment, it is to have a hope that is secure. It is to know that effort is not vain, that things are not hurrying to a worse confusion. Only in that hope can one rise again, and set one's face heavenward after every failure; only in that hope can one throw oneself into the cause and service of humanity. If we are fighting uncertainly, we might as well give over. If we are beating the air, our toil is mockery. If there is no kingdom that is on its way, then let us eat and drink, for tomorrow we die. But if we believe in a prevenient God, who in love has willed the end in the beginning, then hope is born, and courage is renewed, and our labor in the Lord is not in vain. God in the past is the source of peace, for He has blotted out our transgressions like a cloud. God in the present is the source of strength, for if God be for us, who can be against us? But God in the future is the source of hope, when you are baffled, and your arm is weary, when sin seems to triumph in the heart, and evil to be victorious in the world. "Bishop," said Carlyle[1] once to Bishop Wilberforce[2] when they were talking after the death of Sterling[3]—"Bishop," said Carlyle, "have you a creed?" "Yes," said the Bishop, "I have a creed, and the older I grow, the firmer it becomes; there is only one thing that staggers me." "What is that?" asked Carlyle. "It is the slow progress," said the Bishop, "that that creed seems to make in the world." And Carlyle remained silent for a moment, and then said slowly and seriously, "Ah, but if you have a creed you can afford to wait." My friend, if you have a creed you can afford to serve; and if you have a creed you can afford to wait. There is no place now for irreligious hurry, and no place at the darkest for despair. If you and I can say, as I trust we all can say, "The Lord God goes before me," then our labor in the Lord is not in vain.

In closing, note that these words are a promise, and that every promise in Scripture is conditional. I do not know one promise in the Scripture that is not conditional upon human response. We are not only fellow workers in the kingdom; we are also fellow workers in the promises. When the Spirit utters the everlasting yea, the Bride has to answer with the great Amen. You have to lift your hand up, if you would feel it grasped; you have to yield your life up, if you would have it sanctified; you have to turn your steps from the far country, if the Father is to fall upon your neck. Just so, if God is to

1. Thomas Carlyle (1795–1861), Scottish essayist and historian.

2. Samuel Wilberforce (1805–1873), bishop of Oxford and Winchester, third son of reformer William Wilberforce.

3. John Sterling (1806–1844), English author and essayist.

be before us, personally, then we must follow on to know the Lord. We must say to Him resolutely and sincerely, "Take my imperfect will, and make it yours." Not grudgingly, but in the gladness of surrender, we must yield ourselves up to Him a living sacrifice, believing that in His will is blessedness, and that He does all things well. There is a beautiful figure in one of Wordsworth's[4] poems of a bird that is swept from Norway by a storm. And it battles against the storm with desperate effort, eager to win back again to Norway. But all is vain, and so at last it yields, thinking that the gale will carry it to death—and the gale carries it to sunny England with its green meadow and its forest glade. Ah, how many of us have been like that little voyager, fretting and fighting against the will of God. And we thought that life could never be the same again when we were carried seaward by the storm. Until at last, finding all was useless perhaps, and yielding to the wind that blows where it listeth, we have been carried to a land that was far richer, where there were green pastures and still waters. You remember the favorite words of Principal Cairns.[5] "You go first," he would say, "I follow." And when he was dying, and his breath was failing, they listened, and he was still whispering that. So you and I can say, facing the future, "You go first, I follow"; for the Lord, He it is that goes before you, and He will never leave you nor forsake you.

4. William Wordsworth (1770–1850), English poet and poet laureate, 1843–1850.

5. John Cairns (1818–1892), Presbyterian preacher and scholar.

Our Savior Jesus Christ . . . hath brought
. . . immortality to light through the gospel
(2 Tim. 1:10).

5

The Singer in the Street

There are two ways in which Christ has worked in His long task of the regeneration of humanity. He has brought among us from heaven what is new, and He has consecrated what was old. There is a widespread tendency in theological thought today to belittle the originality of Jesus, just as once there was the opposite tendency to ignore Jesus' relation to the past. But both extremes are not only false to Scripture, but they are also false to Christian experience, which always blends the new and old together. If any man be in Christ, he is a new creation. There are ten thousand lives that can testify to that. There is something original and fresh and new in every truly regenerate experience. And yet the grace that has inwrought the new takes into its bosom all the old, and uses it for the service of the kingdom. Old tendernesses begin to live again. Old hopes lift up their faces to the morning. Chords that were broken begin again to vibrate with a music that whispers of the long ago. So in Christian experience, as in the Scripture, there is ever the mingling of the new and the old; new power, and, through the inflow of that power, old hopes and yearnings and longings realized.

Well, now, among these yearnings of humanity, one of the deepest is that for immortality. Christ did not bring it here, He found it here, deep in the shadowy places of the soul. We have read of instances in which a great musician has heard a beautiful voice out in the street. It was that of some poor girl singing for bread in the kindly shadow of a London twilight. And recognizing the beauty of the voice, the master has had it trained at his own cost, till it became a thing of joy to multitudes. In some such way, out in the crowded thoroughfares, our Master heard the voice of immortality. And He recognized the range and beauty of it, undisciplined and uncultured as it was. And so tonight, upon this Easter evening, the question which I want to ask is this, How did Christ train that singer of the street? In other words, what difference has Christ made to the yearning of the heart for immortality? What is the contribution of our Lord to the belief in a life beyond the grave? I think, laying aside what is debatable, we may sum it up in these three propositions. First, Christ has confirmed the hope of immortality. Second, Christ has enriched the thought of immortality. Third, Christ has enhanced the power of immortality.

First, then, Christ has confirmed the hope of immortality.

Now I do not think, friends, that I speak unguardedly when I call the hope of immortality a universal hope. We light upon it in the remotest ages, and find it among the most barbarous peoples. It was this faith that built the pyramids. It was this that reared the mighty Etrurian tombs. It was this that led men to embalm their dead, and to lavish art and treasure on embalming. It was this that placed the food within the coffin, and the piece of money in the corpse's hand; which slaughtered the horses of the departed warrior, and burned the widow on her husband's pyre. It was this that made Socrates despise his poison as something that could not touch his real self. It was this that drew Plato to his loftiest argument, in words that thrill and throb to this hour. From the lowest depths of damp and sunless forests, to the heights of intellectual and spiritual genius, people have cherished the hope of immortality. The strange thing is that that undying hope has never, out of Christ, become a certainty. It is an instinct of all untutored hearts, and yet an instinct that never has been verified. And this is the first great service of the Lord to that universal hope of immortality, that He has turned it, for all who trust in Him, into a full and glorious assurance.

If, then, you ask me how He accomplished that, I reply that the answer is twofold. He has done it first by the doctrine He has given us of the relationship of God and man. Christ's proof of immortality is not our instinct; Christ's proof of immortality is God. If we are His children, and if He truly loves us, it is incredible to Christ that we should cease to be. Once realize the Fatherhood of God, as Jesus was never weary of proclaiming it, and on the bosom of that Fatherhood there nestles the immortality of man. There is no proof that I am an immortal being merely because God is my Creator. He is the Creator of these myriad creatures that dance and die upon a summer's evening. But if God be my Father, and if He loves me with the splendor and passion of a father's love, then I am His and He is mine *forever.* Here for instance is an earthly father, standing beside the deathbed of his child. And he bows his head over a breaking heart, and he strives to say, "Thy will be done." But ah! had he the power to baffle death, and to drive him across the threshold of the home, with what a will would he exercise that power. My brother and sister, God *always* has that power, and if He loves as an earthly father loves, death will never rob Him of His child. It is thus that Christ has confirmed our human yearning. He has rooted it in the Fatherhood of God. He has taught us that at our worst we are so dear to God that nothing shall ever separate us from Him. Christ's proof of immortality is not an argument built on the disproportions of humanity. His proof is a love that will not let us go.

But Christ has not only confirmed it by His teaching. He has also confirmed it by His life. The life of Jesus, for the seeing eye, is the crowning argument for immortality. One of my acquaintances in Glasgow is a German gentleman who has been resident in Scotland thirty years. Well, when I spend an evening in his company, his fatherland grows very real to me. One of my old friends who was at college with me is now an honored missionary in Livingstonia,[1] and there is nothing more living for me than Livingstonia after an hour or two with Donald Fraser. Now that was the kind of impression Jesus made. He irresistibly suggested heaven. He lived so near the frontiers of eternity that the glory of it smote Him on the face. And people awoke to feel that all their yearning for a life that was larger than the life of time was answered in the life of Jesus Christ. He satisfied the longing of the heart. He was the confirmation of its surmise. He carried in Himself, for all who knew Him, the overwhelming proof of a beyond. And it is this, sealed in the resurrection, that has touched the flickering hope of all the world, and turned it into the certainty of Christendom.

---

1. Present day Zambia.

In the second place we have to consider this, that Christ has enriched the thought of immortality.

Now I hesitate to make broad and sweeping statements when I am so conscious of imperfect knowledge, but there is one broad statement I can make, I think, without any fear of contradiction. It is that in the ancient, as in the savage world, immortality has always been a dreary prospect. It has never thrilled with any sense of joy, but rather with a sense of desolation. It has never been thought of as a life enriched, but always as a life impoverished; never as a life to be desired, but rather as a lot to be endured. There are one or two passages in the Old Testament that rise magnificently into a clearer air: "In Thy presence is fullness of joy"; "I know that my Redeemer liveth." But these are the utterances of glorious souls, who saw like Abraham the day of Christ, and the usual outlook is different from that. The future is a shadowy realm of silence. It is a lonely, desolate existence. There is no vision of God in sheol, nor any voice of praise, nor any human warmth or cheerfulness. And you cannot wonder, when you remember that, how the saintliest Jews should have shrunk from it with horror, and cried in agony when death approached, "Deliver me from going down to the pit."

My friend, I need hardly say to you how radically Christ has altered that. If He has deepened the shadows for all who are impenitent, He has banished them for all who are His own. Just as God, when He takes some sluggish creature and enriches it with new wealth of being, gives it a new capacity for joy, but also a new capacity for pain; so Christ, taking the thought of immortality, left it no longer dull and rudimentary, but capable of all the blessedness of heaven, and all the anguish and bitterness of hell. Enrich the great idea of patriotism, and you shall have blood in it as well as triumph. Enrich the great idea of home, and you shall have anguish there as well as love. Enrich the great idea of immortality, and you shall have joy and glory in its compass, and also, by a law inevitable, the possibility of awful woe. Now that is exactly what Jesus Christ has done. He has heightened and deepened immortality. He has made it far more glorious than before. He has made it far more dreadful than before. He has filled it for the finally impenitent with an agony of remorse that is appalling, and He has filled it for every childlike heart with a bliss that is beyond compare. Eternity can never be colorless again for anyone who has heard the word of Jesus. Either it is unutterable loss, or else it is unutterable gain. And that is what I mean when I suggest that Christ has enriched the thought of immortality, as He has enriched the thought of motherhood and home.

The third thing I touch upon is this, that Christ has enhanced the power of immortality.

Now, of course, all hopes must have a certain power. Men and women are always molded by their hopes. The kind of thing you long for in the shadow always affects and influences character. But it is singular, and has often been observed, that among all the hopes which people have cherished, few have been so powerless out of Christ as the universal hope of immortality. As if a child at play should find a diamond, and look on it merely as a curious pebble, and only understand its priceless value when one passed by who had the eye to see, so in the garden of the heart people found eternity, and never understood the riches of it, till Some One came along whose hands were pierced. The most that the future had ever done for men and women was to fill them with a vague and haunting fear. It had never inspired them, never come with comfort, never upheld them when the way was weary. And what I say is that Jesus took that yearning, lying unused in every human soul, and turned it into one of the mightiest powers that have ever been brought to bear upon humanity. Let me indicate the truth of that in two directions, and so close.

Think, for example, of how the Christian faith has brought immortality to bear on work. It has given an impulse to all honest toil that has practically changed the face of Christendom. If all our striving is to cease at death—if every effort is to be ended there, well might we ask, when effort costs so dear, whether all our effort were worth while. But if all we have striven to do, and all we have failed to do, is to be perfected in the eternal morning, then in the dreariest we pluck up heart again. Our toil is not a task of three score years. Our toil is a task that has eternal issues. Every capacity that we have fought our way to, we shall carry over into the beyond. So in the thick of it there steals upon the ear the music of the distant triumph song, and we thank God and take courage by the way. Divorce our duty from our immortality, and duty becomes incredibly hard. It is when a man can say, I am *forever*, that he can say with a glad heart, I *ought*. And that is why duty has blossomed like the rose, since Jesus lived, and died, and rose again, because He has touched it with the hand of the forever.

Think, lastly, how our Christian faith has brought immortality to bear on sorrow. It has given beauty for ashes, the oil of joy for mourning, the garment of praise for the spirit of heaviness. You young people, who have not drunk of sorrow yet, will think I am using exaggerated language. To you it is Glasgow which is intensely real, and the beyond which is the pageant of a dream. But there is someone sitting beside you here tonight, who has laid her treasure in a little grave, and for her it is Glasgow that is the place of shadows, and the one intense reality is heaven. The one thing love refuses to believe is the foolish doctrine of annihilation. Love wants the loved one not for twenty years. Love wants the loved one forever and forever. And now comes Christ to every breaking heart, and says, "Let not your heart be troubled. In My Father's house are many mansions, I go to prepare a place for you." What is all your philosophy to that, splendid though be the triumphs of philosophy? Do you think philosophy will climb the garret stair and give its comforts to that lonely widow? Yet that is what Christ is doing every day, in the lone hut and in the crowded Babylon, to Queen Alexandra[2] mourning for her brother, and to the laborer mourning for his child. And we do not sorrow as those who have no hope. We are begotten into a lively hope. "In My Father's house are many mansions. If it were not so I would have told you." Death is no journey into the obscure night where the wild beasts are crying in the dark. It is the passing for all who are in Christ into a larger and a brighter room.

2. Alexandra Feodorovna (1872–1918), Russian empress, consort of Nicolas II.

Baptizing them in the name of the Father, and of the Son, and of the Holy Spirit (Matt. 28:19).
This is my body, which is broken for you (1 Cor. 11:24).

6

The Sacramental Idea

There have been few controversies in the church so bitter as those which have raged around the sacraments. This feast of love has witnessed sorer strife than any other object of the faith. So pitiful indeed has been the warfare that has torn Christendom into hostile camps over the sacraments that men have wondered in all reverence why Christ should have instituted sacraments at all. One answer to that difficulty is that sacraments are a great help to Christian character. There are certain elements in the Christian character which call for the sacramental idea to nourish them. And that is why Jesus of Nazareth sent a sword, and instituted what was so fraught with peril, and said, "This do in remembrance of me. "I would like, then, to dwell for a little time on some of the moral influences of the sacraments. I would like to show you that the sacramental idea has its place in the formation of the Christian life.

In the first place, then, the sacraments stand for this, that all that is highest and holiest is a gift. In language eloquent because it is pictorial, they speak of religion as of something offered. Weary with striving for some dim ideal; worn with the struggle for a better life, the sacrament, in simple silent beauty, reminds us that what we crave for is a gift. Think of the sacrament of baptism. How helpless—how passive is the little child! It is all unconscious of what is going forward; it does not understand, nor does it need to. But as it lies there in its father's arms, and as the water is sprinkled on its brow, and as the minister utters the solemn words, "I baptize you in the name of Father, Son, and Spirit," surely there is not one of us but feels that here, at the very dawn of life, is the emblem of a grace that is a gift. I have baptized in my ministry not a few adults, and it has been a very solemn service. There is something deeply impressive in a service when a man bows the knee and is baptized. But still more impressive, for those who have eyes to see, is the sprinkling of water on a little child, for it tells of a grace that is stooping down to us, and of a heavenly love that is a gift. Not when we begin to think and ponder—not when our minds are wakening to reflect—not then do we lift ourselves into the love of God, and rise into the circle of His family. But when we are helpless in our opening days, when we would perish but for the love of home, then does the love of heaven stoop down upon us, and in the sacrament bestow its seal. That, then, is one outstanding feature of what I might call the sacramental idea. It lays no emphasis on human effort. It is not a picture of any human striving. It is the emblem of a love that is bestowed—of a gift that is royally and freely offered—it tells us that before we have discovered God, God in His mercy has discovered us.

Now that being so, I think we can perceive the vital importance of sacramental teaching. It proclaims forever that the Christian life is rooted in a heavenly deed of gift. Not by the labors of our hands, however strenuous—not by our zeal, although it knows no respite, not by these alone can we be fashioned into the likeness of the Lord Jesus Christ. We must receive before we can accomplish; we must be planted if we are to grow; we must begin by opening the heart to the offer of the grace of God in Christ. The Christian life does not begin in effort. The Christian life begins in receptivity. It does not start in an impassioned struggle; it starts in a glad reception of a Savior. And it is when we are in danger of forgetting that, and thinking that all depends upon our toil, that like a silver bell above the stir of things comes the sweet music of the sacrament. We see the water touching the child's forehead, and we know that the child is but a helpless innocent. We see the bread broken and distributed—offered to us by other hands than ours. Till half insensibly we come to feel that at the back of everything we yearn for, there is a life that is ours as a free gift. Now it has never been easy, I believe, to have that receptive and responsive heart. But I question if it was ever harder than in the times in which we live today. For this is a time of progress and discovery—a time when everything seems possible to man—a time when man might well be proud of the secrets he has wrested from the universe. We all have something of the age in us, and we carry it over into our religion. And we fill our churches with strenuous activities till they become as bustling as the marketplace. And we forget, or if we do not forget we are at least in peril of forgetting, that what is most vital in the religious life comes to the human soul by way of gift. Therefore it is that in an age like this the sacraments must never be despised. In words so plain that he who runs may read, they meet the peril of the prevailing temper. They tell us that the Christian life does not take its rise in any Godward yearning, but in the fact that God loved, and that He gave.

Secondly, in the Christian experience, the sacraments have this peculiar value, that, in a very marked degree, they sustain and animate the life of feeling.

It is distinctive of the Christian life that it is essentially a heart-life. It is not born in the region of the intellect; it is born in the region of the feelings. Centering as it does in the Lord Jesus Christ, it is always a life of personal relationship. From Him it flows—to Him it returns again—in fellowship with Him it is maintained. It does not rest on intellectual certainty; it rests on a Savior who lived and died for us. And so on our part it is a life of love, and of adoration, and of gratitude. It is not by quickening the intellect that Christ has conquered; it is rather by quickening the pulse of being. When Jesus spoke with the two going to Emmaus, they said, "Did not our heart burn within us?" They were not only enlightened by Christ's words; they were also profoundly affected by Christ's words; and from that hour on to this present day that has been the power of the gospel. For you may enlighten a man's mind with truth, and still may leave him uninspired and cold. If you would kindle him to any sacrifice, you must have the power of getting at his heart. And if the church, with all her faults, has ever been a missionary church, it has not been because her creed was deep, but primarily because her Christ was love. We love, because He first loved us. There is the sum and substance of it all. Take that away—that personal relationship—and the glory of the gospel is departed. No more will there be enthusiasm in service. No more will the poor have the gospel preached to them. No more will lives be joyfully surrendered for the evangelization of the world. Only when feeling, then, is deep and strong, do we catch the peculiar spirit of the gospel. Men and women are not saved by understanding Christ. They are saved by loving and by following Christ. They are saved by loving Him with an adoring gratitude, by serving Him in personal surrender, by trusting Him utterly when the shadows deepen and the heart is weary with the way.

But the fact is that as the ages pass that primacy of the heart is apt to be imperiled. For a man cannot leave his intellect behind him when he comes into living fellowship with Christ. No thoughtful person can worship and adore without the desire to know whom he adores. It is the deepest instinct of his being to justify his ardor to his intellect. Hence does faith ever tend with passing years to be stated in terms of the intelligence, and the vision to be embodied in the creed. Just as the human mind can never rest in adoration of the world of nature, but by its very constitution is impelled to the investigation of the properties of matter; so can it never rest with any gladness in childlike adoration of the Christ, but must ever be striving to interpret Him. That this is inevitable and altogether worthy, I need not take time this evening to discuss. We are not only to love God with all our hearts; we are to love Him also with all our minds. And yet, as the vision passes into doctrine, and the living Christ is interpreted in creed, there is always one subtle and peculiar peril. It is the peril of giving to clear thinking the primacy that Christ has given to love. It is the tendency to intellectualize religion, and make it depend upon accepted dogma. It is the danger of being proud of argument, and of all the deep things of the Catechism, and of forgetting that everything is useless without the yielding of the heart to Christ. In other words, as faiths grow ancient, it is increasingly hard to keep the feelings tender. It may grow easier to comprehend, but it does not become easier to adore. And, therefore, the ever-deepening need, when the vision of Christ has passed into the creed, that the heart be quickened, and the affections warmed, and the life of feeling given its own place.

My friend, if anything is certain it is that God has provided for that need. He knows our frame and remembers we are dust, and is touched with the feeling of our infirmities. He has provided for it in the world of nature, which fills us with adoring wonder. He has provided for it in sanctuary music, which so often opens up the fount of tears. And He has provided for it also in the sacraments, where there is so little to satisfy the mind, and yet so much that wins unerringly into the very secret of the soul. For the sacraments lift up no voice to preach. They move in a realm where argument is silent. They are a simple picture, drawn by the hand of heaven, and such as the eyes of a child delight to dwell upon. And so do they lead us to the childlike spirit, where trust and wonder and love are all-embracing, and where the greatest and most real of things are the things that never can be proved. Again as the water drops upon the infant we see the grace that is so free and boundless. Again as the piece of bread is broken we see the body pierced upon the cross. And looking at it we rise above all theory of how the atonement may have been accomplished, and we say simply, *The Savior died for me.* And then as our memories of Christ are kindled other memories come stealing in. And we think of our children and we pray for them. And we think of those who sat beside us once. And we recall the voices we shall never hear again, and the hands that never shall be grasped in ours, till the day break and the shadows flee away. Ah, brethren, in our whole round of worship is there anything that can take the place of this? Where is the service that can so reach the heart, and make us filial and brotherly? And that is one reason why Christ gave the sacraments—to shield us from a dry and barren faith, and to guard us, by flow of tender feeling, from becoming doctrinal and hard and cold.

Thirdly and lastly, in the sacramental idea there is a constant safeguard against worldliness.

It is not easy when we speak of worldliness to define precisely what we mean. It is one of those things so easy to be noticed and yet so difficult to be described. It is not dependent upon great possessions, for many wealthy people are not worldly. It is not excluded by narrowness of means, for the poverty-stricken can be intensely worldly. Probably we get nearest to the meaning of it if we think of it as absorption in the world—the world of power, or the world of fashion, or the world of social opinion or convention. He who is worldly takes these as his end. They are not his instruments; they are his all. For them he lives—by them he judges—beyond them he has no vision and no interest. And what the worldling needs above all else, if he is to be lifted above his poor miserable vanity, is something that will spiritualize the secular, and help him to see the ideal at its heart. Now nothing but the grace of God will achieve that. Only in His light shall we see light. Think not, I pray you, that there is any magic in the simple ritual of the Christian faith. But unquestionably one of the surest means to illumine and transfigure the material is the idea that was authorized by Christ—the deep and beautiful idea of sacrament. For we sprinkle water upon the little child, and the water speaks of a love that is divine. And we take a piece of bread into our hands, and see a Savior crucified on Calvary. Till, for the heart grasping such sweet mystery, and feeling the meaning of such common elements, all life becomes the sign and seal of God. Taught through the bread to see the death of Christ, man sees in his wealth the means of serving Christ. Trained through the cup to see redeeming blood, he finds in every meal a kindly providence. Led through the sprinkled water to see love, he goes into a world where are a thousand waters, and every wave that laps upon the shore is sacramental of the voice in heaven. Once let that spirit be realized, and no one can be worldly any more. We can use all things now as not abusing them, for all have a message from a realm unseen. And every place in our journey is a Bethel, with a ladder rising from it to the throne, and angels descending and ascending on it.

James the son of Zebedee, and John his
brother . . . mending their nets (Matt. 4:21).
The God of all grace . . . make you perfect
(1 Peter 5:10).

7

The Net Mender

We have all seen fishermen upon a summer morning mending their nets on the seashore. With a patience and a skill that we have envied, we have watched them busy at their task. These bronzed faces, and strong and vigorous frames, tell of many a year upon the deep. We can picture the men handling their boats magnificently when the wind is freshening into angry storm. And now in the quiet of the summer morning, when the waves are idly lapping on the beach, they are busied with the mending of their nets. It was thus that James and John were busied when they received the call that changed their lives. Their boat was rocking in the shallow water, and they were chatting, and working as they chatted. And then came Jesus, and claimed them for Himself, and called them into the service of discipleship, and they left everything and followed Him.

Now you will wonder why, with that Highland scene, I have associated these words of Peter. Well, the reason is a very simple one, although perhaps not lying on the surface. The word that Peter uses here for "make you perfect," is the same word as is used for mending of the nets. It is as if Peter had said, The God of grace, whatever else He may do, will mend your nets for you. And when you remember that Peter was a fisherman, and had spent many a day upon the Sea of Galilee, it seems impossible that he should have used the word without some recollection of his craft. Our calling, whatever it may be, has a way of coloring the words we use. It touches language with old associations, and gives it some of the music of the past. So Peter, in the throng and stir of Babylon, writing his letter of comfort to the churches, flashed back in thought again to the old days, when the water was lapping on his boat. The God of grace will make you perfect. The God of grace will mend your nets for you. Our nets are sorely broken in the boat, and the God of grace is the great net mender. It is on that figure I want to dwell tonight, and to try to discover some of its significance, for that it was often present to the first disciples there cannot be a shadow of a doubt.

Now first, how are nets usually broken? That is a question which is worth considering. Well, I was talking to an old fisherman this summer, and the gist of what he said was of this nature.

Sometimes, he told me, nets are broken by the *ordinary wear and tear* of fishing. They get worn out here, and they get worn out there, through the rough handling of the common day. There is no reason to suspect that they were bad nets. They may have been purchased from the finest maker. Nor have they met with any accident, such as may happen to the most skillful fisherman. But fishing is rough work at the best of it, and the handling of tackle never can be gentle; and so as the days pass—now here, now there—the fisherman comes to find his nets are broken. There are points where the net is very apt to break, but it is not always there the breakage happens. Sometimes in the least expected quarter, unexpectedly, a rent appears. And so, my brother, in these lives of ours is there often a breaking down through wear and tear, and sometimes the breaking is at the very point where you and I might never have expected it. There are men who have never been great sinners, as we put it. They have never had extraordinary trials. They have only had the wear and tear of life—the strain of business and the stress of home. And yet sometimes that very wear and tear has spoilt all that was finest and most beautiful, and the temper is irritable, and the heart is sullen, and the net, so delicately made, is broken.

Again he told me that nets are often broken through *the encountering of some jagged obstacle*. They are caught by some obstruction in the deeps, and, clearing themselves free of it, are torn. It may be a piece of wreckage in the sea, jagged, and with iron spikes upon it. It may be the sharp edge of some familiar reef, that has been swept clear of its seaweed by the storm. But whatever it is, the net goes dragging over it, and dragging over it is caught and rent, and tearing itself free in desperate effort it gapes disfigured like some wounded thing. Are there no human lives like that? No nets mystical that are so broken? It may be a hidden and surprising sin that does it; it may be a sudden and overwhelming sorrow; it may be the ruin of a cherished friendship, or the wreckage of a love that meant the world, or some swift insight into another's baseness, where once we dreamed there was sincerity. In such an hour as that the net is rent. There is a tearing of the very heartstrings. And faith is shattered, and God is but a name, and life seems the most shallow of all sophistries. For always, when we lose our faith in man, there falls a shadow on our faith in God, so that the very stars seem masterless, and goodness but the mockery of a dream.

And then he told me that nets are sometimes broken through *the very wealth of the sea that they enclose.* And he did not need to tell me that, for I had read it as a child in Holy Scripture. I remembered a scene on that same sea of Galilee when the disciples had toiled all night and had caught nothing. And then in the morning came the Master—it is always morning when the Master comes. And He bade them cast upon the other side, and casting so, their nets were filled with fishes—filled with such a great abundance of them that the nets, as we read, began to break. My friend, it seems a thing incredible that the gifts of a good God should break the nets. Does it not seem unlike divine compassion that the very wealth of heaven should lead to ruin? Yet are there lives on every hand of us—God grant that yours and mine be not among them—where nets are broken just because God is good. What I mean is, that life has been so easy that all that is best and noblest has decayed. Prosperity has had a hardening influence, and luxury has contracted every sympathy. Powered with everything that makes life rich—surrounded with all imaginable comforts, how many there are who have never done a hand's turn to leave the world better than they found it!

So far then on the breaking of the nets. Now will you think of the loss when they are broken? Well, to begin with, remember it is the loss of the most important possession of the fisherman. If his cottage is burned he can still ply his calling, and be out providing for his wife and children. If a blight falls upon his little garden, it is hard, but it is not unbearable. But if his nets are useless all is useless, and his very livelihood is swept away, and other boats shall hoist their sails tonight, but his shall rock idly in the harbor. There are some losses that are insignificant, and only a foolish man will trouble over them. But there are other losses that are vital, and affect everything, and are determinative. So with a fisherman is a lost net, and so with every man is a lost life, which is not lived to the glory of its Maker, and has never known the joy of doing good. All other losses, matched with that, are comparatively insignificant. The loss of health may be a bitter thing, and the loss of a fortune may be very terrible. But the one loss that cuts down to the quick, and calls for mercy in the heart of heaven, is not lost health nor lost prosperity: it is lost life and opportunity. It is a mighty thing to save the soul; but we want to save the life as well as save the soul. We want to have sin conquered, and habits brought to heel, and time redeemed, and something worthy done. And it is just when we are doubting of all that, and wondering if there be any hope for us, that the Bible comes to us, a seaborne people, and says, The God of grace will mend your nets. He will do it by His pardoning mercy, that forgives everything for Jesus' sake. He will do it by His upholding power, that will never leave us nor forsake us. He will do it perfectly, and do it now, and do it for the weakest and the worst, for the God of all grace will make you perfect.

But not only is it a vital loss. It is a peculiarly distressing loss, for this reason. The loss of the rent net entails the missing of riches that are at hand on every side. If one of our whalers were to be wrecked off Orkney,[1] it would lose a harvest that was far away. There are a thousand miles between the whaling ground and the wild cliffs and stormy seas of Orkney. But when a net was rent upon the sea of Galilee, it meant not the loss of a far-distant harvest, it meant the loss of what was just at hand. *There* were the shoals of fish in the blue waters. They were in the very depths where the boats lay. They were not far away in other seas; they were where Peter was, and John and James. And that was the pity of the useless net, that all that was precious was so near at hand, and yet, for all the power to take it, might have been a thousand miles away. My friend, the God of grace will mend your nets. He will give you the wealth that is lying near at hand. He will mend your nets, not for some distant fishing—but for the fishing where your barque is tonight He will redeem for you *your* opportunities, and show you new meanings in

1. northeast Scotland

your daily task, and give you the wealth that is on every hand of you, although it may be you have never dreamed of it. Home will be different from what it has ever been; it will be so full of peace and happiness. Work will be different from what it has ever been, for it will all be done with new ideals. And on every hand of you, all unsuspected once, will be opportunities of doing good, and of helping someone who has need of help, although you never saw that need before. The God of grace will make you perfect. The God of grace will mend your nets for you. He will sweep into your poor barren life the riches that are there just for the taking. For the gladdest things are never far away, nor hidden in distant oceans inaccessible, but they are here where you and I are living, and where eyes of love answer to our own.

And so we come to the work itself of net mending, and I ask in closing what kind of work is that? Well, in the first place, you will agree with me that *it is a work that calls for very perfect skill.* Have you never been amazed at the deft fingers of some rough old fisherman upon the Clyde? Those hands of his, so brawny and so powerful—they could hoist any sail and manage any sheet. But the beautiful thing is that these very hands, all rough and seamed and hardened with the weather, will work as delicately as a woman's hands in the fine work of mending nets. Were you and I to try it—what a failure! What a hopeless tangle we would make of things! We have our own bit of work that we can do, but the one thing we could never do is that. Yet he, with hands as deft as any woman's, and with an eye that sees right through the tangle, makes his gear ready for the deeps. I have often thought that God's hands were like those hands. They too are powerful, and can grasp tremendously, when the wind is high and when the waves are raging. But they, too, with a delicacy infinite, and with a tenderness surpassing that of women, can mend the broken net upon life's shore. The hand of Christ was mighty to command. When it was lifted up, the devils trembled. Yet that same hand, with what unerring skill did it ply its task upon the brokenhearted! It touched the weary, and they took heart again, and it was laid on the hopeless, and their hope was kindled, and it fell with a healing that was irresistible on lives that shrank from every other touch. That was the ministry of Christ on earth. That ever since has been His ministry. When wisdom has failed, and learning been inoperative, Christ has succeeded, and is succeeding still. For He knows our frame, and remembers we are dust, and He is infinitely strong and gentle; and He alone, if we but trust Him, can mend the broken net and make it perfect.

But it is not only a work that calls for skill, *it is a work that calls for patience* also. There are tasks you can hurry through, and get them done, but you can never hurry the mending of the net. That is indeed a recognized distinction between a first-rate fisher and a bad one. The one, impatient, will patch his nets up anyhow, that he may have leisure for the public house. But the other makes it a leisurely affair, and settles down to it, and is deliberate—so deliberate sometimes that you and I are inclined to be irritated at his slowness. But the man is not working for our shallow praise. He is working with a higher thought than that. For he loves that net of his with a strange love that you and I could never understand. So with a leisureliness that is old-fashioned now, in this age of telegraph and aeroplane, he works at the mending through the summer morning. There is a patience that is born of cowardice, and there is a patience that is born of love. The one is the patience of a broken-spirited people who have been crushed for ages by some tyrant. But the other is the patience of our fishermen, and it is also the patience of our God, who through length of days, as Newman sings, elaborates a people to His praise. If you and I are ever to be perfect, it will take infinite patience to achieve it. We are so backward—so ready to forget—such foolish scholars in the school of heaven. Blessed be God, that love which gave a Savior will never weary in its appointed task, till that has been made perfect which concerns us.

And then, in closing, this work of net mending, *is it not a work that involves hope*? There would be little use in mending any net if there were no hope of a harvest of the sea. Sometimes around the coasts of Scotland fish take what the fishermen call a flight. One year they are there in plenty, then unaccountably they disappear. And I know little towns upon our northern coasts where that has happened, and where hope was killed, and where the nets, so finely mended once, have hung upon the shore until they rotted. Always, when a net is mended, it means that there is hope for coming days. And always, when a life is mended, it means there is a harvest yet in store. And that is why, when a man yields up his will, and gives himself into the hand of God, hopes that were quenched begin to shine again, and the heart thrills with what is yet to be. We have sinned, and we have sinned exceedingly. We have done our very best to spoil our lives. We have wasted time, and squandered opportunity, and been unloving and utterly unworthy. Thanks be to God, spite of all that, and of things that may be darker far than that, the broken net is going to be mended. He forgives us even to the uttermost. He is pledged to save us even to the uttermost. Deeper than our deepest need are the infinite depths of His compassion. It is in such a faith that this September evening we give Him our lives which are so rent and ragged, assured that His grace will be sufficient for us, and His strength made perfect in our weakness.

Unto us a child is born (Isa. 9:6).
Before Abraham was, I am (John 8:58).

8

The Eternal Son

At Christmas, in common with all Christendom, our thoughts go gladly journeying toward Bethlehem. We see the manger, and the little Babe within it, and the shepherds listening to the song of angels. A birthday is always a great day, and Christmas is the greatest birthday of the year. There was no sounding of trumpets in any court about it, yet it was mightier than any birthday of the Caesars. We have only to think of all that Christ has been—we have only to think of all that Christ has done, to be thrilled by the ineffable grandeur of the hour, when to us a child was born.

Yet when we come to study the New Testament, there is one thing which very soon impresses us. It is that the birth of Jesus in its pages does not occupy the place we should have looked for. We might have expected that apostolic writers would have dwelt on it with adoring wonder. In every letter we might have thought to find unnumbered references to the birth of Jesus. Yet as we read the apostolic literature that is certainly what we do *not* find. There is many a thought flashed upward to the throne. There are very few flashed backward to the manger. It is not that Bethlehem is ignored. Still less is it that Bethlehem is denied. The impression rather is that it is lost in the full light of an overwhelming truth. It is lost, as it were, in the wonderful assurance that as their Lord is alive forevermore, so forever had He been alive in the bosom of the eternal Father. The fact is, we are out of touch a little with the apostles' conception of the Savior. For them His earthly life was like a valley between two peaks that rose into the heavens. And we are so fond of lingering in that valley that we almost forget the heights that close it in; but they, every hour that they lived, lifted up their eyes to the hills. So profound was the spiritual impression that Christ had made on them, that they could not conceive of Him as just another man. So overwhelmingly had He suggested God to them, that they could not think of a time when He began to be. Hence they who had lived with Him and seen His glory did not dwell on Bethlehem and the manger, but wrote "In the beginning was the Word, and the Word was God." To me it seems a very idle business to discuss the borrowing of that Logos doctrine. I shall be delighted if one shall prove to me that it was borrowed from the Alexandrian philosophy. To me the wonderful thing is that John *did* so find it as the expression of the divine activity, and felt in a flash it was a fitting category for the lowly prophet he had known in Galilee. He had no august traditions to uphold. He had no orthodox doctrine to maintain. He had only the memory of the beloved Master upon whose bosom he had lain at supper. And yet he felt as he remembered Him that nothing was so true to that remembrance as to say, "*In the beginning was the Word, and the Word was with God, and the Word was God.*" The one thing the apostles never do is to date the career of Jesus from His birth. For them, with all their marked divergencies, He was the eternal Son of God. They knew the gladness of the prophetic message, "For unto us a child is born," but they knew also with undimmed assurance that "Before Abraham was, I am."

Now if that were only apostolic doctrine, there are many who would treat the matter cavalierly. They would find for it historic parallels, and call the writers the children of their age. But the singular and indeed inexplicable thing is not that Christ's preexistence is apostolic doctrine, but that unquestionably it had its place in the mature consciousness of Christ Himself. Christ does not speak of Himself as being born. He says, "I am come," or "I was sent." "Father, glorify Thou Me," He says, "with the glory, which I had with Thee before the world was." And then there is the second of our texts tonight, a word that always thrills me when I hear it, "Before Abraham was, I am." My friend, if words mean anything at all, these words imply personal preexistence. You cannot explain them by thinking of the Son as eternally present to the thought of God. And remember it was not Paul who uttered them, nor Peter, nor the beloved John; it was Jesus, and Jesus was the truth. Well now, tonight what I want to do is this: I want to show you the bearings of that doctrine. I want to show you how all the joy of Christmas is really involved in its acceptance. I want to show you how vitally it touches all that is deepest and richest in the gospel, all that has won the heart and changed the life of innumerable thousands of mankind.

But before doing so there is one difficulty that I should like to dwell on for a moment. It is a difficulty that often has been felt, and perhaps especially at Christmas time. Was Christ conscious of that former life of His? Was it present to Him when He was a child? As He played in the village street of Nazareth did the glory He had left lie open to Him? I think that everyone of us must feel that any such consciousness of preexistence is fatal to the simple human charm of the infancy and youth of Jesus. Doubtless He had His childish dreams of that kingdom where time and space are not. Heaven lay about Him in His infancy as it lay about all of us when we were children. But to think that He was vividly conscious as a child that He had lived forever with the Father, is to pluck the heart of childhood from His bosom, and the innocent wonder of childhood from His eyes. I think that His birth was a sleep and a forgetting, though trailing clouds of glory He had come. I do not imagine that this knowledge reached Him by any easy way of reminiscence. I think that it was slowly formed within His mind as the choicest fruit of His filial obedience; that it emerged for Him into a perfect certainty out of the depths of His fellowship with God. When He was a child He thought as a child, for to us, we read, a *child* is born. And then He grew in knowledge and in wisdom, and was baptized with the Holy Spirit. Until at last His consciousness of sonship became so overwhelming and intense that it transcended time, and rose above beginning, and showed itself as an eternal thing. The closer that any being lives with God, the more does he feel that time is but a dream. Beginnings and endings are but incidents when there is the grip of the everlasting arms. And it was when Jesus, through the Holy Spirit, entered into all the riches of His sonship, that He realized in that absolute relationship something that had no beginning and no end. Only thus, I think, can you preserve unsullied the perfect childhood of our dear Redeemer. Only thus can you believe at Bethlehem that the Word was made flesh and dwelt among us. Only thus with all the joy of Christmas can we say, "For unto us a *child* is born"; and yet go out into the night and whisper, "Before Abraham was, I am."

What, then, are the spiritual values of Christ's preexistence? Let me indicate to you the three that are most evident. And the first is that *when we lose our hold on it, the love of God is dimmed.* For God so loved the world, not, that He *thought*—God so loved the world, not, that He *said*—God so loved the world that He *gave* His only-begotten Son for you and me. And the simple fact is that if Jesus Christ began to be in the hour when He was born, then in heaven there was no Son to cherish, and none in the fullness of the time to give. I learn the depth of a true mother's love from her unfailing spirit of self-sacrifice. I learn how dearly the patriot loves his country from his readiness to fight for it and die for it. And so alone do I learn the love of God, not from the beauty of the summer meadow, but from a deed of sacrifice more wonderful than ever mother or patriot achieved. It is not enough to tell me that God loves me. Life is far too tragically for that. You must show me a God giving His dearest for me if you would persuade me that I am dear to Him. And that is the one thing you can never show me if in the Godhead there was no society, no Son to love before the stars were kindled, and none in the fullness of the time to give. Take away the Lord's eternal being, and the love of God is but a speculation. I have to gather it from broken syllables, some of them far too bloody to be legible. I have to do my work and face my music and bear my suffering and meet my death, sustained by nothing in this world of shadows but the shadow and surmise of desire. My friend, it is not thus that men are conquerors. We are more than conquerors through Him who loved us. We need to know, not merely to conjecture, that in the heaven of heavens there is love. And of that transcendent fact there is no certainty, such as can be of service in the shadow, save the assurance of the heart that knows that the Word was made flesh and dwelt among us. I turn to nature, and ask, "Is God love?" And nature shows me the earthquake at Messina.[1] I turn to life, and life throws back the napkin from the cold faces of these little children in Dundee.[2] I turn to the earthly experience of Jesus, certain that there the love of God will shine, and lo, a cross, and a very bitter cry from it, "My God, My God, why hast Thou forsaken Me." Ah yes, but God so loved the world that He gave His

1. which destroyed the city in 1908.
2. A reference to some unidentified tragedy in Dundee, Scotland.

only-begotten Son. Once believe *that* to be the heart of history, and everything else can wait until the morning. Yet that is meaningless, and has no place in heaven, and ceases to be real as life is real, if Christ began to be when He was born.

Again, *if we lose our hold upon Christ's preexistence, then the glory of the life of Christ is dimmed.* It may still win us as a life of beauty, but it has ceased to awe us as a life of grace. For the grace of our Lord Jesus Christ is certainly *not* the fact that He was poor. The grace of our Lord Jesus Christ is this, that *though He was rich*, for us He became poor. It is this which has thrilled and awed the hearts of men—not that He whom they worshiped was a servant, but that being in the form of God, He took on Him willingly a servant's form. When the supper was ended, He laid aside His garments, and took a towel and washed His disciples' feet. It is a little picture, perfect in its outline, of the life of ministry that was so near its close. And what has awed men in that life of ministry has never been simply its lowliness of toil, but the thought that Christ in bending to His toil had laid aside His garments of eternity. Date everything from the birth hour at Bethlehem, and you have nothing left but the poverty of Christ. He is only another of that roll of heroes who have served heroically in a narrow lot. My friend, however inspiring that may be, it is certainly not the inspiration that has founded Christendom, and changed the hearts of men, and kindled the adoration of the ages. You know the grace of the Lord Jesus Christ, that though He was rich, for us He became poor. The conquering wonder of it all is not the poverty; it is the infinite wealth that was given up for poverty. It is not the manger—it is not the cross—it is the stooping from heaven to manger and to cross that has thrilled men as they never could be thrilled by any tale of patient, quiet endurance. In other words, remove the preexistence, and you lose the infinite grace of the Redeemer. There were no riches to be given up if Christ began to be when He was born. And therefore if you would know the joy of Christmas, it is not enough to say a child is born; you must launch out into the deeps and whisper, "Before Abraham was, I am."

Lastly, *if we lose our hold of Christ's preexistence, the glory of our humanity is dimmed.* We have lost our historical and abiding argument for the nobility and dignity of man. There was a time when that was easily credited, for man was the tenant of a mighty world. His world was the fixed center of God's universe, and the stars in their courses were its obedient servants. It was for man that the sun arose in splendor; it was for man that the hosts of heaven were marshaled; it was to tell the petty secrets of man's destiny that the kindly planets moved into conjunction. Citizen of such a noble kingdom, there could be little question about man's nobility. Waited on by all these glittering servants, man was only a little lower than the angels. But now the world has lost her proud centrality, and heaven has shifted and gone far away, and sun and stars have other work to do than to tell strange stories of the death of kings. Heaven is removed and become astronomical. There is no Jacob's ladder that can reach it now. The earth, to which all creation did obeisance once, is now but an atom on creation's outskirts. And all this knowledge has so impressed the mind with the insignificance of this our dwelling place, that there has stolen on the heart, like a dark shadow, the possible insignificance of man. "What is man that Thou art mindful of him"—a creature of a day upon a distant satellite? What is man whose life is as a vapor, on a far atom of a boundless universe? My brother, from all such sense of nothingness, there is no argument so mighty to redeem as the argument that God so loved the world that He gave His only-begotten Son for you and me. Christ took not on Him the nature of angels. He took on Him the seed of Abraham. He, the eternal Son of God, was found in fashion as a man. Why, sir, if that be historically true, then, son of man, stand upon thy feet! for you, child of an atom and a grave, are great and honorable forevermore. Seasons come when we all feel our greatness, but we need more than *feeling* for assurance. We want to have feeling in its loftiest hours confirmed by the witness of historic fact. And this I find, like the sound of some great bell, swinging slow across the driving storm, in the deep and solemn music of the truth, that the Word was made flesh and dwelt among us. Never again can I belittle man, if the eternal Son became man. Never again can I despise humanity, if He was found in the likeness of humanity. And never again can I be quite so certain of the infinite value of mankind to God, if Christ began to be when He was born. *Unto us a child is born*: yes, the gladness of Christmas is in that. It has hallowed home, and sanctified the child, and given new radiance to the eyes of motherhood. But remember that deep is calling unto deep, where the little infant is crying in the manger—and so go out into the night and say, "*Before Abraham was, I am.*"

Stay me with flagons, comfort me with apples (Song 2:5).

9

The Old Orchard

When I was in Mentone in the south of France last year, there was one eminent man who was often in my thoughts. It was Mr. Spurgeon, that honored minister of Christ, who in his years of weakness lived much at Mentone.[1] I used to look at the hotel he stayed in, and think of his courage when everything was dark. I used to think of the little companies who would gather there, while he broke the bread and preached the Word to them. So he, being dead, yet lived in grateful memory, for never surely have we had in England one who preached with greater power or fullness the unsearchable riches of Christ Jesus. Well, the other evening, turning over some old pamphlets, I chanced to light on an address by Mr. Spurgeon. It was an address delivered at Mentone to a little company upon this chapter. And in the course of it, and in a single sentence, he threw out a hint upon these words of ours, which has been working in me ever since, so that I have no help but to get it uttered. That is why I have chosen this strange text, and not at all because it is a strange text. What, think you, is at the heart of it, giving it a

1. The influential English Baptist preacher, Charles Haddon Spurgeon (1834–1892), who often recuperated at Mentone in southeast France.

spiritual significance? Well, this is what Mr. Spurgeon found in it, in his own imaginative and illuminative way, and you will see its force at once when I suggest it to you.

The speaker in this exquisite chapter is a beautiful and simple country maiden. The home of her childhood has been a country home; her lot has been cast in sweet and pleasant places. Over her head the apple trees are bowing, rich in their wealth of blossom in the spring. Under her feet there is no marble pavement, but God's embroidery of the green grass. And it is there, where life is pastoral, and habits are simple, and eyes are big with innocence, that her mysterious lover woos and wins her. I call him mysterious, because, foreshadowing Christ, he is no peasant, but a prince disguised. He is the son of a king, although she knows it not, when she opens her heart to him and takes him in. But the hour comes when he declares himself, and whispers in her ear his royal lineage; and then he brings her into his banqueting house, and the banner over her is love. From that moment the old life is gone, and a new life has now become inevitable. No longer is she a simple country maiden; she moves amid the halls of a royal palace. And it is now, not shrinking from her station, but quite unable to banish tender memories, that her thought flies back to the old rustic days, and she cries, "Comfort me with apples." Amid all the splendors of the palace, her thought goes yearning back to the old orchard. She sees the blossom on the trees again, and the lush grass where as a girl she played. And all the lights, and all the stately music, and all the pomp and pageantry of kings cannot quite fill up that tender heart that once was happy in a simple peace. Stay me with flagons—nay, they will never do it. Hence with the flagons—comfort me with apples. Let me get back again what I have forfeited in this glittering and artificial life. So does she yearn after a lost simplicity, when God was near, and when delights were innocent, when all that she needed to be supremely happy was the sunshine, and the streamlet, and the grass.

Now it seems to me that this same yearning is audible in many spheres of life. We have it, for instance, in many different accents, in every highly civilized society. Of all the gains that civilization has won for us, I am fully and gratefully aware. It has enabled man to realize himself to an extent undreamed of in an earlier day. Yet in different accents, some of them pathetic, and some of them thrilling and throbbing with revolt, you may catch the yearning, in civilized society, for something that in the progress has been lost. Men scarce can see the forest for the trees now, they are so immersed in multifarious duties; life is elaborate and artificial, and there is constant excitement, and no rest; and at the heart of all that stir and glamour, often, if you have ears to hear, you shall detect the note of this fair Shulamite, crying in palaces, "Comfort me with apples." You have it in every social craze for an unhampered and a simpler life. You have it in that love of gardens, which is so characteristic of today. You have it in the new interest in children, with their hearts of wonder and their eyes of innocence, from whom at their one word God is not far away, when of such little immortals is the kingdom. All these features of artificial life are but the different echoes of one yearning. They are the quiet reverting of the heart from the hall of banqueting to the old orchard. They are the craving for that sweet simplicity, and leisured peace, and reverence and love, which are so hard to find and hard to cherish in the jostle of the city street. Stay me with flagons—that is the cry of man to the wealth and luxury which time has won. And wealth responds, and builds him noble houses, and gives him costly and exciting pleasures. And then the human heart, a little weary, and not quite satisfied with all its getting, sees the old orchard where the grass was green, and whispers, "Comfort me with apples."

The same thing is also often seen in what we call a prosperous career. It has often been noted with what a wistful fondness men hark back again to struggling days. You get a man who has succeeded in life; who has fought his way from poverty to riches. You get him alone, when he is at his best, and when he is sure of a sympathetic hearer. And you know how often, when the tongue is loosened, it is not his present prosperity he dwells on; it is rather on these stern and struggling days, when the only gold was the mystic gold of dreams. He will tell you the hard story of his boyhood—of his rough handling and of his sorry lodging. He will tell you of how he rose to study, and of how he starved himself to buy a book. And he will tell you perhaps of some true heart that loved him, and sent him singing through the hardest of it, and made his home, though it was poorly furnished, a shelter from the storm and a shadow from the heat. *Now* he has everything that wealth can give; every luxury that riches can command. There is no denial now; no anxious questioning before the purchasing of this or that. And yet in these moments, when the deeps are opened, with what a tender and affecting wistfulness does he look back out of the house of banqueting to the old and vanished orchard days. He has won much, but he has lost a little, and with all his gains he knows that he has lost it. That hope unclouded—that love which was so sweet—that eager heart which sang in the gray morning. And though he does not murmur nor repine, for God has been wonderfully good to him, yet are there times when he too, like the Shulamite, yearns for the greenness of the summer grass. Stay me with flagons, is his cry. And wealth supports him with all her staying power. She gives him every comfort in the world, and power with men, and countless opportunities. Yet he too, like the maiden in the palace, where pillars were marble and where cups were golden, may sometimes whisper, Comfort me with apples.

Do you remember how Russell Lowell[2] puts that?

When I was a beggarly boy,
And lived in a cellar damp,
I had not a friend nor a toy,
But I had Aladdin's lamp;
When I could not sleep for cold,
I had fire enough in my brain,
And builded with roofs of gold
My beautiful castles in Spain.

Since then I have toiled day and night,
I have money and power good store,
But I'd give all my lamps of silver bright
For the one that is mine no more.
Take, fortune, whatever you choose,
You gave, and may snatch again,
I have nothing 'twould pain me to lose,
For I own no more castles in Spain.

The same craving again is very evident in the long history of the church of Christ. Ever and anon the church has been rekindled into a passion for a lost simplicity. I do not know if any of you happen to have read a great biography that was published recently. I refer to the biography of Cardinal Newman,[3] that subtle, sensitive, spiritual genius. Well, one thing which grows clear in that biography is Newman's devotion to the medieval church, and what a magnificence that church enjoyed the readers of his pages will discover. It had been brought into the banqueting house, though its banner was

2. James Russell Lowell (1819–1891), American poet.
3. John Henry Cardinal Newman (1801–1890), English theologian and writer.

scarce that of love. And its ritual was splendid, and its cathedrals wonderful, and its worship mysterious and awful; yet at the heart of all that ornate splendor, shining gloriously across a darkened Europe, what an unquenchable desire there was for a more still and reverent simplicity. It showed itself in the monastic cell, where men went to be alone with God. It showed itself in sweet and simple hymns, which with adoring hearts we are yet singing. And it showed itself in the fullness of its power, when the appointed time of reformation came, and when hearts that all the splendor had not comforted, were comforted by the simplicity of God. Out of the heart of that medieval church there rose the cry, Comfort me with apples. There was born the craving in it for a life in God which should be simpler than all that magnificence. And it was that craving which was divinely answered when the season of reformation came, and when every believing heart was recognized as the sanctuary of the Father in Christ Jesus. For the simplest hymns are after all the best hymns, and the simplest prayers are after all the best prayers, and the simplest preaching, if it be true to Christ, is after all the preaching which has power. And sooner or later, out of all magnificence, the church comes back to that and is at rest, as to the orchard where the sun is warm, and the morning shadows are sleeping on the grass. Stay me with flagons, cries the soul of man, and the church answers with her golden chalices. And she clothes her priests with many-colored vestments, and lights her candles, and rings her silver bells. Yet even the poorest heart is far too wonderful ever to remain satisfied with that, and sooner or later out of the hall of banqueting there comes the yearning, Comfort me with apples. Give me back again the simple prayer that is more than the echo of a printed book. Take away that concert music, and give me music that rises from the heart. Speak to me, not in the Latin tongue, but in the tongue that I can understand, when life is difficult, and ways are dark, and heart and flesh are fainting in the valley. Such were the hymns of apostolic times. Such were the prayers of apostolic times. Such was the preaching of the Word, and such the sacrament, in the days when the church was mighty and prevailed. And always from the midst of ornate worship and elaborate ritual and costly ceremonial there rises heavenward the cry unquenchable of the Shulamite in the palace of her lord. For the church is not only saved by going forward. The church is also saved by going backward: backward through all the growth of centuries to the sweet simplicities of early faith; back to the day when there was no cathedral, nor pulpit, nor loud resounding organ, but only a living and a burning faith that Jesus Christ was risen from the dead.

I have often thought, too, that this same yearning was to be traced in reference to the Bible. From all the wealth and glory of our literature men find themselves craving for that old book again. I will make bold to say that there is no one here tonight who loves good literature more than I do. I will make bold to say that there is no man here who better knows all its sustaining power. Yet God so orders this strange life of ours that for most men sooner or later comes the season when the one book that saves us from despair is the book that we read from at our mother's knee. It is not that other books have got no message. If they are living books they are the gifts of God. And they hail us as with the voice of comradeship when we are wrestling forward to the sunrise. But life, even the poorest life, has needs so deep, and mysteries so mighty, that there come seasons when the word of man is powerless, and the only power is the Word of God. Do you remember what Coleridge[4] said about the Bible? It is a very significant confession. He, a voracious and extensive reader, said it found him as no other book had done—found him in the secrets of his heart, and in the needs that he could never utter, and in the questionings that are forever rising in the steady pressure of the great realities. Let a man ignore his Bible for long years. Let him read nothing but the novel and the newspaper. Yet I shall tell you what so often happens in a land where we breathe the Christian air from birth. Sooner or later comes to him a day when novel and newspaper are ineffectual, and his heart yearns, as did the bride of Solomon, for the green pastures of the Word again. Need I recall to you the words of Scott[5] as he lay dying where the Tweed[6] made music? "Lockhart," he said, "read to me from the Book"; and Lockhart[7] said to him, "Which book, sir?" And then Sir Walter, the same great, simple gentleman in death as he had been in life, said, "My dear, there is only one Book." What a poorer world it would have been for some of us without those glorious novels of Sir Walter. And what a poorer world it would have been for him without his ballads and his Shakespeare and his Dryden. Yet when the hand of Almighty God had touched him, and

---

4. Samuel Taylor Coleridge (1772–1834), English poet and literary critic.
5. Sir Walter Scott (1771–1832), Scottish novelist and poet.
6. The river Tweed in southeast Scotland.
7. John Gibson Lockhart (1794–1854), Scottish lawyer and biographer of Scott.

when deep was calling unto deep, "My dear," he said, "there is only one Book." That is why our grave and reverent forefathers always spoke of the Bible as *the Book.* "Bring me the Book," and the wife brought the Book, and there was family worship in the cottage. From scenes like these old Scotia's grandeur springs—from hearts that were proud that sons should be book learned, yet knew that for the depths as for the heights there was but one book worthy of the name. My younger brother, I who love all literature earnestly counsel you not to neglect the Bible. I who can lose myself for hours in Shakespeare beg of you not to leave the Book unread. For it can find you as no other book can, and it can guide you as no other book can guide you, and it can put its mighty arms around you when other hands are but groping in the gloom. Stay me with flagons, we cry out to literature, and literature answers in her royal way. And she brings the wine of Shakespeare and of Milton, and of Tennyson[8] and of Browning[9] and of Meredith.[10] Yet still the heart, in that royal house of banqueting, where the poorest student shall sit and feast with kings, has somewhat of yearning in it still unanswered, and cries like the Shulamite, Comfort me with apples.

And then lastly, and in a larger sense, I think that this is true of all our spiritual knowledge. Life has a way of bringing us back again to a few simple and elemental things. Just as a man, when years are passing over him, likes to revisit the scenes of happy childhood, and, coming home from Australia or from Canada, will go to see the village where he played; so often, after many a high adventure, and crossing of the deeps into far regions, do men come home again to a few simple truths that shine for them in the light of long ago. You remember how true that was of Paul as we read his history in the New Testament. Paul was converted on the Damascus road and brought there into the fellowship of Jesus. And then with a spiritual daring that was splendid Paul pressed forward into the grace of Christ, and scaled the heights and sounded all the depths of the liberty wherewith Christ had made him free. What mighty themes he handles in his letters! What profound mysteries he grapples with! Verily in these same letters there are things hard to be understood. And yet as we read the story of the Acts, when the days of his activity were well-nigh over, we find him coming back, with glow-

8. Alfred (Lord) Tennyson (1809–1892), English poet.
9. Robert Browning (1812–1889), English poet.
10. George Meredith (1828–1909), English novelist and poet.

ing heart, to the early days on the Damascus road. On that all his theology was built. From that all his experiences sprung. Ever acquiring more and more of Christ, that day still shone in all its early wonder. And so at the end we have no loftier argument than just the telling of the Damascus story, when the light shone on him, and when the voice was heard, and he was led by the hand into the city. In some small measure, according to our years, we all have a life-history like that. For all of us, if we be really living, ought to be sounding the deep things of God. And yet how certainly life brings us back again, out of all mystery and all perplexity, to some few simple elemental truths, rich in the memories of long ago. "What is the greatest discovery you ever made?" said one to Sir James Simpson,[11] who discovered chloroform. "What was the greatest discovery I ever made?" he answered, "It was the discovery that I had a Savior." And amid all the triumphs of his years, well-won, with a heart as brave as that of Paul, on that he rested, and to that returned, as the one rock for the foot of mortal man. If there is one thing for which I thank my God, it is that ours is not an easy faith. I should distrust with all my heart an easy faith, in a life and in a universe so difficult. But if there are problems in it that we shall never solve and deeps in it that we shall never penetrate, I do rejoice that at its very heart is the saving power of a redeeming love. Stay me with flagons, I cry to my religion, and it offers me the cordials of the strong. It bids me drink of the chalice of election, and of the two mysterious natures in one person. And then when, a little weary of it all, I cry like the Shulamite, Comfort me with apples, it says to me, My child, you are a sinner, and Jesus in His love has died for you. So am I back in the orchard once again, though now my dwelling be in the house of kings. So do I hear the wind among the branches when the music of the palace is beyond me. So out of every massive argument, stately and noble as the hall of princes, do I steal away in heart to the quiet shadow, and say, My beloved is mine and I am His.

---

11. Sir James Young Simpson (1811–1870), distinguished Scottish medical scientist.

Two of them went that same day to a
village called Emmaus (Luke 24:13–35).

10

The Road to Emmaus

Of all the appearances of the risen Christ, none has a stronger hold upon Christendom than this one. It has brought light to many darkened hearts, and comfort to innumerable souls. Christ revealed Himself to Mary in the garden, and that will always be precious to the church. He revealed Himself to the Eleven, and to Thomas, and to Peter and to John beside the Sea of Galilee. But this meeting on the Emmaus road, with its revelation of the living Savior, is engraven on the universal heart.

Who these two were we cannot tell. We know nothing about them except the name of one of them. And we are not at liberty to associate that name *Cleophas* with the *Klopas* who is mentioned in the gospels. That they were not of the eleven disciples is certain, for it was to the Eleven that they hurried with their news. They were clearly on intimate terms with the apostles, for they knew where they lodged when they went straight to them. But beyond that we know nothing of the men, neither their story in the days before the cross, nor yet their service in the coming years when the Holy Spirit was given at Pentecost. They were in no sense distinguished persons. They were not outstanding in their zeal or love. They occupied no place of proud preeminence among those who had been followers of the Lord. And I take it as characteristic of the Lord that in the glory of His resurrection life He gave Himself with such fullness of disclosure to those unknown and undistinguished men. It reminds one vividly of that earlier hour when He had talked with the woman of Samaria. She too was nameless, and utterly obscure, yet with *her* had He lingered in the richest converse. And now the cross has come, and He has died and risen, yet being risen He is still unchanged, for He still reveals Himself to lowly hearts. Here is the Savior for the common man. Here is the Lord who does not spurn the humble. Here is the Master of all those obscure lives that are yet precious in the sight of heaven. Had these two travelers been John and Peter, we might have hesitated to take home their rich experience, but being what they were, they are our brothers.

First then let us try to understand the state of mind of these two travelers. And in the first place this is notable *that these two travelers had lost their hopes.* There was a time, not so long ago, when their hopes had been burning brightly like a star. They trusted this was He who would redeem Israel—that was the glowing conviction of their hearts. And as they followed Jesus in His public ministry, and saw His miracles, and heard His words, brighter and ever brighter grew the hope that this was the Christ, the Son of the living God. Even the cross itself had not dispelled their hopes, for they remembered that He had talked of that. They remembered that He had said, "Destroy this temple, and in three days I will raise it up again." But now the third day's sun was near to setting, and darkness was soon to fall upon the world, and a great darkness, heavier than sunset, was beginning to cast its shadow on their hearts. It was true that some women had come hurrying in, bearing the tidings that the tomb was empty. But it was one thing to be told the tomb was empty, and quite another to believe that Christ was risen. And even the women had confessed, when questioned, that they had not seen the Lord Himself, but only an empty grave, and the stone rolled away, and certain mysterious shapes they took for angels. Clearly, then, their Master had not risen. He was still sleeping somewhere beneath that Syrian sky. They would never see Him again, nor hear His words, nor follow Him through any village street. And so that evening, journeying to Emmaus, they were men convinced that they had lost their Lord, and having lost Him they had lost their hopes. Are there any here who are like these men? Any who have lost their hope in Christ? Any to whom Christ was very real once, and who now have a name to live and yet are dead? My brother and sister, if that be your condition—if once you had a hope that now is dimmed—you are like these two journeying to Emmaus.

Then in the next place this is notable, that *these two travelers had lost their gladness.* "What are you speaking of," said Jesus to them, "as you walk together and are sad?" Sometimes, as we pass along the streets, we meet a face of unutterable sadness. Sorrow is stamped on every lineament of it, all the more tragic because a smile is there. And when we see it, amid the crowd of faces that bear no trace of any great experience, it haunts us so that it is long ere we forget it. Now that is what our Lord seems to have noticed, graven deep upon the faces of these travelers. "What are you talking about," He said to them, "as you walk together and are sad?" The utter absence of joy upon their faces—the look of melancholy and of sorrow—touched at once His tender loving heart. And can you wonder that their looks were sad, when all that brightened life for them was gone? A hopeless heart may be a very brave heart, but I never heard that it was a merry heart. So these two disciples, having lost their hopes, had lost that gladness which is the child of hope, and as they walked together they were sad.

So long as Jesus Christ had been alive, there had been a great gladness in their hearts. Only to see Him had been like music to them, as it always is with anyone we love. That they had had their troubles just like other people is only to say that they were human. Perhaps they were farmers struggling with short harvests, or fishermen who had often toiled and had caught nothing. But this was certain, that in Jesus' company their deepest experience was a great gladness, a joy that they never could quite fathom, and yet which they knew to be intensely real. Always in His society there was delight. There was a feeling of peace and of security. When He was with them all their care and worry took to itself wings and fled away. But now their Lord has passed beyond their knowledge, and it was like the passing of the sunshine for them, and as they walked together they were sad. Now sadness is of many kinds. There is the sadness which the exile feels when he is far away from home and kindred, and when in the thronging of the crowd around him he catches no glimpse of a familiar face. There is the sadness which the aged feel, when they remember happy days now gone forever; and there is the sadness of the open grave. All these are elements of our mortality, but there is a spiritual sadness different from these, and the cause of it is an absent Lord. When in prayer the heavens seem as brass, when the Bible loses its fragrance and its dew, when spiritual books begin to pall on us, when the services of the house of God become a weariness, then is the heart of the true disciple sad. Then does one feel as if Jesus had not risen, and as if all one's hopes in Him had been a mockery. Then do men cry the exceeding bitter cry, "They have taken away my Lord, and I know not where they have laid Him." And should there be any of God's children here this evening who are suffering from such spiritual desertion, I beg of them to remember that their frame of heart is like that of the two journeying to Emmaus.

But there is one thing more that is notable, and it is this, that *these two had lost none of their desire*. They had lost their hope and they had lost their gladness, but they had lost none of their desire. That afternoon, walking to Emmaus, their talk was all of the Lord Jesus Christ. And from a hint in the original, we learn that their talk was animated, intense, and eager. They were talking loudly, and the words were being flung one to the other, for out of the fullness of the heart the mouth was speaking. Someone has said, and there is truth in it, that our friends are never really ours till we have lost them. Only then, undimmed and unobscured, does the vision of them arise within our hearts. And as it is with those whom we have loved, and who have left us and passed into the shadow, so was it with these disciples and their Lord. They never understood how much they needed Him until the day when they thought that He was gone. They never understood how much they loved Him, till the shadow of parting had fallen on their love. But now they knew it, and so, that dreary day, their talk as they journeyed was all of Jesus Christ, and the deepest desire of their hearts was this: O that I knew where I might find Him! Are there any here this evening who in the secret of their souls are saying that? Careless and prayerless, backsliding and worldly, are you coming to feel you cannot live without Him? If so—if as the hart for the waterbrooks, unsatisfied, you thirst for the living God—remember you have a kinship with these two.

Such then was the spiritual condition of these men, and now we want to know how Jesus dealt with them. We want to follow the successive stages by which He gave them back their joy and peace.

In the first place, then, and passing by minor matters, He showed them the supreme necessity of His death. "Ought not Christ," He said, "to have suffered these things, that so He might enter into glory?" We may take it for certain that these two disciples had never really grasped the need that Christ should die. They had shared in the common hope that He would reign, and it was a throne they were dreaming of and not a cross. If any dark surmisings had arisen in them, stirred by the mysterious words of Jesus, they had crushed them as something too terrible to contemplate. That He whom they loved should die a felon's death was something too awful to believe. And when it happened—there, before their eyes—it seemed a hideous and irreparable calamity. It was as if there had been some mistake in heaven; as if the will of the Eternal had been baffled; as if powers were abroad defying the Messiah, and hurrying His triumph into tragedy. And then Christ met them, and spoke about His death, and they learned that the crucifixion was no accident. It was no longer the greatest of calamities; it became the greatest of necessities. Ought not Christ to have suffered these things? And they saw its moral and spiritual grandeur, and it dawned upon them that the cross they loathed was something more wonderful than any crown. It was *then* that their hearts began to burn within them, and the light to break upon their darkened souls. And everything looked different to them now when they saw the meaning of the death of Jesus. And I venture to say that it is always so with hearts that are hungering for the living God—the primary step toward fellowship and peace is to come face to face with the death of Jesus Christ. That I am a sinner and cannot save myself—that God has provided an all-sufficient Savior—that He has died for me, and that I die in Him, and through His death reach up to heaven again, all this, so simple that a child can grasp it, and yet so deep that angels cannot fathom it, is the basis of our peace with God. Think not to comprehend all that it means. The deepest we can never comprehend. Call it a substitution if you will—call it an atonement, call it anything. The vital thing is not what you may call it; the vital thing is to grasp it and to feel it, and feeling it to find that in the blood of Christ there is peace of conscience and fellowship with God.

Then the next step our Savior took was to lead them back to the Word of God again. "Beginning at Moses and at all the prophets, He expounded unto them the things concerning Himself." We know from the gospels how Christ had loved the Scripture in the days of His ministry before the cross. We know how He used it when He was tempted, and how He preached from it in the synagogue of Nazareth. And it is a sign to us that He is still the same, though He has passed into the resurrection glory, that He still goes back to the old familiar Scripture which He had learned beside His mother's knee. It is a singular thing that, after He was risen, Christ never once appeared to His mother. The name of Mary is never mentioned once in the forty days of our Savior's resurrection. But I sometimes think that when she heard these two rehearsing all that He had taught them from the Scripture, she would have her own sweet secret memories of the old home, and would be quietly certain she was not forgotten. Had these two travelers, then, been neglecting their Bibles? I do not think that that is the least likely. Probably they knew Moses and the prophets far better than any of us in the church tonight. But I want you to think what Scripture must have meant to them in all manner of unexpected depth and fullness, when the interpreter of it was the Lord Jesus Christ. You and I may have listened to some saintly preacher drawing out the inner meaning of God's Word. And as we did so, our hearts burned within us, and we saw what we had never seen before. And if that be so with an erring, sinful minister, I want you to try to think what it must have been when the risen Son of God handled the Scripture, and showed these two the meaning of it all. Once again they heard of the Paschal Lamb, and of the brazen serpent in the wilderness, and of the smitten shepherd in the book of Zechariah, and of the suffering servant in Isaiah. But hearing it all interpreted by Christ, the Bible became a living book to them, and in the hour when it became a living book, they found that Christ Himself was by their side. Once more do I venture to suggest that it is always so in the experience of the soul. One of the surest signs that Christ is nigh is when He makes the Bible live again. It is a living Christ who makes a living Scripture, and when He is going to reveal Himself to us, passages that we have known since we were children begin once more to live and burn for us. If Christ be absent, then all the lore of ages will never make the Word a living book. If Christ be dead for us, in heart and conscience, then is the Bible always a dead book. But when old texts take a strange grip of us, when they haunt us through the market and the street, when we cannot silence some gracious invitation, when we cannot shake off some oracle of warning, when promises come like music to the ear in days of despondency or hours of peril, when some great text that we have long ignored reaches out its loving hands to us—I say that when *that* happens to a man, the risen Savior is not far away. That was what the two disciples found. The Bible became a living book to them. And their hearts burned within them as they heard again the echo of the old familiar passages. And it all meant that He whom they thought vanished was not vanished but at their very side, though their eyes were holden, and they did not know Him.

And then He revealed Himself in the breaking of the bread, and it seems like an anticlimax, does it not? After all this marshaled preparation, shall we not look for something far more glorious? We shall have some vision that will strike the senses? We shall have some flash of glory on the eye? But He revealed Himself *in the breaking of the bread.* It was in no sense a sacramental meal, as we use that word *sacrament* in our theology. It was a frugal supper in a village home of two tired travelers, and another. Yet it was then—in the breaking of the bread, and not in any vision of resurrection splendor—that they knew that their companion was the Lord. How that discovery flashed upon their hearts, the Bible, so wonderful in its silences, does not tell. It may have been the quiet air of majesty with which He took at once the place of host, when they had invited Him in to be their guest. It may have been the familiar word of blessing that awakened sweet memories of Galilean days. Or it may have been that as He put forth His hand after the blessing to take the bread and break it, they saw that it was a hand which had been pierced. However it was, whether by word or hand, they felt irresistibly that this was He. Some little action, some dear familiar trait, told them in a flash this was the Christ. Not in some vision of resurrection glory, but in some characteristic movement of the fingers, maybe, they recognized that they found their Lord. In daily life we are always meeting that—the revelation of the insignificant. A certain trick of speech—a tone, a look—and someone whom we have lost is at our side again. And so when a man has spiritually lost his Savior, and is being restored to the joy of his first love, it is often so that the Lord reveals Himself. Our commonest mercies come to gleam on us as the most wonderful of all created things. Our sicknesses, our trials, our disappointments, are all transfigured with a Father's love. Until at last though we have seen no vision, and have only had common meals and common mercies, we too are thrilled and say, "It is the Lord." When that deep certainty once fills a man it seems as if nothing else could ever matter. When that deep certainty once fills a man, in a real sense for him to live is Christ. When that deep certainty once fills a man he will hurry like these two disciples to Jerusalem, and tell out, though he may not say a word, that he has seen the Lord.

But call to remembrance the former days
in which, after ye were illuminated, ye
endured a great fight of afflictions
(Heb. 10:32).

11

The Anguish of the Light

This is a very remarkable conclusion to a verse that suggests the blessings of the light: it is one of those suggestive anticlimaxes that are so familiar to students of the Scriptures. No blessing is nobler than illumination. It tells of the benediction of the light. It speaks of a life that has arisen from darkness, and moved into the glorious shining of the sun. And yet, when we expect to hear of summer's gladness, and to catch the sound of music in blue heaven, we hear of battle, with its blood and misery, and the cry and agony of wounded men. After illumination a great joy? We should have looked for some conclusion such as that. After illumination a great sense of liberty, and a peace that the world cannot take away? Scripture does not deny these blessed consequences, but in its splendid fidelity to all experience it says that after illumination may come battle. It is on that aspect of things I want to dwell tonight.

Think first, then, of the illumination of the intellect, and of all that follows on the light of knowledge. That is not always liberty and power: it is sometimes a conflict which is very terrible. When Eve in the virgin paradise of God ate of the tree of the knowledge of good and evil, her eyes were opened, and she was illuminated with the light that never was on sea or land; and yet that light did not bring peace to Eve, nor gladness, nor any rest of heart, but only the sorrow of a weary struggle. The more we know, the more we want to know. The more we know, the more we cannot know. And doubts are born, and speculations rise, and much that once seemed certain grows unstable. Until at last, wearied and in perplexity, not through the power of darkness but of light, a man begins to realize how grim is the struggle that succeeds illumination.

We see that on the larger field of history in such a movement as the revival of learning. There came a time when Europe was illuminated with the knowledge which she had lost for centuries. Once more she woke to the glory that was Greece. Once more she felt the grandeur that was Rome. And the night vanished, and the morning came, with all the tingling of the life of dawn. And then, following hard on that enlightenment, and born of the very glory of it all, there came a story of confused fighting that can be read upon a hundred battlefields. Old interests went out to battle with the new. Old ideals were very loath to go. Old institutions, buttressed by the dark, felt the terrific power of the light. And homes were rent, and churches cleft in twain, and countries hurried into civil war, and all as the issue of illumination.

Nor is that consequence less notable in the lesser field of personal experience. There are those here who can recall the struggle that followed the clear shining of the light. Here for instance is a young man, a student, who has been trained in a pious Scottish home. There he accepted without serious questioning the faith of his father and his mother. Their character commended it to him—he saw it lived and therefore felt it true—and in a faith that never had been shaken, he joined in worship and bowed the knee in prayer. There are many who never lose that childhood's faith. They grow as the lily and spread their roots as Lebanon. It is no necessary witness of superiority that a man should have come to his own by way of agony. But oftentimes, with all that light of knowledge which the years bring to most of us today, there falls a different story to be written. Illumination comes by what we read: it flashes upon us in our college lectures. And the world is different, and God and man are different, from all that we cherished in our childhood's days. And then begins that time of stress and strain, so bitter and yet so infinitely blessed, through which a man must fight his way, alone, to faith and peace and character and God. There is a strife that is nobler than repose. There is a battle more blessed than quiescence. There is a stress and strain which comes when God arises, and cries to a young heart "Let there be light." All which, so modern that it seems of yesterday, is yet so old that Scripture understands it, hinting not vaguely in our evening's text of the struggle that succeeds illumination.

Think next of the illumination of the heart. The illumination of the heart is love. Just as the light of the intellect is truth, so the light of every heart is love. Without love the heart is always dark, and with love the heart is always light. The most common dwelling becomes a palace with it, and there is sunshine for the dreariest day. And all the wealth "of Ormus and of Ind," and all the joy of fame, and whirl of fashion, can never irradiate these hearts of ours like love. He who dwells in love dwells in God, and he who dwells in God is in the light. The luster of the heart is always there, but it is unlighted until love comes in. And now call to remembrance the former days in which, after you were illuminated, you endured a great fight of afflictions. Long years ago some of you mothers here gathered your firstborn child into your arms, and there was such gladness in these eyes of yours that every neighbor saw your life illuminated. And now as you look back upon it all, and think of all that has come and gone since then, you know the sorrows that have followed love. What sleepless nights—what hours of weary watching—what seasons of agony when death was near! What struggle to do that which was hard to do, when wills were rebellious and lips untruthful. All this has followed the illumination that came when the love of motherhood was born, and all this is the anguish of the light. Let a man love his work, and in that light he shall be led to many a weary wrestling. Let a man love his land, and in that light he shall take up burdens that are not easily borne. Let a man love his risen and living Savior, and in that light his life shall be a battlefield, as he wrestles daily not with flesh and blood but with the principalities and powers of darkness. Love has its triumphs, but it has its tortures. Love has its paradise and it has its purgatory. Love has its mountains of transfiguration, and its olive gardens where the sweat is blood. Love is the secret of the sweetest song that ever was uttered by human lips, and love is the secret of the keenest suffering that ever pierced the heart.

Then once again I ask you to observe how true this is of the illumination of the will. For the will like the intellect has its great hours, when in the light of heaven we see light. It may be we have been groping in the darkness, not seeing clearly what our duty was. And choice was difficult, so much depended on it: there was so much to win, so much to lose. And then it may be in one radiant hour, never to be forgotten through the years, we heard as it were a voice behind us saying, "This is the way: walk ye in it." Very probably we had prayed about it, for it is in such seasons that men learn to pray. We cried, "It is not in man that walketh to direct his steps: Lord, lead me, for I know not which is best." And then, perhaps by some word from friendly lips, or by some providence or disappointment, clear as the sun shining in mid-heavens we saw what for us must be the path of duty. Such hours of high and resolute decision are among the greatest hours of human life. There is not a power or faculty we have that is not illuminated by the glory of them. And yet the struggle and torment that preceded them, when we were stumbling and groping toward decision, may not be half so terrible and searching as the struggle and the strain that follow after. Never are things forsworn so sweet to man as in the season when they are forsworn. Never is the alternative so winning as in the hour when it has been rejected. Never do things renounced appeal to us so sweetly and so subtly and so secretly as in the season when we have turned our backs upon them, and set our faces bravely to the morn. The most difficult task in life is not to win; the most difficult task is to keep what we have won: never to falter, when the shadows deepen, from the verdict of our high and radiant hours; never to go back on our decisions, never to listen again to any voices which in our worthiest and purest moments we knew to be the voices of the Enemy. That is the reason why great decisions ought to be reinforced by prayer. There is no weapon on earth like prayer for helping us to keep what we have won. For prayer unites us to the living Christ, and touches the vilest of us with the touch of heaven, and brings to our aid that power of perfect living which was witnessed long ago in Galilee. Tasks in hours of insight willed must be through days of gloom fulfilled, but in the gloomiest day a man may lift his heart up, and draw for his need out of the grace of Jesus. And so the highest comes back to us once more, and we see it and love it again for all our faltering, and on us too the angel faces smile which we have loved long since, and lost awhile.

And then in closing I want you to take our text in regard to the illumination of the conscience. Do you remember when conscience was illuminated what a great fight of afflictions you endured? That may have happened many years ago, when you were young and ardent and impressionable: and yet so unsearchable are the ways of God, that perhaps it is happening to some of you tonight. Tonight, after all these years—prayerless, careless, hardening years—perhaps it is happening to some of you tonight. You recall how David after a great sin hardened his heart and justified himself. And then by the word of Nathan the prophet there flashed on his conscience the light of a holy God. Whereupon that mighty soul, after he was illuminated, broke out into that penitential agony which has come ringing down the ages, and shall ring on forever: "Create within me a clean heart, O God, and renew within me a right spirit. Wash me with hyssop and I shall be clean: purge me and I shall be whiter than the snow." That is not the crying of despair, nor of the soul that has forfeited the everlasting mercy: it is the eternal crying of the human conscience that has been irradiated by the light of God. My brother and sister, if God has so come to you, He will never leave you nor forsake you. He has a purpose of peace toward your soul tonight that has been destined from the bosom of eternity. He has begun His saving work in you which only awaits the fullness of response, to issue in the blessedness of power, and in the rest and liberty of heaven.

I am not sent but to the lost sheep of the house of Israel (Matt. 15:24).
I, if I be lifted up . . . will draw all men unto Me (John 12:32).

12

The Cross and the World

We have but to read the record of the gospels to find confirmation of the former of these texts. The whole activity of Christ on earth shows Him as sent to the lost sheep of Israel. Within the boundaries of Israel He was born, and within the boundaries of Israel He died. With the one exception of the journey here recorded, He never in His maturity left the Jewish land. His twelve disciples were of the Jewish faith; His friends were inhabitants of Jewish homes; His enemies were not the Romans, but H*is own*, to whom He came and they received Him not. For His teaching He sought no other audience than the men and women of the Jewish villages. For His retirement He sought no other solitude than the solitude of the Galilean hills. And all His miracles, with certain rare exceptions, which were recorded because they were exceptional, were wrought for the comforting of Jewish hearts, and for the drying of tears in Jewish eyes. The whole story of the gospel, then, is a witness to the truth of our first text. In the fulfilling of His earthly ministry Christ confined Himself to Jewish limits. And He did so because of His assurance, reached in ways we cannot now consider, that He was sent to the lost sheep of the house of Israel.

But as we study the words of our Redeemer, one thing gradually grows very clear. It is that He anticipated a ministry that should be wider than these Jewish limits. I am not thinking just now of any words He spoke after He was risen from the dead. I am thinking only of His recorded utterances in those crowded years before the cross. And what I say is that no reasonable man can study the discourse of the historic Jesus without discovering that He foresaw a ministry which was to be as wide as the whole world. There is, for instance, the second of our texts today—"I will draw all men unto me." There is that beautiful word of an earlier chapter, "Other sheep I have which are not of this fold." There is that utterance at Simon's table, when the woman broke the alabaster box, "Wheresoever this gospel shall be preached in the whole world, this that she hath done shall be told of her." I ask you to observe that these great sayings have stood the test of the most searching criticism. They are so germane to the mind of Christ that they have come triumphant through the fires. And they tell us this, that through the earthly ministry, confined as it was within the house of Israel, Christ had the outlook of an approaching lordship over the nations of mankind.

But these utterances tell us more than that, and to this I specially invite attention. They tell us that in the mind of Jesus His death and His worldwide empire were related. So far as we can learn the mind of Christ, we can with reverence say this about it. It was when the cross was clearest in His thought that the worldwide empire was most clear to Him. If you will think of the texts which I have cited, and consider the occasion of their utterance, you will understand quite easily what I mean. Take for instance that most beautiful word, "Other sheep I have which are not of this fold." What are the words which immediately precede it? "The good shepherd giveth his life for the sheep." At the very moment when the thought of shepherding kindled the vision of the shepherd's death, at that very moment there flashed upon the Lord the vision of the sheep beyond the fold. Take again the scene at Simon's feast where Jesus spoke of a gospel for the world. "Wheresoever this gospel shall be preached in the whole world, there this deed that she hath done shall be remembered." And what was it that the woman had done under the interpreting eyes of Jesus Christ? She had anointed His body for its burial. In other words that womanly act of hers had spoken to Jesus of His coming death. Over the table where the guests reclined, it had cast the awful shadow of the cross. And it was *then*, anointed for His burial by an act which no one else could understand, that

Christ in vision lifted up His eyes and saw the gospel preached to the whole world. Clearly, then, Christ looked upon His death as the great secret of a worldwide empire. When the one grew vivid in His thought, there rose on Him the vision of the other. And that to me is a matter to be brooded on, as one of the most momentous of all truths, by every man and every woman who is interested in the world empire of the Lord. Now the question is, can we follow out that thought, and see even dimly where the connection lies? It is that which I should like to attempt to do this evening.

In the first place, it is the death of Christ which supplies the motive of missionary enterprise.

We must ever remember that when we speak of the death of Christ, we speak of a death different from our own. Our deaths bring the cessation of activity: Christ's was the crown and climax of His life. "I have power to lay it down," He said, and that is a power no other man has shared. We die when the appointed hour comes, and when the hand of God has touched us, and we sleep. But Christ never looked upon His death like that, as something inevitable and irresistible. He looked on it as the last free glorious service of a life that had always been a life of love. Here in one gleam, intense and vivid, was gathered up the light of all His years. Here in one action which we name His dying was gathered up the love in which He wrought. And it is just because of the power of that action, concentrating all the scattered rays, that Christ could say, "I, if I be lifted up, will draw all men unto me."

How true this is as a fact of history we see in the story of the Christian church. There is the closest connection in that story between the death of Christ and missionary zeal. There have been periods in the church's history when the death of Christ was practically hidden. The message of the cross was rarely preached; the meaning of the cross was rarely grasped. And the gospel was looked on as a refined philosophy, eminently fitted for the good of men, inculcating a most excellent morality, and in perfect harmony with human reason. We have had periods like that in Scotland, and we have had periods like that in England. God grant that they may never come again with their deadening of true religion. And always when you have such a period, when love is nothing and moral law is everything, you have a period when not a hand is lifted for the salvation of the heathen world. For it is not morality that seeks the world; it is religion centering in love. It is a view of a divine love so wonderful that it stooped to the service of death upon a cross. So always, in evangelical revival, when that has been apprehended in the wonder of it, the passion to tell it out has come again, and men have carried the message to mankind.

And may I say that it is along these lines that the road must lie to a deepening of interest. To realize what it means that Christ has died is to have a gospel that we must impart. There are many excellent people who, in their secret hearts, confess to a very faint interest in missions. They give, and it may be they give generously, and yet in their hearts they know that they are not interested. They know almost nothing about mission fields, and are never seen at missionary meetings, and take the opportunity to visit a sister church when a missionary is advertised to preach in theirs. With such people I have no lack of sympathy, for I think I understand their position thoroughly. I have the gravest doubt if any good is done by trying excitedly to lash up their interest. But I am perfectly confident that these good people would waken to a new and lively interest, if only they realized a little more the wonder of the love of God in Christ. What think you, my brother and my sister, is the most wonderful thing that ever happened? It is not the kindling of the myriad stars, nor the fashioning of the human eye that it might see them. It is that once the God who is eternal stooped down from heaven and came into humanity, and bore our burdens, and carried our sorrows, and died in redeeming love upon the tree. Once realize what that means, and everything else in the world is insignificant. Once realize what that means, and you *must* pass it on to other people. And that is the source of missionary zeal—not blind obedience, nor any thoughts of terror, but the passing on of news so wonderful that we cannot—dare not—keep it to ourselves.

In the next place, the death of Christ interprets and answers a universal longing. It meets with perfect satisfaction the deepest need of all the world. One of the great gains of this age of ours is that it has drawn the world together so. There is an intermingling of the nations now that but a few decades ago was quite impossible. Thanks to the means of transport we possess, and to the need of expansion on the part of nations; thanks to the deathless spirit of adventure, to the gains of commerce and to the march of armies, there is a blending now of the whole earth such as was undreamed of once. Now one result of all that intermingling has been a new sense of the oneness of humanity. No longer do we delight in travelers' tales, such as captivated the Middle Ages. Men push their way into untraveled forests, and they come to us from Arabia and Tibet, and under all that is strange they bring us tidings of the touch of nature that makes the whole world kin. We realize today as men had never done how God had made all nations of one blood. Deeper than everything that separates there are common sorrows and elemental hopes. There is one common heart by which we live; one common life in which we share; one common enemy awaiting all, when the pitcher is broken at the fountain.

But especially has this oneness of humanity been made evident in the religious life. That has been one incalculable gain of the modern study of comparative religion. It has investigated a thousand rites, and found at the back of them a common longing. It has touched the foundations of a thousand altars, and found they were built upon a common need. It has gathered from Africa, from India, from China, the never-failing story of religion, and always at the very heart of things it has discovered one unchanging element. It is not enough to say that all men have religion. That is now an accepted commonplace. Something far more wonderful and thrilling has been slowly emerging into prominence. It is that under a thousand different rites, from those of Patagonia to those of China, there lies the unquenchable desire of man to get into right relationship with God. Deeper than all sense of gratitude, though gratitude is very often there—deeper than unreasoning terror, though heathen religion is always big with terror—deeper than that, this fact stands out today, based on exhaustive and scientific study, that the deepest longing in the soul of man is the longing to get right with God. It is that in the last analysis which explains sacrifice, and where is the heathen tribe that does not sacrifice? It is that which explains the sway of heathen witchcraft, of which the evils can never be exaggerated. The religious life is the deepest life of man, and in that life, over the whole wide world, the one determining and vital question is, how can mortal man get right with God?

My brother, I almost ask your pardon for having taken you so far afield. But you see, I think, the point which I am driving at, and from which there is no possible escape. That very question, so vital to humanity, is the *question which the atonement answers*. It answers the cry that is rising to the heavens from every heathen rite and heathen altar. It tells men in language that a child can grasp, yet with a depth that angels cannot fathom, how sinful man by an appointed sacrifice can be put right with the eternal God. I believe with all my soul in educational missions, but at the heart of missions is more than education. I believe with all my soul in medical missions, but at the heart of missions there is more than healing. Christ never said, "My teaching shall draw all men," nor yet, "My healing power shall draw all men" He said, "I, *if I be lifted up*, shall draw all men, "and this spake he of the death that he should die." That means that in the atoning death there is the answer to man's deepest need. It means that the deepest cry of all humanity is answered in the message of the cross. And I venture to say that all we have learned today in the modern study of comparative religion, corroborates, and authenticates, and seals that certainty upon the lips of Jesus.

Then, lastly, we have the thought that the death of Christ has liberated His influence. It has opened the window of the ark, if I might put it so, that the dove might fly abroad over the waters. "It is expedient for you that I go away," He said, "for if I go not away the Comforter cannot come." Now the Lord is that Spirit, says the apostle—it is that same Jesus glorified and liberated. So by the lifting up upon the cross Christ was set free from local limitation, to pass into a spiritual ministry that would be coextensive with the world. No longer can any village of far Galilee claim the present monopoly of Christ. No longer can loving hearts in Bethany say, "He is our guest and ours only for tonight." He is as present now by the lake shores of Africa as He is within this house of God this evening, and present so because He lived and died. We often talk of the *story* of the cross as if in that story lay the world's redemption. But I beg of you to remember that while that is true, it is far from being all the truth. Christ spoke not a word of the story of the cross. He said, I—persisting through the cross—I, the living Christ, will draw the world—I whom death is powerless to hold. In other words, when our missionaries go forth, they go with something more than a sweet story. They go with Him of whom the tale is told, so wonderful, so unspeakable, so moving. They go with Him who, having tasted death, is now alive and lives forevermore, and who is able to save unto the uttermost all who come to God by Him.

Be of good courage, and he shall
strengthen thine heart (Ps. 27:14).

13

The Quality of Courage

There are three qualities, says Emerson[1] in a familiar essay, which attract the wonder and reverence of mankind. The first is disinterestedness, the second is practical power, and the third is courage. Every mythology has got its Hercules.[2] Every history its Wallace[3] or its Cid.[4] There is nothing that men will not forgive to one who has exhibited conspicuous gallantry. Even the dumb animals are ranked by us according to their possession of this quality, the bravest being nature's aristocracy. There are peoples who make a jest of truth, but there is no people which makes a jest of courage. The love of it, from Orient to Occident, is the touch of nature which makes the whole world kin. And that is why war will never cease to fascinate, spite of all proofs of its illogicality, because there is in war a matchless stage for the display of courage.

Nor can we wonder at this admiration when we remember the universal need of courage. There is no lot, no rank, no occupation,

---

1. Ralph Waldo Emerson (1803–1882), American poet and essayist.
2. Hercules, mythical son of Zeus and Alcmene, famous for his extraordinary strength and courage.
3. Most likely William Wallace (1272?–1305), Scottish patriot and hero.
4. Rodrigo Díaz de Vivar (d. 1099), Spanish national hero.

in which one of the first requirements is not fortitude. When we are young we admire the showy virtues, and we put the emphasis upon the brilliant gifts. We are all enamored of what is glittering then, and we think that life is to grow great that way. But as the years roll on, and life unfolds itself, and we look on some who mount and some who fall, we come to revise our estimates a little. Then we discover that a certain doggedness is far more likely to succeed than brilliance. Then we discover that cleverness means much, but that the courage which can persist means more. Then we discover what the Master meant, when at the close of the long years of toil, He said, Well done, not, good and brilliant, but Well done, good and *faithful* servant. Courage is needed by the mother in the home, it is needed by the young man in the office. Courage is needed for the hills of youth, and for the dusty levels of our middle age. There is a courage peculiar to the pulpit, and another peculiar to the football field, and another peculiar to that darkened chamber where the head is throbbing and the lip is parched. Let a man have all the talents without courage and he will accomplish little in the world. Let a man have the one talent and a courageous heart, and no one can tell what things he may do. Probably when the story of our lives is written, our gifts will be found less diverse than we thought, and it will be seen that what set us each apart is the distinguishing quality of courage.

For courage is not an isolated virtue, so much as the ground and basis of the virtues. It is like the tingling of health in a man's body, which makes itself felt in every activity. When I travel in one of our electric cars, I cannot but wonder at that electric current. It drives the car; it lights it in the evening; it rings the bell when we want the car to stop. One single energy, and yet that single energy shows itself powerful in all these different forces, and so are the forces which God has given a man fed by the single energy of courage. If you could get deep enough down among our vices, you would probably find they had a common source. Somewhere deep down in the unfathomed darkness there is one spark of hell that sets them all afire. So with our virtues and all that makes us men, there is one spirit that kindles and sustains them, and that enkindling energy is fortitude. For you never can be patient without courage, and without courage you never can be pure. It calls for a little courage to be truthful, and it calls for a little courage to be kind. And sometimes it takes a deal of courage just to say out that which we ought to say, and sometimes it takes more courage to say nothing. My brother and sister, in this strange life of ours, never forget that fortitude is victory. There is no final failure for the man who can say, I am the master of my fate. Never to tremble at the looming shadow, never to shrink from the unwelcome duty, never to despair when things seem hopeless, is the one road to the music and the crown. Do you know the most common command in Scripture? The most common command in Scripture is, Fear not. Times without number in the Word of God rings out upon us, Thou shalt not be afraid. For courage is at the roots of life, and it is the soil in which every virtue flourishes; it is no isolated or independent grace, but is the nursing mother of them all.

Now if this be so, it is at once apparent that the truest courage is an unobtrusive thing. There is nothing spectacular or scenical about it; it sounds no trumpet before it in the streets. I grant you there come moments in some lives when courage flashes into dramatic splendor. There are hours, for men, of crowded life which are worth an age without a name. When the soldier dismounts to save a wounded comrade—when the fireman risks his life to save a child—there is something in that which strangely moves the heart. That is the courage which thrills, and it is splendid, but the courage which thrills is rarely that which tells. No voices cheer it; no papers give its chronicle; no medals reach it from any millionaire. It moves in the shadow of our dreary streets, and dwells in the shelter of our humble homes, and carries the crosses which every morning brings in a quiet and happy and victorious way. I suppose there was never anyone on earth quite so courageous as our Savior Christ. Yet give a pagan that life of His to read, and I do not think he would say, How brave He was! He would say, How loving He was—how infinitely patient—how radiantly peaceful in the teeth of calumny;[5] yet love and patience and radiance and peace were but His matchless courage in disguise. The courage which tells is not the courage which clamors. The courage which tells is the courage that is quiet. It sounds no trumpet; does not strive nor cry; never lifts up its voice in any street. It only does things when it feels least like them, anoints the head for every hour of fasting, comes to the cross in such a smiling fashion that others scarce suspect the cross is there.

We see also along this line of thought that courage is different from insensibility. Courage is not the absence of fear; courage is the conquest of fear. One man, in some hour of peril, may feel that his

5. personal slander

heart is beating like a sledgehammer. Another, in an hour precisely similar, may scarcely be conscious of a quickened pulse. And yet the former may be the braver man if he does resolutely what the hour demands of him, for he has felt what the other never felt, and feeling it has brought it to subjection. I often think of that fine old story of Henri IV,[6] king of France. At the siege of Cahors, when he was young in arms, his body began to tremble like an aspen. And he cried to his body, so that all who were near him heard, "Vile carcass," he cried, "thou tremblest, but thou wouldst tremble worse if thou but knew where I am going to take thee in a moment." So saying, with a body trembling like an aspen, he flung himself into the thickest of the fight. I have heard of two young men who had a cliff to scale, and one of them was very white about the cheeks. And the other looked at him, and with a sneer said, "Why, I believe you are afraid." "Yes," he replied, "I am afraid, and if you were half as afraid as I am, you'd *go home*." The fact is, that as you rise in being you rise in the nobility of courage. It is those who are capable of being most afraid who are capable of being most courageous. You will never fathom the bravery of Christ unless you bear in mind that Christ was sinless. For sin is always coarsening and deadening—"it hardens a' within, and petrifies the feeling." And it is when we think that Jesus Christ was sinless, and being sinless was exquisitely sensitive, that we come to realize the matchless fortitude that carried Him without a falter to the cross. I beg of you not for one moment to believe that because you feel afraid you are a coward. Moses and Paul and Jesus Christ Himself knew in its bitterness the shrinking of the flesh. Courage is not the absence of dismay; courage is the conquest of dismay. It is how a man deals and grapples with his trembling that makes the difference between strong and weak.

It is one of the glad things, too, in human life that courage grows easier as life advances. If we are living well, and doing our work faithfully, we grow more equal to our problems with the years. A child begins by fearing almost everything because it begins by knowing almost nothing. Every shadow may be a horrid specter, and every shuttered room be full of ghosts. But the years pass, and we enter many a shadow, and the abhorred specters are not there, and so do our childish terrors pass away. I knew an officer who in the

---

6. Henry of Navarre (1553–1610), first Bourbon King of France, who abjured Protestantism upon his succession.

thick of battle was reckoned among the bravest of the brave, and yet that man would blanch if he found himself in the presence of diphtheria. And I know scores of ministers within our city who would never think twice of visiting diphtheria, and yet I warrant you they would be ghastly spectacles within the fighting lines of Adrianople.[7] The fact is that, far more than we imagine, courage is a result of habit. The soldier who trembled in his first engagement will enter his twentieth without a thought. And so is God kind to us as life advances, and the fiery ardors of our youth decay, for with ripening knowledge some things become harder, but it does not become harder to be brave. The dash is gone. The youthful fire is gone. We are not heroic as at twenty-one. The old man cannot storm the heights of life with the reckless enthusiasm of the cadet. But he has seen such goodness of the Lord to him, and had such through-bearing in trial and difficulty, that he can lift his heart up, and go forward gently, where youth would grow quite tragic and despair.

There are two open secrets of true courage to which I would call attention as I close, and one of them is self-forgetfulness. Just as the open secret of all happiness is never to think of happiness at all, but to forget it, and to do our duty quietly, and to take the longer road that leads through Galilee, so the open secret of all courage is to forget there is such a thing as courage, in the gladness and the glow of an ideal. When David fought with the lion and the bear, he never thought of the lion and the bear. He only remembered that he was a shepherd, and that his duty was to guard the sheep. So doing his duty in a fine forgetfulness, courage came to him like a bird upon the wing, and sang its morning music in his heart. When Captain John Brown, that fine American hero, was asked why others were conquered by his regiment, "Well," he replied, after a moment's thought, "I suppose it is because they lacked a cause." They had nothing to fight for that was worth a stroke, and having nothing to fight for or to die for, it followed as the night the day that they were ineffectual in battle. The most timid creature will face tremendous odds when danger threatens its defenseless offspring. The Roman slave girl will throw herself on martyrdom when she is animated by the faith of Christ. The woman, in her self-forgetful love for the infant that she has suckled on her bosom will dare to starve and even dare to die. That is why love is such a nurse of courage, and that is where love is different from passion. For passion is selfish,

7. In western Turkey during World War I.

and seeks its own delight, and will ruin another if only it be gratified. But love is unselfish, and seeks not her own, and hopes all things, and believes all things, and like John Brown's regiment is always ready, because for the battle it never lacks a cause. Desdemona, in the play of Shakespeare, is

> A maiden never bold,
> Of spirit so still and quiet that her motion
> Blushed at herself,[8]

yet standing at Othello's side, Desdemona confronts her father and her world, and she confronts them because she loves Othello so. Love for her fledgling makes the wild bird brave. Love for her baby makes the mother brave. And now comes Christ, and by His life and death writes that word *love* upon the gate of heaven. And so has He made it possible for thousands, who otherwise would have faltered in the shadow, to pluck up heart again, and play the man, and to be strong and of good courage by the way.

And the other secret of the truest courage is a strong and overmastering sense of God. When you get deep enough I think you always find that in every life that has been greatly brave. When Peter was separated from his Lord awhile, then he denied Him with a fisher's curses. With no one near but the soldiers and the servants, he was as a reed shaken with the wind. But when the Lord came in and looked on Peter, Peter went out into the night and wept; and so repentant, became a man again. When I can go to my labors saying God is with me—when I can lie on my sickbed saying God is here—when I can meet my difficulties saying This is God—when dying I can whisper, He is mine—then in communion with that power and goodness I am no longer tossed and tempest-driven, but in the storm and shadow I am strong. It is that conviction Jesus Christ has brought to the weakest heart in the most dreary street. Prophets and psalmists might believe it once, but the poorest woman can believe it now. To be in communion with God through Jesus Christ—to know that He is ours and we are His—is the victory which overcomes the world. Such courage is not based on fancied power. It is based on the absolute and the eternal. It is not kindled by any glow of anger. It is kindled and kept by the eternal spirit. So can the weakest dare to stand alone, and dare to live alone, and dare to die alone, saying, The best of all is, God is *with us*.

---

8. From *Othello* by Shakespeare.

The Creator of the ends of the earth
(Isa. 40:28).

14

The God of Nature

Attentive readers of the Old Testament have often noticed one very striking feature of it. It is the manner in which the writers of it fall back for comfort upon the God of nature. Never was there a nation in the world more jealous of religious privilege than the Jews. They stood to God in covenant-relationship which no man could share in save through circumcision. And the strange thing is how often their great writers, when they are seeking comfort or direction, fall back, *not* on the covenant God, but upon the Lord of heaven and earth. They knew, and in hours of trial they had tested, the strengthening efficacy of their own Jehovah. They never forgot that He whom they adored was the God of Abraham and of Isaac and of Jacob. But it is wonderful to find how often their petition goes right away beyond a covenant God, to Him who laid the foundations of the universe, and kindled the nightly shining of the stars. "I to the hills will lift mine eyes," says David. "Lift up your eyes to the heavens," cries Isaiah. In hill and glen, in sunshine and in star, prophet and psalmist find their ground of hope. And I say it is a thing very significant that in a people whose God was so intensely national, there should have been such frequency of outlook to the God who made the heavens and the earth.

Now if this is true of the Old Testament, it is still more notably evident in the New. There is a place there far larger than we think sometimes for the God who fashioned the valleys and the hills. One might have thought that the fatherhood of God would have swallowed up everything in the New Testament. It was a truth so thrilling and so new that we would not have wondered had it swept the field. And yet these very men whose lives were changed by Christ's deep doctrine of God's fatherhood, never ceased to turn for help and comfort to Him who made the heavens and the earth. Christ Himself had led the way in that. He was never weary of so proclaiming God. "I thank Thee, Father, Lord of heaven and earth," He said. And "He maketh his rain to fall on the evil and the good." And so the apostles, having learned of Him, went out to the world to proclaim a Father-God, who was none other than the God of nature. "It is he who giveth the rain and fruitful seasons," is one of the practical arguments of Paul. In the city of Phidias,[1] with its marble temples, he preached of a temple that was not made with hands. And Peter, when he would comfort his vexed readers and encourage them to cast their care on God, bids them commit their souls to Him, because He is a faithful creator. Such then is the attitude toward creation that you find in the Old and New Testaments. Nature is never handled scientifically nor is she treated of aesthetically. Nature is the woven garb of God, whereon we look as on a royal vesture, and looking learn many a thought of help about Him with whom we have to do. What then is it that creation teaches? What does it enforce about its maker? Viewed solely in the light of Scripture, what has the world to tell us about God? It is on that thought that I should like to speak a little this evening.

In the first place, all through Scripture, nature enforces the unity of God.

There is one truth which all history teaches, and which at once, I take it, will command assent. It is that no real religious life is possible save under the deep sense that God is one. Real religion at the heart of it is the feeling of dependence upon God. It is the resting of the human soul upon the infinite and eternal arm. But if in the region that is beyond the veil there be a hundred warring arms instead of one, anything like dependence is impossible. To have many gods, however beautiful, is as fatal to real faith as to have

---

1. In Athens where the great sculptures of Phidias (c. 500–c. 432 B.C.) were displayed.

none. There can never be any unity of heart if there is no such thing as unity in heaven. And that is why nations in polytheistic stages have always been irreligious nations, untouched by any worthy reverence, and unsupported by any worthy faith. To have many gods may be the way to art, as it was once, long ago in ancient Greece. It may inspire the sculptor in his toil as the thought of the one God could never do. But art, even the art of Greece, is purchased at a price that is too great, when it is purchased by the uneasy loss of the deep and quickening sense of the divine. That is why the great religious souls in Greece broke through the pantheon and reached the one. Neither Socrates nor Plato could find rest in a heaven that was swarming with divinities. Nor ever has the human heart found rest there, nor inspiration, nor comfort in distress, but only in the thought that God is *one*.

Now that the Bible proclaims the unity of God is of course known to every Christian child. And it proclaims it on a twofold witness which is called in to attest that revelation. The one is the witness of the human conscience that is always restless in a divided heaven. This voice within gives an uncertain sound when it is but the echo of a thousand voices. And the other is the witness of creation which, even to the unscientific Jew, spoke of the unity of the creating mind as audibly as it speaks to you and me. What is the first word of the creation story? In the beginning, God. You may smile at the childish picture of six days, but if you are wise you will never smile at that. And how does the gospel of St. John begin—the deepest book that ever mortal penned? "In the beginning was the Word, and *all things* were created by the Word." That is the uniform attitude of Scripture, and I say that that attitude is very wonderful. Surrounded by nations who saw rival powers in nature the Jew never faltered in seeing only one. There is one power of the sunshine, said the Persian, and another power of the shadows of the night; but "I form the light and I create the darkness," says the Almighty of the Jewish covenant. The God of the hills on which the snow is resting is the God of the valleys where the harvests are. The earth is the Lord's and the fullness thereof, the sea also is His because He made it. The clouds are His chariot, and the flame of fire; He rides upon the wings of the wind; yet it is He who clothes the lilies of the field, and providentially caters for the sparrow.

In the second place, keeping close to Scripture, nature enforces the majesty of God.

It is a strange thing to say, and yet I say it boldly, and believe you will come to agree that I am right: I say that as God grows richer for us personally, His majesty is apt to be obscured. Luther in his homely way used to assert that there was a great deal of religion in the possessive pronouns. He meant that when a man can say My God, he has advanced far in the religious life. And this is the joy of our faith in Jesus Christ, that with a fullness of appropriation once undreamed of, we can look heavenward in every hour of need, and say with a full heart, My God. Now that is the very flower of religion, and that is what Luther meant by his possessive pronouns. And yet have you not seen, have you not felt sometimes, the peculiar peril of that appropriation? Filled with the personal love of God to us, and touched with the wonder of His condescension, sometimes we are on the borders of forgetting that He is a God of infinite majesty. In the gleam of heaven which the prophet caught there were cherubim round the eternal throne. And they veiled their faces in the sight of God, and they ceased not crying, Holy, Holy, Holy. But now, in Jesus, God has come so near us, and is so pitiful with all a father's pity, that the voices of the cherubim are still. I hear men speaking about God today in a way that reverent lips should never use. I hear men praying to God today with a familiarity that makes one shudder—or rather it would make one shudder if we did not remember what was at the heart of it, a sense of the nearness of God in Christ so vivid, that to be with Him is to be at home.

Now the Holy Scripture in its wisdom foreseeing as it were this coming danger, takes infinite pains in every part of it to safeguard the majesty of God; and one of its chosen ways of doing that, and of showing that He is infinitely great, is to take us by the hand like little children and lead us out into the world of nature. "I to the hills will lift mine eyes," that is how the psalmist puts it. "Behold who hath created these things," that is how the prophet Isaiah puts it. He takes up the isles as a very little thing, and all the nations before Him are as nothing; and He orders all the armies of the sky, and the stars in their courses fight against His enemies. I have always thought that this was one great purpose of the nature-miracles of Jesus Christ. Over against the miracles of healing they reassert the majesty of God. They tell us that He who was of such compassion that He would not break the bruised reed, was yet of a majesty that could command the storm, and call the waves to the surface of the sea. The heavens declare the glory of God, and the firmament shows forth His handiwork. When I consider the heavens which You have framed, then say I, What is man that You are mindful of him? So are we led out of our little life into the largeness and liberty of nature, to feel again what we are prone to lose—the awful majesty of the eternal. The more you are a humble, loving Christian, the more you need that ministry of nature. The nearer God has come to you in Christ, the more you need the message of creation. You need it amid your boundless privileges which have made God your father and your friend, that you may still be hushed and reverent.

Lastly, keeping close to Scripture, nature enforces the faithfulness of God.

There is perhaps no attribute of God harder to credit than His faithfulness. He who can set to his seal that God is true, is on the highroad to the morning and the crown. It is not hard to credit God's omniscience, nor is it hard to accept His omnipresence. It is not hard to believe, if we have hearts at all, in His providential and general benevolence. But just quietly to believe that God is faithful, through all life's tangle and all its disappointment, that, I say, is one of the hardest tasks that has ever yet been set to mortal man. I shall suggest to you three considerations why it is hard to credit the faithfulness of God.

One is, and I put it first, that *we are all of us ourselves so unfaithful.* We are unfaithful to our own ideals, and we are unfaithful to our own resolves. Now we know that God made man in His own image, and we are here worshiping tonight because that is so. But there is a deep sense, I speak with reverence, in which man also makes God in his own image. For he has ever taken that which was deepest in him, and that which was most characteristic of his life, and carried it up into the gates of heaven, and set it to be worshiped on the throne. If constancy then had been a human virtue, it would have been easy to think of God as constant. Had we ourselves been faithful to the highest, then would our God have been faithful to the best. And it is just because we are not faithful, but are ever sinning, and falling from our vision, that it is hard to credit the faithfulness of God.

Another consideration that explains the difficulty is *the wonderful nature of God's promises.* The more we meditate upon these promises, the more astounding they become. There are certain promises which men make which it is easy to believe will be fulfilled. They cost no trouble, and involve no sacrifice, and are in no way impossible to keep. But the promises of God, the more we study them, rise to such heights and pass into such deeps, that it takes something more than human wisdom quietly to believe that they are true. When Jesus said to Simon Peter, On this rock I will build My church, I should scarcely wonder if to Simon Peter that stupendous prediction seemed incredible. And yet the fact is that to the poorest sinner, whose will is spoiled and sapped by evil habit, as wonderful promises are made tonight as were ever made to the apostle Peter. If we knew what God is, we could believe them all, but then we only know a little of what God is. But if we only know a little of what God is, we know a great deal of what we are ourselves. And it is that, and all the glaring contrast between the promise of heaven and our hearts, that makes it hard to credit the faithfulness of God.

And the third consideration is this, that *God dwells in heaven and we do not see Him.* It is hard to believe in the unfailing interest in us of those whom we never can set eyes upon. They may legislate for us in the way of government, but that is the care of the many, not of the one. They may remember us with kindly help sometimes, but we all need help more intimate than that. Just to believe that those we never see are constant to us in their every thought, is never in a world like this an easy business. Now insensibly, but very really, such incredulity affects our heaven. No man has seen God at any time, yet our only hope is to credit His fidelity. And it is that absence from all sight and touch which is inevitable since God is spirit, which makes it difficult to grasp that He is faithful.

Now in the Holy Scripture there are many proofs of the faithfulness of God, but there is no proof so evident and easy as that which is gathered from the world of nature. The Jew knew nothing of the laws of nature of which we speak such a vast deal today. He would have looked at you with quiet amusement had you spoken of the uniformities of nature. But he saw that the night succeeded to the day, and he reaped the harvest spite of storm and rain, and he lifted up his heart to the eternal, and said to himself, He is a faithful God. How did Isaiah close his word of cheer to men who thought God had quite ignored them? He is the *Creator* of the ends of the earth, he said, who faints not, neither is weary. How did Peter comfort the poor church which thought that God had forgotten to be gracious? Commit the keeping of your souls to Him, he cried, as unto a faithful *Creator.* As I moved through the country a few weeks ago it was a sorry sight that met the eye. Here was water lying in great pools, and there were the crops beaten to the ground. And then I read that certain clergymen, who are a disgrace and dishonor to their calling, had intimated to their helpless people that there would be no harvest thanksgiving this year. He that believes shall not make haste. While the earth remains there shall be seed time and harvest. Lift up your eyes, for the fields are white unto harvest, and a harvest more bountiful than we have had for years. So once again when all the ground is dank, and heaven is cloudy, and reaping seems impossible, I shall take sides with the old Jewish heroes, and believe in the faithfulness of God.

15

The Reawakening of Mysticism

At a period not far distant from the present, and well within the memory of some of us, it was the fashion to decry all truth that was not reached by the action of the intellect. The only interpretation reckoned valid was the intellectual interpretation; the only methods which were regarded seriously were the logical and scientific methods; the only truths deemed worthy of acceptance were such as were capable of comprehension, and could be verified by scientific processes.

For this insistence on the comprehensible there were reasons which are readily apparent. There was that wonderful awakening of the intellect that marked the nineteenth century in England. There were those marvelous discoveries of science which gave to science a certain lordly arrogance, as if there were no truths she could not come by, and no secrets which she could not penetrate. All that was only a little while ago, and yet one is conscious of a subtle change today. The sense of the mystery which broods on things is far more vivid than thirty years ago. Men are awakening as to haunting presences which are ever near us, yet eluding us; they feel that there are more things in heaven and earth than are dreamed of in our philosophy. There is a growing belief that in the universe are secrets which are not intellectual at all. There is a strengthening trust in the verdict of the feelings, and in the illumination of the will. There is a deepening sense that all that is most real can never be demonstrated by any logic, but must be felt, where argument is hushed, in the silence and shadow of the soul. Now this new attitude of men and women is what may be called the attitude of *mysticism.* He who feels so, although he may not know it, has been touched by the flaming of the mystic torch. And it is on that mysticism, and the gains of it, in the peculiar circumstances of the hour, that I wish to speak a word or two tonight.

Taken in its most general sense, mysticism may be defined in some such way as this. It is the attitude of mind that feels intensely the wonder and the mystery of things. There is a little poem by Tennyson which I may read to you as beautifully illustrative of this attitude—

> Flower in the crannied wall,
> I pluck you out of the crannies;
> I hold you here, root and all, in my hand,
> Little flower—but if I could understand
> What you are, root and all, and all in all,
> I should know what God and man is.[1]

Well now, in regard to nature, that is the typically mystic attitude. The mystic's finger is on the skirts of God when he touches the flower in the crannied wall. The botanist classifies it in the realm of nature; the artist revels in its perfect coloring; the mystic finds in it, beneath its beauty, the shadow of the unseen and the eternal. For him there is a spirit eager to express itself in every bird that flies, and every flower that opens. For him there is more in the cataract than water, and more in the sunshine than a kindly heat. For him all nature is a sacrament, the outward sign and seal of the invisible, the charactered garment of the eternal God, woven exquisitely upon the loom of time. The mystic has no quarrel with the man of science—he may himself be a scientific man. But he holds that reality has many aspects, of which the scientific aspect is but one; and he claims for all these other aspects, which appeal to

1. From *Flower in the Crannied Wall* by Alfred (Lord) Tennyson (1809–1892).

feeling rather than intelligence, a place in the interpretation of the whole. The mystic knows that all the sounds of music are but so many vibrations of the ether. He knows that the whole range of melody can be thus scientifically accounted for. But when he listens to the boyish chorister whose voice goes ringing through the vast cathedral; when he hears the pealing of the solemn organ, and the psalm that rises from a thousand hearts; when he hears the music of the forest, or of the "lav'rock lilting wildly down the glen," he knows there is more in music than vibrations. He does not doubt the scientific fact, but that fact is not the truth for him. For him the truth is all that flow of feeling that is liberated by the touch of melody. It is the wistful longing—the dim and vague regret—the visions of peace and purity and God that rise upon him out of the obscure night when the sound of music steals upon the ear. For the true mystic these are the realities, and all that he touches and sees is but a shadow. The everlasting hills are not so real to him as the mysterious peace of God which they convey. Someone is calling where the winds are sighing; someone is moving where the leaves are rustling; someone is yearning toward the human heart where the waves are breaking on the shore. For the true mystic that is not idle poetry; for the true mystic that is the reality. The call of the sunset is far more real to him than the crimson and the gold which are its pageantry. He feels, though he can never prove it, that God is not far away from anyone of us, breathing in every wind upon the corn, and brooding in love on every lonely valley. That was what Wordsworth felt amid the dales of Cumberland.[2] That was what Boston felt among the hills of Ettrick.[3] That was what Sir Isaac Newton[4] felt, and General Gordon in desolate Khartoum.[5] And that, I think, is what is coming back again, and falling like a dew on countless hearts, and leading men nearer to Him in whom are all things, and by whom all things consist.

But mysticism is something more than that, if we take it in its religious sense. It is the doctrine that God is to be sought and found in

2. William Wordsworth (1770–1850), the English poet, found much of his inspiration in the Lake District in northern England.

3. Thomas Boston (1677–1732), Scottish minister and writer who served at Ettrick in Scotland.

4. Sir Isaac Newton (1642–1727), English philosopher and mathematician.

5. Charles George Gordon (1833–1885), British commander killed by Muslim forces in the Sudan.

the secret places of the soul. Not in the outward world, however beautiful, is the true vision of God to be attained. Sunrise and sunset and the evening star—these are but the outskirts of His ways. It is in the soul within us—in the hidden sanctuary—in the silence and secret of the human heart, that the union which is true blessedness is won, and the vision is granted which is peace. For this end, says the mystic, must a man learn to withdraw into himself. He must learn to practice, whatever pain it cost him, the spiritual method of detachment. He must shut the gates on every chariot wheel, and close the lattice against the show of things, and so, in silence and alone and self-absorbed, shall he awaken to the fact of God. As on a summer day on the hillside we watch the ships that are sailing on the sea, and mark the cottage smoke that clambers heavenward, and follow the wagons on the distant road, and so gradually we fall adreaming, and the active power of vision is relaxed, and then and not till then there steals upon us the murmuring as of a million wings; so as we lose our hold on what is outward, seeing everything as it were yet seeing nothing, does there steal on the soul the mystic sense of God. At first it may only be an intuition—a feeling inexplicable that He is here. For most of us—poor worldlings that we are—it may never be anything more wonderful than that. But for the heaven-born mystic that inward sense of God attains to such a glory of assurance that, like the apostle, he is caught up into heaven, and hears what human lips can never utter. In such a rapture there is no place for prayer, for prayer is the speaking of one to another. In such a union there is no place for praise, nor for any handling of sacramental elements. In such a rapture no proof of God is needed, for the one intense reality is God, nearer than breathing, closer than hands and feet, in the perfected adoration of the soul. Then everything in the universe grows shadowy under the vivid consciousness of God. Nature herself, with all her glorious pictures, seems but the unsubstantial pageant of a dream. The one overwhelming reality is God, not reached by argument, nor seen in outward things, but felt as a burning and a living presence in the silent and secret chambers of the soul. Just for this reason the deepest fact of mysticism can never be conveyed from soul to soul. That which is deepest in it can never be communicated in the set and formal terms of human speech. It is like that pleasure in the pathless woods—that rapture by the lonely shore—which, as Byron[6] has it, we can "ne'er express, yet cannot all conceal."

6. George Gordon (Lord) Byron (1788–1824), English poet.

Now it is just here that the difference comes in between all pagan and true Christian mysticism. And this is a matter of such profound importance that I would give much to make it clear to you. The great accusation leveled at the mystic is that he has no room for Jesus Christ. Alone with the infinite in secret rapture, the figure of the historic Jesus vanishes. But it has always seemed to me that this objection might equally be urged against the grace of prayer, for I question if anybody, when he prays to God, is actually conscious of the historic Christ. We do not go back in thought when we are praying to Him who walked among the fields of Galilee. We lift up our hearts, without a thought of Galilee, to the infinite and eternal God. Yet in so doing we glorify Christ Jesus, for all that we seek and all that we find in God is what we have been taught to seek and find in the life and in the words of Christ. Now as it is with the exercise of prayer, so is it with the attitude of mysticism. A pagan mystic withdraws into the silence alone, unbefriended, unaccompanied. But a Christian mystic withdraws into the silence with all that he has learned in Jesus Christ, of a God who has a father's heart, and who knows the yearning of a father's love. Like the poor prodigal, the Christian mystic says, I will arise and go to my Father. And so he arises from the world of sense, and goes to the quiet homeland of his soul. And there he is met in silence and in secret not by a cold and unintelligible spirit, but by a Father who has never ceased to love, and, loving, has never ceased to hope. There may be no consciousness of Jesus there, yet all the time Jesus is glorified. It is His God the Christian mystic meets, and not any spirit of universal nature. And what I impress on you, dear friends, is this, that it is just at that point that the Christian mystic differs, with a difference unspeakable, from every pantheist and Neoplatonist.[7] That is the mysticism of St. Paul, and that is the mysticism of St. John. The pagan mystics, whom they knew so well, entered the secret place with empty hands. But they, out of the garden of the church, went in, and locked the door, and were alone; but each carried on his breast the Rose of Sharon, and in his hand the Lily of the Valleys.

One great service which mysticism renders is to keep religion from rigidity. When the church is in danger of becoming hard, mysticism exerts a softening power. There are times when the church is very dry and doctrinal, with clear-cut answers to every human problem, and men may seek refuge for the life of feeling then in the

---

7. Third-century A.D. philosophical school founded by Plotinus.

beauty of ritual or the joy of praise. But the true salvation from a cold dogmatic is the breath of a mystical spirit in the church, and the opening of eyes of awe upon the infinite, and the wondering spirit of a little child. When I was sent, a young minister, to Thurso, I found myself in a very strange environment. I found myself among a people to whom the doctrines of the faith were everything. And gradually, true Scotsman that I was, I found myself reveling in these dogmatic things, and able to split a hair with any of them on election and foreknowledge and freewill. But I had one friend there who was a perfect mystic, as surely as he was a perfect gentleman. He is still there, rich in the inward light, though he has fallen on loneliness and blindness. And I bear my witness how that mystic saved me when my religion was becoming intellectual, and showed me how, with all our definitions, we must yet be still and know that He is God. In some such way, I think, in every age has mysticism been a blessing to the church. It has softened outlines. It has moved the heart. It has kept the truth from being stern and rigid. It has gone out from council and assembly, where creeds were fashioned and heresies condemned, and it has remembered that even at the cross there was darkness from the sixth hour to the ninth.

In mysticism again there is a refuge from our modern critical unsettlement. In a day of unsettlement and bewilderment like this, it is a refuge from the storm and a shadow from the heat. There was a time not so long ago when the record of Holy Scripture was unquestioned. Every page was verbally inspired, and every statement had a divine authority. But now that old security is gone, and a thousand questions are asked about the Bible, and much that seemed fixed as the eternal hills is felt to be contingent and provisional. It was easy once to have a living faith, based on the impregnable rock of Holy Scripture. It is easy still for all who play the traitor to the light which knowledge is pouring on the Word. But it is not easy for the honest man, who welcomes light whatever it discloses, and yet who feels that life is simply meaningless without the fellowship of Jesus Christ. How to be certain when all things seem uncertain—how to be fixed when everything is shifting—that is the difficulty which thousands feel who are touched with the critical spirit of today. And it is just there, as it seems to me, that Christian mysticism has its place and value, making it possible, amid all unsettlement, to have a life of joy and power and peace. For mysticism does not go to Holy Scripture with any theory of inspiration. It does not go to find any doctrines there, or to prove or disprove anything at all. But it goes to the Bible with a childlike heart, bent upon finding Someone who is calling, and, having found Him, it opens wide the heart to Him, and says, "Come in, You blessed of the Lord." As when a storm is raging on the sea, and in that storm is someone whom we love, and we can hardly see him for the driving mist, and yet we know he is yonder on the waters, and so are we fearful and smitten to the heart till he makes the shore, and we clasp him in our arms, and then we are no longer fearful but can look on the crested waters and be still; so when once out of the stormy sea we have drawn Christ into the secret place, then for us there is no terror in the tempest. And remember that that is always possible, no matter what our views of Scripture be. There is Christ, arising from its pages, mysterious, ineffable, sublime. Take Him in, my brother, to your heart. Do not ask if the Bible be the Word of God. The Bible is the Word of God to you, if it brings you face to face with Jesus Christ.

Do you remember how Principal Shairp puts that?

I have a life with Christ to live,
But ere I live it, must I wait
Till learning can clear answer give
Of this and that book's date?
I have a life in Christ to live,
I have a death in Christ to die—
And must I wait till science give
All doubts a full reply?

Nay rather, while the sea of doubt
Is raging wildly round about,
Questioning of life and death and sin,
Let me but creep within
Thy fold, O Christ, and at Thy feet
Take but the lowest seat
And hear Thine awful voice repeat
In gentlest accents heavenly sweet,
Come unto Me, and rest;
Believe Me, and be blessed.[8]

Lastly, and in a word or two, there is this further need today for Christian mysticism. It is God's corrective for that intense activity

8. "I Have a Life with Christ to Live" by John Campbell Shairp (1819–1885), Scottish author and professor of poetry at Oxford.

which is so characteristic of the modern church. Whatever men may say about the church, she is tremendously active and energetic now. At home—abroad—in the slums of every city, she is toiling with an inspired assiduity. And ministers have such multifarious engagements that hardly can they snatch a quiet hour, and men and women have so many meetings that they have scarcely time to meet with God. Of all the blessings of this immense activity there is no one more thankfully cognizant than I am. It has called into action innumerable gifts, and made many a wilderness blossom as the rose. And yet in the glow and fervor of that service there is one peril that is always imminent, and that is the peril lest the church forget that she must be still and know that He is God. It is so much easier to bustle than to brood—so much easier to strive than to be still—so much easier to take the outward road than deliberately to take the inward road. And it is thus that a true Christian mysticism is needed to balance our clamorous activities, for in quietness and confidence shall be our strength. I look with all the desire of my heart for the spiritual revival that is coming. I am confident that I shall live to see the day when like doves to their windows men shall flock to Christ. But of this I am sure that that day will not dawn till we have less faith in outward organizings, and a far deeper and more powerful faith in the brooding of the Holy Spirit. Whenever the church relies on her committees—whenever she begins to be proud of her machinery—whenever she forgets, in social zeal, to wonder and to be still and to adore, then mysticism comes, and like a breath from heaven falls on the cheek of all her fevered striving, and bids her seek the beatitude of rest. Be still and know that I am God, mysticism says. He leads the sheep by waters that are still. Not in the whirlwind is God manifested; He speaks to the weaned heart in the still voice. And when He speaks, and when at last we hear Him, the thirsty land shall become springs of water, and the ransomed of the Lord shall come to Zion with songs and everlasting joy upon their heads.

Thy gentleness hath made me great
(Ps. 18:35).

16

The Gentleness of God

What exactly may be meant by greatness is a question that we need not linger to discuss. It is enough that the writer of this verse was conscious that he had been lifted to that eminence. That he had been in very sore distress is clear from the earlier verses of this chapter. His heart had fainted—his efforts had been vain—his hopes had flickered and sunk into their ashes. And then mysteriously, but very certainly, he had been carried upward to light and power and liberty, and now he is looking back over it all. That it was God who had so raised him up was, of course, as clear to him as noonday. He had sent up his cry to heaven in the dark, and to that cry his greatness was the answer. But what impressed him as he surveyed it all was not the infinite power of the Almighty; it was rather the amazing and unceasing gentleness wherewith that infinite power had been displayed. Thy gentleness has made me great, he cried. That was the outstanding and arresting feature. Tracing the way by which he had been led, he saw conspicuous a gentle ministry. And so tonight in brotherhood with him, and interpreting in the light of Christ that old expression, I should like to speak on the gentleness of God.

Let me say in passing that that wonderful conception is really peculiar to the Bible. I know no deity in any sacred book that exhibits such an attribute as that. Of course, when you have many gods, it is always possible that one of them be gentle. When the whole world is tenanted with spirits, some of them doubtless will be gentle spirits. But that is a very different thing indeed from saying that the one Lord of heaven and earth has that in His heart which we can dimly picture under the human attribute of gentleness. No prophets save the prophets of Israel ever conceived the gentleness of God. To no other poets save these Jewish poets was the thought of heavenly gentleness revealed. And so when we delight in this great theme, we are dwelling on something eminently biblical, something that makes us, with all our Christian liberty, debtors unto this hour to the Jew.

Now if we wish to grasp the wonder of God's gentleness, there are one or two things we ought to do. We ought, for instance, ever to lay it against the background of the *divine omnipotence*. You know quite well that the greater the power, the more arresting does gentleness become. As might advances and energy increases, so always the more notable is gentleness. It is far more striking in a mailed warrior than in a mother with her woman's heart; far more impressive in the lord of armies than in some retired and ineffectual dreamer. The mightier the power a man commands, the more compelling is his trait of gentleness. If he be tyrant of a million subjects, a touch of tenderness is thrilling. And it is when we think of the infinite might of God, who is King of kings and Lord of lords, that we realize the wonder of our text. It is He who calls out the stars by number, and makes the pillars of the heaven to shake. And when He works, no man can stay His hand, nor say to Him, What are you doing? And it is this ruler, infinite in power, before whom the princes of the earth are vanity, who is exquisitely and forever gentle.

Again, to feel the wonder of it, we must set it against the background of *God's righteousness*. It is when we hear the seraphs crying Holy, that we thrill to the thought of the gentleness of God. There is a kind of gentleness—we are all familiar with it—that springs from an easy and uncaring tolerance. It is the happy, good nature of those characters to whom both right and wrong are nebulous. Never inspired by any love of goodness, and never touched by any hate of evil, it is not difficult to walk the world with a certain smiling tolerance of everybody. Now there have been nations whose gods were of that kind. Their gentleness was the index of their weakness. Living immoral lives on their Olympus,[1] why should

1. Mt. Olympus in Greece, legendary home of the Greek gods.

they worry about man's immorality? But I need hardly linger to point out to you that the one radical thing about the Jewish God—the one unchanging feature of His being—was that He was infinitely and forever holy. He was of purer eyes than to behold iniquity. The soul that sins, said the prophet, it shall die. And He visits the sins of the fathers on the children, even to the third and fourth generation. All this was graven on the Jewish heart, and inwrought into the Jewish history; yet could the psalmist sing in his great hour, Thy gentleness hath made me great. I beg of you therefore never to imagine that the gentleness of God is but an easy tolerance. Whatever it be, it certainly is not that, as life sooner or later shows to every man. Whatever it be, it leans against the background of a righteousness that burns as a fire does, and I say that helps us to feel the wonder of it.

Well now, if the gentleness of God be a great fact, we shall expect to light on traces of it everywhere. And I think that the more we dwell upon His handiwork, the more clear to us does it become.

Think, for example, of the realm of nature—of this spacious world in which we dwell. It is not only eloquent of power; it is eloquent also of the hiding of that power. Men used to think, in bygone days, that the universe was all created in one week. There was the fiat of divine omnipotence, and lo, the birds were singing on the trees. But now we know, thanks to the toil of science, that the ways of the divine were not like that, but were far more wonderful than that. Not in one hour did God adorn His cosmos, but through the patient toil of countless ages. Unbaffled and undeterred and undismayed, He held to His purpose of a world of beauty. Until at last, by a handling so delicate that the tiniest despised weed rejoices in it, every tree has its distinctive grace, and every bird has its distinctive song. Creation in a day may tell of power, but I want to know more of the Creator than just power. I want to trace in the broad world around me foregleams of that God I find in Christ. And it is when I learn how the Creator moves in infinite delicacy through countless ages, that I find in nature something more than power; I find there the gentleness of God. There is not a daisy in any summer meadow but could say, Thy gentleness hath made me great. There is not a bird that flies across the heaven but could take up and carry on the cry. For bird and flower and sun and moon and star are what they are, not because God is mighty only, but because the hand of God through ages has been unceasingly and exquisitely gentle.

The same jewel upon the bosom of omnipotence flashes out as we survey the Bible. The Bible is really one long record of the amazing gentleness of God. Other features of the divine character may be more immediately impressive there. And reading hastily, one might easily miss the revelation of a gentle God. Yet so might one, walking beside the sea, where hammers were ringing in the village workshop, easily miss the underlying music of the waves ceaselessly breaking on the shore. But the waves are breaking although the hammers drown them, and the gentleness of God is always there. It is there—not very far away—at the heart of all the holiness and sovereignty; it is there where the fire of His anger waxes hot and His judgments are abroad upon the earth, and men are crying, It is a fearful thing to fall into the hands of the living God.

Take, for instance, that opening Scripture of Adam and of his sin and exile. Whatever else it means, it means unquestionably that God is angry with disobedient man. And yet at the back of it what an unequaled tenderness, as of a father pitying his children, and loving them with a love that never burns so bright as in the bitter hour of necessary punishment. Losing his innocence, in the love of God Adam found his calling and his crown. He fell to rise into a world of toil, and through his toil to realize his powers. So looking backward, through that bitter discipline, unparadised but not unshepherded, he too could surely say with David, Thy gentleness hath made me great.

Or think again of the story of the Exodus, that true foundation of the Jewish race. It took one night to take Israel out of Egypt, but forty years to take Egypt out of Israel. And while that night, when the firstborn were slain, was dark and terrible with the mighty power of God, what are those forty years of desert wandering but the witness of the gentleness of heaven? Leaving Egypt a company of slaves, they had to win the spirit of the free. Leaving it shiftless, they had to win reliance; leaving it cowardly, they had to learn to conquer; leaving it mean, as slaves are always mean, they were to reach to greatness by and by, and looking back on it all what could they say but this, Thy gentleness hath made me great. Never forget that in its age-long story the Bible reveals the gentleness of God. Hinted at in every flower that blossoms, it is evidently declared in Holy Scripture. It is seen in Adam and in Abraham. It is seen in the wilderness journey of the Israelites. It is found in the choicest oracles of prophecy, and in the sweetest music of the psalms.

I think, too, that as life advances, we can all set to our seal that

that is true. We all discover, as the psalmist did, how mighty has been the gentleness of heaven. In the ordinary senses of the word, you and I may not be reckoned great. We have neither been born great, nor have we come to greatness, nor has greatness been thrust upon us. And yet it may be that for you and me life is a nobler thing than it was long ago, and truth is more queenly, and duty more august, than in a bypast day we can remember. We may not have won any striking moral victories, yet has our life leaned to the victorious side. We have not conquered yet all that we hoped to conquer, yet our will is serving us better through the years. There are still impurities that lift up their heads, and still passions that have to be brought to heel, yet it may be that you and I tonight are nearer the sunrise than ten years ago. If, then, that be so with you, I bid you halt a moment this Sabbath evening. I bid you look back on the way that you have come, and think of all that life has meant for you. For if you do it, and do it in sincerity, I believe that you, like the old psalmist, will go out into the lighted streets and whisper, Thy gentleness hath made me great. Think of the temptations that would have overcome you had not God in His gentleness taken them away. Think of the courage you got when things were dark; of the doors that opened when every way seemed barred. Think of the unworthy things that you have done which God in His infinite gentleness has hidden, of the love that inspired you, and of the hope that came to you, when not far distant was the sound of breakers. You, too, if you are a man at all, can lift up your eyes and cry out, God is just. It may be you can do more than that, and lifting up your voice say, *God is terrible*. But if you have eyes to see, and a heart to understand, there is something more that you can say, for you can whisper, "To me, in pardoning, shielding mercy, God has been infinitely and divinely gentle." If every lily of the field, lifting its head, can say, Thy gentleness hath made me great; if every sparrow chirping on the eaves is only echoing that meadow music, then I do feel that you and I, who are of more value to God than many sparrows, owe more than we shall ever understand to the abounding gentleness of heaven.

Now it seems to me that this gentleness of God reveals certain precious things about Him. It reveals, for instance, and it is rooted in, His perfect understanding of His children. There is a saying with which you are familiar; it is that to know all is to forgive all. That is an apothegm, and like all apothegms, it is not commensurate with the whole truth. Yet as a simple matter of experience, so much of our harshness has its rise in ignorance, that such a saying is sure of immortality—to know all is to forgive all. How often you and I, after some judgment, have said to ourselves, If I had only known. Something is told us that we knew nothing of, and instantly there is a revulsion in our hearts. And we retract the judgment that we passed, and we bitterly regret we were unfeeling, and we say we never would have spoken so, had we but known. The more we know—I speak in a broad way—the more we know, the more gentle we become. The more we understand what human life is, the more does a great pitifulness reach us. And I take it that it is just because our heavenly Father sees right down into the secret heart, that He is so greatly and pitifully gentle. For He knows our frame, and remembers we are dust, and He puts all our tears into His bottle. And there is not a cross we carry and not a thought we think but He is acquainted with it altogether. And all we have inherited by birth, of power or of weakness, of longing or of fear—I take it that all that is known to the God of Abraham, of Isaac, and of Jacob.

And then again it reveals this to us—it reveals our abiding value in His sight. It tells us, as almost nothing else can tell us, that we, His children, are precious in His eyes. There are certain books upon my shelves at home with which I scarcely trouble to be gentle. I am not vexed when I see them tossed about, nor when they are handled in an untender way. But there are other books that I could never handle without a certain reverence and care, and I am gentle because they are of value to me. And the singular thing is that these precious volumes are not always the volumes that are most finely bound. Some of them are little tattered creatures that a respectable servant longs to light the fire with. But every respectable servant of a booklover comes to learn this at least about the master, that his ways, like those of another Master, are mysterious and past finding out. For that little volume, tattered though it be, may have memories that make it infinitely precious—memories of school days or of college days, memories of the hillside where first we read it. It may be the first Shakespeare that we ever had, or the first Milton that we ever handled, and we shall handle it gently to the end, because to us it is a precious thing. So I take it God is gentle, because you and I are precious in His sight. He is infinitely patient with the worst of us because He values the worst of us so dearly. And if you want to know how great that value is, then go home and read this text again: For God so loved the world that He gave His only begotten Son, that whosoever believes in Him should not perish.

Lord, suffer me first to go and bury my father (Luke 9:59).

17

The Conflict of Duties

There has been very considerable discussion as to the precise import of this incident, but the moral significance of it is unmistakable. Here is a man whose difficulty lay in the pressure upon him of conflicting duties. On the one hand he felt the claims of home. He had his duties which he owed a father. On the other hand he heard the call of Christ, bidding him come away and follow Him. And all his difficulty in that great hour, when the windows were opened and the deeps were broken up, was how to reconcile in his own conscience these two competing and conflicting duties. He was not torn between the right and wrong. He was torn between the right and right. He hesitated between two rival claims, both of them stamped with the seal of the divine. For on the one hand there was his filial piety, and his passionate reverence for the honored dead; and on the other hand, imperious and urgent, there was the call of the Lord Jesus Christ.

Now the primal and most bitter conflict of mankind is the conflict between what is good and what is evil. Into that heritage we are all born, and there is no escape from it to the last hour we live. "O wretched man," cries the apostle, "who shall deliver me from the body of this death?" Paul knew, through all his fellowship with Christ, what it was to be clutched at by the beast. And there is no strife of any civil war, or of cross and crescent, or of east or west, that is so terrible and long as that. I had a young friend who came back from Keswick[1] once as if it was going to be singing all the time, and full of his happiness and new-found ecstasy he went to see my venerable father, Dr. Whyte.[2] And Dr. Whyte looked on him and laid his hand upon him, and said with all the intensity of love, "Sir, it will be a sair warstle to the end." My brother and sister, you may lay your reckoning that it will be a sair warstle[3] to the end. For we wrestle not against flesh and blood, but against principalities and powers of spiritual darkness. And yet, as many here can testify, the battle of every day may end in victory, when a man has learned that the strength he has to keep him is the strength of a risen and a living Christ.

But as life advances and deepens and enriches, there is another conflict which emerges. It is not the conflict between right and wrong. It is the conflict between right and right. All of us stand in various relationships, and life is rich in proportion to relationships. To be utterly alone were to be dead, for no man lives to himself. And these relationships, as they enlarge our being, and heighten our personality indefinitely, so do they carry with them, in their widening circles, an ever increasing complexity of duty. As life grows richer, gladnesses increase. As life grows richer, duties are augmented. Every new tie that man or woman forms carries its burden as surely as its blessing. Every new plighting of troth in holy wedlock, every new opening of an infant's eyes, carries its claim as well as its delight. Send a man out into some savage wilderness, and you limit his duty to himself and God. Give him his place in family and state, and family and state lay hands upon him. And so as life advances in complexity, and grows more intricate and rich and wonderful, duties are born which we accept from God, and which are yet very hard to reconcile. So to the conflict between right and wrong there is added the conflict between right and right. New voices call us, new claims press in upon us, and they seem to jar with the old familiar voices. There are men whose most bitter and sorest struggle is not the fight between duty and disloyalty. It is the secret battle of the spirit between one clear duty and another.

---

1. Evangelical Bible conference held annually in northern England.
2. Alexander Whyte (1837–1921), professor at New College, Edinburgh, and Scottish Free Church clergyman.
3. a difficult struggle

On the field of history that is strikingly exemplified by the conflict between military and religious duty. Right down the ages we have signal instances of this moral collision in the soldier's life. No duty is more sacred than a soldier's duty. He is bound in absolute loyalty to his king. For him obedience is the crowning virtue, and disobedience the depth of criminality. And hence for him, bound by his soldier's oath, the awfulness of the problem that confronts him when the obedience he owes his king clashes with his obedience to his God. The Jews realized it when, as Josephus tells us, they were ordered to help to build the heathen temples. In the Roman Empire it was the trial and tragedy of many a soldier who became a Christian. And sometimes in Catholic countries, when our Scottish regiments were bidden to present arms when the Host was passing, loyalty to King George was hard to reconcile with loyalty to the Lord Jesus Christ. It was this conflict in 1857 that gave us the horror of the Indian Mutiny. For never were soldiers more superbly loyal than the Sepoy regiments who wrought the havoc.[4] And all the awful horror of that time, and the carnage, and the tottering of our empire, sprang from the conflict in these souls between military and religious duty.

The same collision in social life is often experienced in another way. It is experienced in the strife that wages between the duties of mercy and of justice. That we are called to be merciful as Christ was merciful is graven deep on every Christian heart. We are to be tender-hearted, forgiving one another, even as God for Christ's sake has forgiven us. We are to bear all things and to believe all things—we are to be patient not to some men but to all—we are to pardon those who have wronged us and defrauded us, not once or twice, but seventy times seven. Now if you have ever tried to live that life you will know something of its tremendous difficulty. If to be merciful were our one duty, it would always be hard for stubborn hearts like ours. But who does not know how its hardness is intensified when, through the crying of the call for mercy, there is heard imperiously and in the name of God the clarion voice that demands justice. If charity is not to grow degenerate, if public life is to preserve its purity, the need of justice between man and man is equally divine with that of mercy. And sometimes the hardest task a man can have is just to reconcile that call for justice with the love in Christ that is always tender-hearted, and pitiful, and ready to forgive. Life calls for the stern word

4. The 1857–58 mutiny of native soldiers (Sepoys) against the army of the East India Co.

as well as for the sweetness of compassion. Life calls for the resolute will and the clear brain as well as for the infinitely tender heart. And there come hours for everyone of us, sometimes at home and sometimes in our work, when the difficulty that drives us to our knees is the difficulty of these conflicting duties.

But still more powerfully do men feel this pressure in regard to the concentric circles of their lives. For all of us live within concentric circles that widen out until they reach infinity. We are surrounded firstly by the home, and the poorest home is always rich in duty. We are surrounded next by the community, by the common life in the heart of which we dwell. And then we are surrounded by the church, and by the teeming life of all the world; and then, for king and peasant and prodigal and saint, the ultimate environment is God. Now one great mark of an advancing life is that it is wakened to the call of these environments. Over the stir and murmur of the self, voices grow audible from further distances. And first they are voices of wife and children, and then of the lives that need us in the city, and then of the great world that lies in bondage, and waits for the redemption of Christ Jesus. Always when we are walking in the light the range of our duties is infinitely widening. If we hear new music in the summer morning, we hear new calling for succor in the dark. And how to say to every voice that claims us, "Speak, Lord, Thy servant heareth," is sometimes harder than to say to Simon, "Get thee behind me, Satan." There is the call of the slums that many a man has heard, "Come down and help us, for we need you so"; there is the call of the wife, sitting alone at home, and of the children there who hardly know their father. There is the call of the great heathen world for missionaries to go abroad and tell of Jesus Christ and then, not less divine than that, the call of a desolate and widowed mother. Ah, sir, if it were right and wrong, we could rise up and make a swift decision. In the strength of Christ we could abhor the evil, and cleave in the Holy Spirit to what was good. But the perplexity and anguish of the heart, and the indecision which is always misery, springs from the clashing not of right and wrong, but rather from the clash of *right* with *right*. In such an hour there is no help for anybody except in personal fellowship with Jesus. All rules are powerless, all maxims ineffectual, and that is why Christ was no trafficker in maxims. Nothing will guide a man in such a difficulty but the living direction of the living Savior, which is intensely personal, and intensely moral, and to the upward lifted heart intensely real.

May I say in passing that this thought illuminates the temptations of our Lord for me? Men have always felt and always will feel the difficulty of thinking of a tempted Savior. That Christ was sinless—infinitely holy—as a reasonable man I must believe. That Christ was tempted in the most real way I could never dream of doubting for an instant. But how a sinless being could be tempted, and feel the anguish and onset of temptation, is very difficult for any mind to fathom. Now I make no pretense to having fathomed it. "God without mystery were not good news" to me. It makes me eager to see Him in the eternal morning, when I think of all He is keeping back to tell me then. But when I meditate on these deep and dark experiences that emerge at the very heart of human life, I begin to see which way the dawn is crimsoning. When I think how the best and holiest I have known have been tempted not with evil but with good; when I think how in some of the most beautiful and saintly lives the sorest battle has been of right with right; when I recall the fact that as life deepens, there may be conflict without one shadow of disloyalty, I see a gleam on the mystery of Christ. If struggle ceased as life became more glorious, then the temptation of Christ would be inexplicable. If conflict ended when sin was overcome, then it would be mockery to think that Christ was tempted. But when we find that with expanding life there comes the new possibility of anguish, then who can tell what blood and tears were possible to that last expansion of life in Jesus Christ.

In closing—for you will remember that I am a Christian minister and not a lecturer on moral problems—in closing will you allow me to show to you the evangelical aspect of these ethics? What I mean is this, that in the Christian gospel that conflict of duties is not confined to man; it is reflected in its full intensity in the life of the eternal God. That God is righteous and infinitely holy, you and I reverently believe tonight. That God is merciful and infinitely loving, you and I have been taught since we were children. And the whole New Testament on its Godward side is but the story of infinite wisdom, reconciling, in a way most wonderful, infinite righteousness and boundless love. How to maintain that law which binds the universe, and yet to welcome and receive the breaker of it; how to reveal the hate of God for sin, and yet to show His love for every sinner—that was the problem which confronted heaven, and which it took infinite wisdom to resolve, and which solved for me, and I do trust for you, the infinite marvel of the cross of Christ. Once I have understood the cross of Christ, I can never doubt the righteousness of God. Once I have understood the cross of Christ, I never can doubt the love of God again. And so in experience, although it baffle thought, I come to feel in the very deeps of being that God hates sin with a consuming hatred, and yet that He loves me with a father's love. Righteousness without mercy cannot save me, for I have broken every commandment. Mercy without justice cannot save me, for the moral law is engraven on my heart. But when I grasp the feet of the Lord Jesus Christ, and let His love flow down into my being, then righteousness and love are reconciled.

No prophecy of the scripture is of any private interpretation (2 Peter 1:20).

18

Inspiration Not Private Interpretation

There are some texts with the words of which we have been familiar since our childhood, and yet we may never have seriously asked ourselves what is their true meaning. Their cadence lingers with us through the years, enriched with recollections of the sanctuary, associated in sweet and tender ways with the worship at the family altar, and yet it may be that all the time we have been misinterpreting the Word of God, or reading into it a sense that was not there. Now this text which I have chosen is one, I think, that is often so misread. The words have a most familiar sound, but have we ever really thought what they imply? It is on that that I should like to dwell tonight, for the subject is one of very deep importance, and rightly understood ought to assist us greatly in our conception of what inspiration is. Observe that *prophecy* is a very large term. You must not confuse it with the word *prediction.* As the priest was one who spoke to God, so was the prophet one who spoke for God. And so the word *prophecy,* in such a place as this, is practically equivalent to our Scripture, which is the revelation of God through man to us.

Well then, our text is sometimes held to mean that you and I must not interpret Scripture privately: that is, we must not take the Word of God and wrest it to our peculiar circumstances. That that is a common mishandling of Scripture every one of us this evening knows. When men are in doubt about some action, they often seize on a text to quiet their conscience. And it is this taking of the large Word of God, and using it for our own private interest, that Peter is supposed to be here speaking of. Now that is a warning which is always timely, and never antiquated nor out of place. It is possible now, as nineteen hundred years ago, to wrest the Scripture to our own destruction. Yet the whole tenor of the passage shows us that it was not that which was in the mind of Peter when he wrote, "No prophecy is of private interpretation."

Again, these words have been taken to mean that we must not isolate the separate words of Scripture. We must not divorce them from the general sense, and give them a private meaning of their own. The word *heresy*, as many of you know, just means such a picking and selecting. A heretic was a man who, out of the whole broad truth, chose out for himself this portion or that portion. And all the evils which have followed heresy, and all the gains which heresy has wrought, have sprung from the false and often passionate emphasis which was laid on the part and not the whole. Now that also is an important truth, for we must never isolate the words of Scripture. We must never take this text or that, and interpret it out of connection with the whole. Yet once again, studying our passage, and looking to the general bearing of it, I think it is clear that that was not Peter's thought when he spoke about private interpretation.

What, then, did the apostle mean? Well, it is clear that he meant something of this nature. The interpretation he speaks of is not yours or mine—the interpretation he speaks of is the prophet's. The writers of Holy Scripture were not analysts; the writers of Holy Scripture were interpreters. Before them passed, as in some vision, the doings of God in providence and grace. And the prophet's work was to interpret these, and to show their meaning, and to convey their message, so that men might be built up in their faith. Now what Peter teaches is that that interpretation was not in any sense the prophet's own. He looked at things, and he saw meaning in them, but it was not his own meaning that he saw. It was not natural insight that conducted him, nor any genius to discern what mattered—all that would have been a private rendering, and a private rendering is not the Scripture. No prophecy is a prophet's own interpreting. It is not given by the will of man. It is the interpretation of events by something different from human genius. It is the interpretation of events by the inspiration of the Holy Spirit, dwelling in men and using every faculty for the glory of God and the blessing of mankind.

Let me say in passing that this view of Scripture is common both to the Old and the New Testaments. I should never dream of building up the doctrine if it had no other warrant than this text. I need not dwell on the Old Testament, for the fact is too patent there to be disputed. "And the word of the Lord came to Joel," that is the attitude of all the prophets. But it may be that you have never noticed how the New Testament adopts that attitude in regard to the testimony of the apostles to Jesus, and to His death and resurrection. Does it not seem a very simple thing to bear testimony to certain facts of history? Could not an honest man with a fair mind have borne witness to the crucifixion? And yet the apostles, who from first to last were witnesses and nothing else than witnesses, are regarded as only fit for that by the indwelling of the Holy Spirit. The Spirit of truth who proceeds from the Father—it is He who is to witness, said our Lord. And we are witnesses of these things, cries Peter in the Acts, and so also is the Holy Spirit. In other words, these men who wrote the Scriptures interpreted the facts, not privately, but through a Spirit given from the Father, who was something other than their genius.

Now this view of Scripture inspiration, which I see not how any can gainsay, sets it apart at once in kind from inspiration of every other sort.

Think, first, of *the inspiration of the historian.* Now a true historian is not an analyst. He is something more than a mere chronicler. It is for him to show the connection of events, and to estimate their importance by their pregnancy. If he does that feebly and confusedly, then we say he is a poor historian. If he does it in a large and illuminative way, we say he has a genius for history. Yet even when there is a genius for history, and logical power, and a grasp of facts, all that we expect in the historian is his personal interpretation of the past. That is why Robertson[1] will treat of a period in a manner wholly different from Hume.[2] That is why Lecky,[3] handling the same facts, will give them a different complexion from Macaulay.[4] They are

1. William Robertson (1721–1793), Scottish historian and principal of Edinburgh university.
2. David Hume (1711–1776), Scottish historian and philosopher.
3. William Lecky (1838–1938), British historian.
4. Thomas Macaulay (1800–1859), British historian and statesman.

inspired, if you care to call them so, using the word in a loose and general way, yet at their best and wisest all they give us is their private interpretation of the past.

Or think of the *inspiration of the dramatist*, as we have it, for instance, in the plays of Shakespeare. We are wont to say that Shakespeare is inspired, and that in a broad sense is true. Well now, suppose you take a play of Shakespeare—take, for instance, the play *Macbeth*. You say that that is an inspired play, and I ask you what you mean by that? Well, there is only one thing you can mean, if your words have any significance at all, and what you mean is something of this kind. You mean that Shakespeare took the few facts of history that he found in the dusty pages of some chronicle, and he touched them with life, and covered them with beauty, and filled them with passion and reality, and this he did with his *own* imagination, and with all the teeming wealth of his *own* brain, and with all the warmth and passion inextinguishable of his own private and peculiar heart. *Macbeth* and *Hamlet* came by the will of man. They are the triumph of individual genius. Their power is contained in this, that they are the rendering of one personality. Were they less private in their interpretation they would never move us as they so profoundly do. They do not live because the facts are facts. They live because Shakespeare is Shakespeare.

Now, brethren, over against all that, there stands *the inspiration of the Scripture*. Unlike all history and every drama, no prophecy is of private interpretation. When a poet is most genuinely inspired, then is he most genuinely himself. When Wordsworth is at his finest and his purest, then is he most emphatically Wordsworth. But what you are taught about Holy Scripture is, that it came not by the will of man, but holy men of God spoke as they were moved by the Holy Spirit. Isaiah did not look at events, and brood upon them, and say, Now this is my interpretation of them. John did not look at the cross and at the grave, and say, This is how it all appears to me. But they looked at every thing under that light of God, which is only kindled by the Holy Spirit, and looking so they saw, and seeing wrote. Mark you, I do not suggest that they were passive: to say that were to misinterpret everything. Probably their powers were never so alive as when they were writing a gospel or epistle. All I say is, and all that Scripture says is, that what you have in the Bible is not genius; it is something different from, and something more divine than, a private interpretation of events.

This fact, let me just say in passing, explains the wonderful unity of Scripture. A deepened sense of that great unity is one great gain of recent Bible study. Men used to argue, and not so long ago, that the Scripture was in arms against itself. They used to argue that John and Paul and Peter were always quietly girding at each other. But I do not know one scholar of authority who would ever dream of saying that today: whatever we have lost in recent criticism, we have gained immensely in the sense of unity. Now if there were ever writers of vigorous and independent personality, I think you may take it that these writers were the men who have given us the New Testament. If there were ever men who would have looked at facts in diverse or antagonistic ways, John and Paul and Peter were such men. In other words, had the Scripture which they wrote been their own personal interpretation, then almost certainly you would have found between them differences that were irreconcilable. And the very fact that these are never found, when they are handling the deep things of God, is a witness to an inspiration different in kind from that of genius. There is the freest play of personality—the writers are penmen and not pens—at the back of every chapter which they wrote is a rich and individual experience. Yet such is the deep and underlying unity in all that is essential to salvation, that the more we study the more we are convinced that the Scripture came not by the will of man. No prophecy is a private rendering. Had it been so we should have had many Bibles. We should have had a Bible of John, where everything was love, perhaps; and a Bible of Paul, where everything was righteousness. And the very fact that the Testament is one, when men so different were the writers of it, speaks of more than individual genius in all its interpretation of events.

Now if this be the scriptural view of inspiration, then we may proceed to ask another question. We may ask, Are there any features in the Scripture which help to corroborate this view? No prophecy is a private rendering. The Scripture came not by the will of man. Are there any features in the Word of God which would incline us to accept that as the truth? In other words, do we find in Holy Scripture what it is almost incredible that we should find, had the writers been consulting their own will? When a man is following his own bent, there are certain things which he avoids. There are aspects of things which from certain standpoints may be highly and naturally uncongenial. And if you find these very aspects dwelt on and expanded and enforced, then you may reasonably conclude that something else is active besides the writer's individual will. Now that is exactly what one finds in Scripture, and finds it the more the more one's knowledge grows. There is a certain curious want of correspondence between the message and the men who uttered it. And I shall close by touching upon that in one or two of its most salient features, that we may see how evident it is that Scripture came not by the will of man.

First, then, I note how often prophetic doctrine contradicts the bias of the will. If there is one thing clear in the prophets it is this, that the truths they uttered were often uncongenial. Now men have spoken uncongenial truths sometimes under a compelling sense of duty. When every interest urged them to be silent, their conscience has compelled them to speak out. But you can never explain that old prophetic fire by saying that it was duty which impassioned it, for duty seemed to point the other way. The call of duty is the call of loyalty. The call of duty is the call of home. The call of duty is the call of patriotism, when the enemy is marching on the gate. And yet how often these old prophetic heroes lifted the voice up in the name of God, and contradicted every such call. Humanly speaking, they dared to be disloyal. Humanly speaking, they betrayed their country. Humanly speaking, they advocated courses that to the wisest seemed to lead to ruin. And if time has showed that they were not disloyal, but the truest patriots in Israel, that only means that in their word of prophecy they were moved by a wisdom higher than their own. They crushed into the dust their private prejudices. They shattered by their speech their private hopes. They flung to the winds, when they lifted up their voice, their private interests and advantages. And what I say is that if the word of prophecy had come to us solely by the will of man, the Bible would have a different tale to tell. No prophecy is of private interpretation. No one would dream it was, who knows the prophets. It is not thus even the bravest speaks when he is speaking at the call of conscience. This is the speaking of men who in their darkness were under the moving of some mighty power, that sat enthroned above the dust of things, and saw the end from the beginning.

The same compulsion, as of some higher power, is seen in the portrayal of great Scripture characters. You have characters set up as an ideal, and then mysteriously that ideal is marred. The Jew had essentially a concrete mind. He loved to see all excellences embodied. He was at the heart of him a hero-worshiper, mightily influenced by old example. And that is one reason why in the Old Testament such a large place is given to biography, in the lives of

Abraham and of Moses and of David. Now remember that a Jewish writer never hesitated to idealize his hero. If he thought it would tell for edification, he would paint a character without a flaw, unhesitatingly. And yet the strange thing is that in the Word of God these grand ideals which are to inspire the world, are dashed with weakness, and tarnished with iniquity, and broken sometimes by the most shameful fall. There was one hero who was the friend of God—what a glorious theme for any Jewish writer! There was another after God's own heart—can you not picture how he would be described? Yet the one—Abraham—descended to mean trickery, and the other—David—fell to the very depths, and all this has been written down for us in the stern pages of the Word of God. My brethren, if the Scripture had come by the will of man, you would never have had anything of that; if prophecy had been a private rendering, you would have had lives like those of the medieval saints. And the very fact that you have falls like these in characters which were meant to lead the world, is a witness to another will than ours. When He, the Spirit of truth, is come, said Jesus, He will lead you into all truth. It was that spirit which came upon the prophets, and led them into the darkest truth unwillingly. Not otherwise can I explain these tragic pages, in writers who knew nothing of historic method, and who would never have hesitated to idealize the past for the glory of their people Israel.

And then, lastly, we trace the same compulsion in the self-revelation of the writers. We trace it in David in Psalm 51, for instance, and we have it manifestly in the apostles. I want you to remember that these apostolic writers were men of like passions with ourselves. They were actuated by the same desires and they knew the pressure of our common hopes. They knew, as every man must know, the desire to stand well with those who heard of them, and to hand on to coming days some not unworthy memorial of themselves. Now the point is that being men like that, they never hesitated to reveal themselves. They wrote of their weaknesses and of their sins in the very record that told the love of Christ. They concealed nothing for the sake of fame; sheltered nothing for the sake of honor; cast no veil on an unworthy hour even in the sacred cause of friendship. Could not Peter have instructed Mark to cover up the tale of his denial? Might not John, being the friend of Peter, have dwelt a little less upon his fall? But the Scripture came not by the will of man, nor is any prophecy a private rendering, and there it all stands written to this hour. There is no hurling of contempt at

Judas—a chapter like that would have been very natural. There is no golden and enhaloed picture of the men who had left everything for Jesus. John knew not what spirit Christ was of. Peter denied Him with a fisher's curses. Judas, in a profound and awful silence, goes to his own place—and that is all. That is not the moving of the will; that is the moving of the Holy Spirit. *That* is the kind of thing which Scripture indicates when it says of itself it is inspired. If there be one thing growing ever clearer, as knowledge widens and the ages pass, it is that Scripture came not by the will of man.

A merry heart doeth good like a medicine
(Prov. 17:22).

19

The Medicine of the Merry Heart

That this is true of a man's self is accepted by everybody nowadays. There is a medicinal value in a merry heart which every physician willingly admits. So strangely knit are we of flesh and spirit, that the one is always reacting on the other. There is the closest intercourse between the unseen spirit and the material organs of the human frame. A certain temper, allowed to rule unchecked, becomes the mother of the most painful maladies; while another temper, diligently cultivated, will do much to keep these maladies away. No prescription, couched in mysterious Latin, and costing a hundred times its real value, is half so medicinal for certain states of body as the possession of a merry heart. And that is why doctors are giving us far less now of things that benefit no one but the seller, and giving us more prescriptions that cost nothing, but make for a certain lightness of the soul. For open windows and exercise and sunshine are not prescribed for their own sake alone. It is not just for their physical effects that such insistence is put on them today. It is also because they have such a powerful influence on that unseen heart by which we live, and which, when glad and radiant and songful, is a better medicine than any on the shelves.

But it was not of that chiefly that Solomon was thinking when he took his pen in hand to write this proverb. He was thinking not of the effect upon oneself, but of the effect of a merry heart on other people. Probably, like many another proverb, it had been struck out in his own personal experience. He had been gloomy one day, and very ill at ease, with a brooding melancholy on his kingly heart. And all the knowledge of which he was the master, and all the delights of which he was the lord, and all the covenant mercies of his father David, could not banish the shadow from that royal brow. And then right down the marble corridor, nearer and nearer, came a singing voice—someone so gloriously happy and lighthearted that the melancholy of the king shone up ridiculous. And then he took his pen and wrote down quickly, on the little roll that was always by his side, *A merry heart does good like a medicine*. So in one moment of a sweet experience did he learn the secret of an abiding truth. So always in our fresh, deep moments have we glimpses of what is valid through the ages. And he is wise, as Solomon was wise, who will never be recreant to that fleeting vision, in hours when the vision is no longer bright, in the clamor and crowding of the street.

There is a beautiful story of Henry Ward Beecher,[1] which some of you may have heard, and which I often think on. One evening, leaving his tabernacle after service, he passed two little urchins at the door. It was a bitter night, and they were raggedly clothed, selling papers to the passersby. And he put his hands on their heads, and gave them a few coppers, and said, "Poor little chaps, aren't you very cold?" And one of them answered, "Yes, sir, we was cold, till *you* passed by." Now there was far more than a merry heart in Beecher; there was a noble, tender, loving, Christlike heart. Still, in some such way as that, in every city street, does the merry heart prove itself medicinal. It heartens men, and puts new cheer in them, and makes them think of the sunshine in November; and in a murky and foggy world like this that is by no means a despicable service. It is a curious circumstance that when one person coughs, others in sympathy start coughing also. But coughing, save in the pessimist's philosophy, has got no monopoly of contagion. Let any man, taking his courage in both hands, go radiant and singing through this world

1. Henry Ward Beecher (1813–1887), American Congregational minister.

of shadows, and he will bring a song on to a hundred lips that otherwise would have been silent as the grave. We are always impressing ourselves on those around us, and doing it most when we least dream of it. We see as much of ourselves in other people, as we ever in reality see of them. And so unconsciously, and in those mystic ways which link our lives into a solidarity, the merry heart, to weary burdened men, does good like a medicine of God. For myself I prefer the lilting of the lark to the most glorious music of any funeral march. For myself I prefer the radiance of June to all the mystery of the November darkness. And for myself, who know something about medicines, I infinitely prefer the merry heart to the most woeful saint who ever scourged himself, thinking to please the Maker of the lilies.

Of course, there is a spurious merriment with which in one form or other we are all familiar. There is a *laughter of fools* occasionally audible, which is as the crackling of thorns under the pot. There came once to the great physician, Dr. Arbuthnot,[2] a very dejected and miserable patient. And Dr. Arbuthnot, examining him, found nothing about the man that called for treatment. "Why," he said, "all that you want is cheering: go and hear tonight that delightful clown Grimaldi." "Alas! Doctor," said the patient, "*I am Grimaldi.*" There are a great many Grimaldis in Glasgow, though one might hesitate to call them clowns. Meeting them you would think they were merry people, yet all the time they have heavy hearts. But sooner or later we detect the trickery, which may be very shallow or may be very brave, and then the merriment becomes pathetic. There is a kind of laughter that can make one weep; there is a jest that brings a lump into the throat; there is a certain gaiety which is supremely pitiful, and makes the eye grow moist. It is like those beautiful flowers that are laid where the dull earth has been heaped upon the coffin, but where everybody knows that the dear dead are lying, under the beauty of violet and lily.

Still more pitiable than forced merriment is the *thoughtless merriment* which we all know. It is the merriment of those who have not been wakened yet to what the Roman poet calls the tears of things. It is the merriment of those who live upon the surface, and have never realized that life is stern, and who will not believe that in every human lot there is a pierced hand not very far away. Such shallow folk are invariably heartless, and therefore our text cannot

2. John Arbuthnot (1667–1735), physician and writer.

refer to them. Solomon says here the merry *heart*—and the simple fact is they have no heart at all. No sorrow of the great world has ever touched them; they have never lifted a finger for a brother; were they to die tomorrow nobody would miss them except the mother whom they have ignored. Such thoughtless merriment does good to nobody. There is no element of triumph in it. There is nothing of help in it for weary people. It never makes any human burden easier. On the contrary, as is the way with selfishness, it makes a great many burdens considerably harder, though love is so loyal that it never speaks of that, but bears all things and is silent.

Indeed, that is one mark of all true merriment—that note of triumph which I have just mentioned. And it is just that element of triumph in it which makes it so largely medicinal to men. In such a life as we all have to live, it is always easy to be heavyhearted. Few of us, as our wives can testify, require to pray heaven to make us irritable. There is no sign of victory about a churlish temper, but rather a certain signal of defeat, and it is by victories and not defeats that battling men and women are encouraged. Whenever a man is dull and heavyhearted, I say that so far he has had the worst of it. He has gone out into the world with all its cares, and the world with all its cares has beaten him. And what men feel about the merry heart is that it too has had to bear the common burdens, and has come through it all in a victorious way, so as never to lose the sunshine and the song. I have known men whose look of triumph was a look of very grim determination. They had to fight the devil in terrific fashion, and the grim look has never left their faces. But the merry heart which in the darkest can still join in the music and the romp of children, is not less certainly a sign of victory than the grim look of the veteran in the field. That, I take it, is why men love it so. It is a note of cheer to them in the hard day. The pity about all worrying souls is this, that by their worrying they help no mortal creature. But the merry heart is the heroic heart, and seeing it men are cheered they know not how, and take themselves bravely to their tasks again.

For merriment, when you come to think of it, has roots that run far down into the soil. It is not a shallow nor a surface thing; it runs away down into self-forgetfulness. Just as the open secret of all happiness is never to think about happiness at all, but to forget oneself in larger interests, and under the glorious leadership of Christ, so the one secret of true merriment, which is as it were the shimmering of happiness, is just to die to ourselves that we may live. I defy any man ever to be merry who is always brooding on his own peculiar troubles. To have a grievance, and to dwell upon it, is one sure way to keep the sunshine out. To give the impression that we have been badly used is not only a tactical mistake in life, but is more likely than any smoke of chimneys to envelop us in a November fog. I read somewhere the other day a fact which impressed me very much. It is that out at sea the organic germs of disease cease in a great measure to exist. A vessel was tested before she left her port to see what the atmosphere was like within her. It was found, as she lay in port, to be literally full of organic germs. But when she was two days out upon the ocean, with the breeze of the open heaven blowing round her, the air was again tested scientifically, and it was found that the disease germs were gone. So always is it when we launch into the deep—and you know who has bidden us launch into the deep. There is nothing in the world like launching out for killing the germs of irritable melancholy. Just to forget ourselves and live in others, and help the lame dog across the stile occasionally, is a better secret for a merry heart than all the picture houses in the city. Let a man be filled with any great enthusiasm, and he will go whistling along the streets. I was never so happy in my life as one great holiday month when I edited the diary of Thomas Boston.[3] I certainly never sang so much before, and I have certainly never sung so much again, which perhaps in the view of my family is a mercy. Quite seriously, for those of us who know Christ, it is just there that Christ does make for merriment. In a unique and an amazing way, Christ does help us to forget ourselves. And so helping us, He does not burden us, but on the contrary gives us a great liberty from the worry and the depression and the heart-sinking that are so incident to our mortality.

But the merry heart is more than self-forgetful; it is also preeminently the trustful heart. It is those who can trust in an all-loving Father who are the genuine Merry Men of God. It is told of Mr. Spurgeon, the great preacher, that driving home to Clapham in his carriage, he suddenly, and without cause assignable, burst out into hilarious laughter. It had suddenly struck him how absurd it was to worry, as he had been worrying that morning, when he had a splendid word like this to lean upon, "My grace is sufficient for thee." *My* grace, and I, the infinite God, before whom the nations are as nothing; and you a child—a creature of a day—a little tiny insig-

3. Thomas Boston (1677–1732), Scottish minister and writer.

nificancy. And so it broke upon him how absurd it was to be going heavy-eyed and heavyhearted, with such a boundless promise for his need. That is the secret of the merriment of children—and except you become as little children. And that is the secret of the merriment of nature, for nature spite of her strife is full of play. The faith which Jesus gives us as our model is not the faith of patriarch or of prophet, but the faith of the grain of mustard seed, which is beautiful in defiance of the storm. Whenever there is distrust between child and parent, there is a shutting of the sunshine out. Whenever there is distrust between wife and husband, the birds on the branches all forget to sing. But whenever there is trust the eyes are bright, and you shall have snatches of music on the stairs, and the best medicine in the family cupboard will be the medicine of the merry heart. It is there again that Jesus Christ comes near us, and gives us the secret of true merriment. For He has given us a God whom we can trust, absolutely, entirely, unconditionally. And when we trust Him, and lean upon Him hard, and lay ourselves down on the everlasting arms, the trees of the forest begin to clap their hands. There never was a merrier heart than Martin Luther,[4] and you recall what his wife did when once he fell abrooding. She put on mournings, and she came quietly in to where he sat with his head between his hands. And "Wife," said Luther to her, "who is dead?" "Why, Martin," she answered, "surely God is dead"—and the big heart of him felt the rebuke at once, and he uprose to play the man again. It is idle to tell me to serve the Lord with mirth unless I can cast my burden on the Lord. It is idle to tell me to have a merry heart unless I am certain that God cares for me. And that is just what Jesus Christ has done, by His words, by His life, by His pierced hands and feet—He has made it absolutely sure to me that God loves me with an everlasting love.

For this reason, let me say in closing, I think the merry heart was dear to Jesus. I would gather from His life that He was fond of it, and knew how finely medicinal it was. You remember the charges that they flung at Christ—a gluttonous man and a winebibber, they called Him. They would never have dreamed of calling the Baptist that—he was so stern, so rigorous, so joyless. And it was just because Christ was different from the Baptist, and was companionable, and loved the haunts of men, that they named Him the friend

---

4. Martin Luther (1483–1546), German theologian and leader of the Protestant reformation in Germany.

of publicans and sinners. The merriest creatures in the world are children, and Jesus passionately loved the children. “Simon, son of Jonas, lovest thou Me?” “Yea, Lord, Thou knowest”—“then go and feed My lambs.” He had always leisure for them in the busiest day; always a place for them when things were darkest; always a thought for the lambs when He was risen, and lambs are the most playful creatures in the world. The Pharisees wanted the children to be men, but Jesus wanted the men to become children—except ye become as little children, ye shall in no wise enter the kingdom of God—not little cherubs with irritating cheeks, but little *children* such as He knew in Galilee, who could be very naughty now and then, but who had always the secret of the merry heart. That secret, as it seems to me, our Savior loved, just because He knew it was medicinal. He knew how it helped men when the way was rough, and how it cheered them when the road was dreary. And He proclaimed that one of life’s great victories was to keep right through it all the childlike heart, and to come smiling from the world’s great snare uncaught. If you do that, my brother, though you do nothing else, you have done far more than you imagine. If you carry your burden in a smiling fashion, you are helping your neighbor more than you have dreamed. And men will take knowledge of you that you have been with Jesus, who was a Man of sorrows, and acquainted with grief, and yet to the end, and amid darkness infinite, spoke with a thrilling heart about His joy.

Love . . . hopeth all things (1 Cor. 13:7).

20

The Hopefulness of Christ

In his admirable monograph on Cromwell,[1] Lord Morley[2] makes a very striking statement. He says that hope burned in Cromwell like a pillar of fire, when it had gone out in all others. When prospects were gloomy, and everything seemed dark, and other hearts had yielded to despair, still, like the burning pillar of the exodus, hope was aflame in the great heart of Cromwell. Now if that be conspicuously true of Cromwell, there is a greater than he of whom it is true also. Unceasingly, unfalteringly, unfailingly, hope burned and glowed in the heart of Jesus Christ. And as they said of Christ, and said with truth, Never man spoke like this man; so with equal truth might we assert, Never man *hoped* like this man. There is not one of us within this house this evening but is an infinite debtor to the *love* of Christ. You may deny it, or you may disregard it, but your indebtedness to His love is still incalculable. But not alone to His love are you indebted—that love which led Him to the garden-grave—you are indebted also to His hopefulness.

Indeed without any exaggeration one might say that hope is the

1. Oliver Cromwell (1599–1658), Puritan statesman, Lord Protector of England, 1653–58.

2. John (Viscount) Morley (1838–1923), British statesman and biographer.

characteristic of the gospel. For the gospel, as it thrills everywhere with life, so does it thrill everywhere with hope. A pagan writer, speaking of the age in which the gospel was given to the world, describes it in words which would be hard to match for pathos and for poignancy. *Moritur et ridet* is his sentence—it laughs with the death-rattle in its throat. It was an age that, for all its boast of conquest and all its inheritance of art and culture, had sunk into the deadness of despair. Then on that world, strangely and unexpectedly, there was breathed the hopefulness of Jesus Christ. And light stole back again into a thousand eyes, and life leaped up within a thousand hearts, till men began to feel that they were saved, not only by a love that bore the cross; they began to feel that they were saved by hope.

Nor is there anything like this, I should like to say in passing, in any of the great religions of the world. In its radiant quality of hope, the gospel of Jesus stands alone. There is a singular tenderness in the true Christian spirit, but I find tenderness also in the Buddhist creed. There is unswerving loyalty to God in the New Testament, but the Muslim is also finely loyal to God. But what neither Buddhist nor Muslim possesses, in virtue of that faith by which they live and die, is a personal and a spiritual hope. No true Buddhist can ever be an optimist; every true Buddhist is a pessimist. He longs to cease, and fade into forgetfulness, and enjoy the dreamless sleep of the nirvana. And not very far away from that despair, though mightily different from it in all practical issues, is the fatalism of every true Muslim. My brother, no Christian is a pessimist, and if a man is a pessimist he is not a Christian. And no true Christian is a fatalist, for Christ is the truth, and the truth has made him free. Over against that dark and dull despair, as a simple matter of historic fact, there stands forever, to inspire mankind, the wonderful hopefulness of Jesus. It was that which filled the first apostles. It was that which thrilled the world when they first saw it. It is that which is written upon the gospel page so that he who runs may read. And tonight I want you to come back to the gospel, and to look at Jesus as we find Him there, that we may appreciate a little better the wonder of the hopefulness of Christ.

We see it, for instance, very clearly in His daily handling of men and women. Christ dealt with people in a faithful way, but always also in a hopeful way. There are times when you and I have spoken hopeful words though there was little hope within our hearts. We have sought to comfort those whose hearts were sore by some little word that had the sunshine in it. But though it was kindly meant, and very easily pardonable, as breathing somewhat of our Father's pity, yet how unerringly the stricken heart reached through the word to the reality! How to be faithful and at the same time hopeful, is sometimes one of the most difficult of problems—how to be true to our own sense of truth, and yet at the same time to keep hope alive. And I say that as you read the life of Jesus you are amazed at His solving of that problem, for never was He less than perfect truth, yet did He always quicken into hope. Never was man so faithful as the Lord. Never one who could so pierce the depths. He never uttered a single word of compliment. He never said anything because it sounded kindly. And the amazing thing is that with that fine fidelity to all that was most sad and all that was most tragical, chords that were broken began again to vibrate under the thrill and music of His speech. Poor women who had fallen to the streets began to hope again, they knew not why. The thief on the cross, after a lawless life, awoke to feel that he might be remembered. In the very hour that they were self-exposed, and found themselves judged as man had never judged them, in that very hour they began to hope. That is always the wonder of Christ's hopefulness. It leans on the bosom of a perfect knowledge. It sees the vilest, and yet does not despair. It knows the worst, and yet it hopes the best. And that is why the hopefulness of Jesus is still moving and mighty in the world, when other hopes, that were all golden once, have passed, broken, into the glen of weeping.

Especially is this hopeful handling evident in Christ's constant treatment of the Twelve. Christ was not only patient with the twelve, He was magnificently hopeful too. Had He lost heart with them as the days passed, I think that no one would have wondered at it. They were so ignorant, these twelve disciples—they were so slow to learn—so irresponsive. Yet always trusting even when things were blackest, and always hoping even when hearts were dourest, He fashioned them at last into that band of heroes who carried forth the gospel to the world. Every one of these men was saved by hope. Had Christ not hoped for them, they had been lost. *They* knew not what spirit He was of, and at the very end they all forsook Him. Yet to the very end He clung to them, and trusted them in the teeth of all the evidence, and hoped them into such a manhood as has made us their debtors to this hour.

This same element of hopefulness is very evident in Jesus' teaching. I know no words of any teacher that are quite so hopeful as the words of Christ. If you read the biographies of preachers, as I have loved to do, you will find one very common feature in them. You will find that almost all the greatest preachers began their ministries with a stern note. From Chrysostom[3] right on to Dr. Parker,[4] I scarcely know one preacher of the gospel who did not begin by lifting up his voice and calling for judgment on a sinful world. The singular thing is that with Jesus the beginning was quite different from that. The old Jewish law began with cursing, but the ministry of Christ began with blessing. "Blessed are they who hunger and who thirst." "Blessed are the pure in spirit." That was the music which heralded the message, and that too was the music of the close. Many preachers lose hope when they grow old. Life lessens hope by its terrible realities. Instead of hope there comes a certain quietude, and the voice of a not unhappy resignation. But Christ the teacher, to the very end, and spite of all that life had meant for Him, still taught in the quiet of the upper chamber with the magnificent hopefulness of youth. Ah yes, someone may say to me, but what about the middle of His ministry? Is it not often in that mid-time period, when the glow is gone, that men lose hope? And so I turn back to the gospel page, and I study the midtime of Christ's ministry, and I shall tell what it is that I find there. I find a story of a coin that was lost, and seemed to be hopelessly hidden in the dust. I find a story of a sheep that wandered, yet was it not left wandering in the desert. I find a story of a prodigal son who cast from him recklessly the ties of home, and who, to every servant in that home, would seem to be lost and lost forever. But the coin was found, and the lost sheep was found, and the son who had destroyed himself was found. It is never with losing, it is always with finding, that the midtime parables of Jesus close. And I call *that* the trumpet note of hope; and the world heard it, and was saved by hope, as you and I, who also have been lost, are saved by hope this very hour.

Let me say in passing how vivid is this feature in the lessons which Jesus drew from nature. Christ dwelt upon the hopeful side of nature in a way which I have never anywhere seen justice done to. In the Old Testament you have many a noble passage which takes you out into the world of nature. Psalmists and prophets were men of open eyes, and they saw the glory of this glorious world.

3. John Chrysostom (c. 344/354–407), bishop of Constantinople and influential church Father.

4. Joseph Parker (1830–1902), English Congregational preacher.

But very generally what touched their hearts, and uttered itself in prophecy and song, was the mighty—the terrible—the awful. They heard the thunder echoing in the mountains—they saw the cedar bowing to the storm—they listened to the tumult of the sea and thought of a voice that was as many waters: so did they dwell on the sublime in nature, finding in it the shadow of their God; but of a gentle, kindly, hopeful nature, they very rarely thought and rarely spoke. Then came Jesus with His open eye, and you detect the difference at once. It is not from storm and tempest that He teaches—there is no sound of cataract or breaker. He speaks of the lily brightening the meadow, of the bird flying in the summer heaven, of the field clad in its golden mantle and bowing delicately in the autumn breeze. He takes the mustard seed, most insignificant, and finds in that the image of the kingdom. He feels the kiss of the wind upon His cheek, and says that the Holy Spirit is like that. He thinks of Mary in the home of Nazareth, hiding the lump of leaven in the meal, and He remembers how to His boyish wonder it wrought mysteriously till the whole was leavened. Everywhere, in all His nature-teaching, you have that glorious element of hopefulness. You have Christ drawing from the book of nature lessons of good cheer for mortal men. And this, mark you, though He must have known that somewhere in that world a tree was growing on which ere long He was to hang in agony, with the nails piercing His hands and feet.

And then again you find this hopefulness in Jesus' attitude toward the future. I think it is in that regard that the hopefulness of Christ is most amazing. I want you to think just for an instant of the kind of treatment which Jesus had from men. Some of them thought He was beside Himself, and others of them thought He had a devil. And His own household did not believe in Him, and His own disciples did not understand Him, and His own people, to crown all, gave Him the last welcome of the cross. If there ever was treatment that might have caused despair, I think it was the treatment Jesus knew. If there ever was ground to think the future hopeless, I think these grounds were in the life of Christ. And yet, my brother, you know as well as I do, how, with a heart calm as a summer sea, Christ seems to have looked right down the ages with a hope that was radiant and unquenchable. Wheresoever this gospel shall be preached, He said, this that this woman has done shall be declared. As often as you eat this bread and drink this cup, you do show the Lord's death until He come. He never doubted, though Simon might insult Him—He never doubted on the verge of Calvary, that men and women to the end of time would gather to His feet and would adore. Spat upon, He never doubted that. Mocked at, He never doubted that. Disbelieved in—hung upon a cross—He never doubted the glory yet to be. And I say that when you think of that, as a simple and authentic fact of history, you feel that Christ, with His unconquered hopefulness, is worth a million melancholy Buddhas.

In closing, and in a word or two, there is one other question that I want to ask. Can we discern with any clearness the sources of this saving hopefulness? Well, there is much that I might say on that, but I shall not attempt to handle it exhaustively. I shall only suggest to you three lines of thought which I regard as scripturally valid.

In the first place, the hopefulness of Christ was bound up organically with His sinlessness. Some evening I am going to preach to you on Christ's sinlessness, but tonight I just want you to take this. What, tell me, in your life and mine is the most deadly enemy of hope? It is not calamity, for if we be men at all, there is something in us that rises to calamity. The deadliest enemy of hope is sin, and every time you and I yield to sin, with all the other miseries it brings, there is always a dimming of the star of hope. Is not that true? I never met anyone who was the slave of sin who did not live on the margins of despair. I never met any victim of a secret habit who was not growing steadily more hopeless. And on the other hand, I never met a man who was living in a victorious way, into whose eyes there was not coming steadily the unmistakable light of a fine hope. Well now, Jesus Christ was sinless. He was tempted, yet He was sinless. He had His battle to fight in full reality, yet at every point of it He stood and conquered. And so out of your own experience I think you will understand me when I say, that in that tempted yet ever-conquering manhood there is one source of the hopefulness of Christ.

But not only was it rooted in His sinlessness; *it was also rooted in His love.* For as we know from what we read tonight, love hopes all things. Think of the father with his prodigal son, how he still hopes in the teeth of all the evidence. Think of the wife of an unworthy husband, how she still hopes for him, although he be a beast. For love remembers as nothing else remembers, and love can see when other eyes are blind, and love can cling with a divine tenacity when other hands are loosened in despair. Now, brother, whatever Christ was, He was wonderfully and infinitely loving. You may have doubts about many things in Christ, but you never can have any doubts of that. And if love, even our poor love, hopes all things of the beloved, then I think that in the love of Christ we find another secret of His hope.

And then, lastly, the hopefulness of Christ was His utterance of the hopefulness of God. It was the revelation of the Father's hopefulness, and saying that there is no more to say. Have you ever deeply or seriously thought about what I call the hopefulness of God? I do wish you would sit and think of it, it is such an amazing thought for social service. In the long story of an evolving universe—in the steady trend of every year to harvest—in the upbuilding of every human life—have you discerned the hopefulness of God? Theologians have talked enough about His anger. We want to talk a little more about His hopefulness. It is unconquerable. It is irresistible. It is undimmed through ages and millenniums. And for us who believe that Jesus knew the Father in a unique and incommunicable way, that hopefulness upon the fields of Galilee is but the transcript of the hope in heaven. Dear friend, there is hope for you tonight. Hope of the best for you—even for you. Strike out that word *despair* from your vocabulary. There is no room for despair where Jesus is. Were I a Buddhist, I should have no such message, but I thank God I am not a Buddhist. I am here as the messenger of One whose power is infinite, and whose hope for you is radiant as the dawn.

With twain he covered his face (Isa. 6:2).

21

The Veiled Faces of the Seraphim

This is the only place in the Old Testament where we find mention of the seraphim. It is the one glimpse we have in Scripture of these strange creatures by the throne of God. In every vision of God vouchsafed to men there are certain features which are universal. Just because God is one, and man is one, all hours of rapture have their common elements. But just because the yearning of each heart is different from that of every other heart, each vision has its peculiar character. To Moses, gazing upward into heaven, there was under the feet of God a sapphire pavement. To dying Stephen, when the heavens were opened, there was Jesus standing on the right hand of God. To Isaiah, in a circle round the throne, there rose these mystical and mighty creatures, crying antiphonally and eternally, Holy, Holy, Holy. They were in fashion as a man, for they had hands and feet, yet each was the possessor of six wings. With twain they did fly, in the ministry of God; with twain in humility they hid their feet. But most subduing of all perhaps is this, that before the dazzling radiance of God with twain they covered their faces. Just as a man who has lingered in the shadows, and steps out suddenly into a blaze of light, puts up his hand before his eyes, instinctively, to shield them from that blinding glare, so these mysterious beings round the throne, returning from their voyaging through the universe, cover their faces in the light of God. There is a radiance which they cannot brook. There is a dazzling glory which would blind them. Gifted with powers more splendid than the angels, they know it is wisest for them not to see. And so do I think they teach us our true wisdom, in regard to many of the mysteries around us, which are so dark, often, with excess of bright. We have such curiously discursive intellects that there is nothing we do not seek to penetrate. We want to gaze into the heart of things, till we have wrested from them their eternal secrets. And then the Scripture shows us these great beings, loftier in endowment than the wisest of us, and with twain of their six wings they veil their faces. They would not be so near the throne of God, unless their attitude were acceptable to God. God has not made us only to interrogate; God has made us also to adore. And I wish to suggest to you tonight one or two matters on which the questionings of man have been so futile, that it may be God does not ask our questioning, but rather the veiled faces of the seraphim.

To begin with, I take the doctrine of the Trinity—the doctrine that there are three persons in the Godhead. It is a truth that seems very remote from us sometimes, and yet it lies at the heart of Christianity. When men go out to serve in the name of Christ, I think they seldom realize the Trinity. I shall venture to say that even when they pray, they are not often conscious of the Trinity. And yet the truth that God is three in one lies at the very basis of our faith, and without it our faith is airy as a dream. For the Trinity is not a speculation; the Trinity is a historical necessity. It sprang not from any musings of the mystics, but from the glowing experience of redemption. It was as men awoke to all that Christ had meant, as an unparalleled fact in the universe of God, that they broke through their passionate monotheism and placed Him with the Father on the throne. Then as the years went by, after the resurrection, they found that the Spirit was the Lord's interpreter. And they knew as reasonable men that what is dead cannot interpret what is *living*. If it takes the living to interpret Plato,[1] and if it takes the living to interpret Shakespeare, much more will it take the living to interpret Christ. Nay more, it will take someone who is akin to Him, for that is a law

1. Plato (428–348 B.C.), Athenian philosopher and pupil of Socrates.

of all interpretation. You must have the poet in you to understand the poets. You must have the prophet in you to understand the prophets. And so men came to feel that that great Spirit, which in their lives was interpreting the Lord, must be living and must be divine. It was along that pathway that the Christian church came to her mighty doctrine of the Trinity. She did not fashion it from abstract speculation; she fashioned it from the experience of redemption. And yet, when we lift up our hearts to heaven, and try to think of God as three in one, is there any man so wise that he can do it? If God be love, as I believe He is, then I can always think of Him as *two in one*. For love implies a giver and receiver, and where love is, two are always one. But to endeavor to conceive of God as *three in one* sends my imagination home with broken wing, and yet it is through that truth I am a Christian. It is in such perplexity that I lift up my eyes, and see the winged glory of the seraphim. With twain they fly on the ministry of God, and so while the day lasts I seek to serve Him. But with twain these great mysterious creatures cover their faces in the dazzling light, and cry continually, Holy, Holy, Holy.

Again this mystical imagery is of help to me when I meditate on the divinity of Christ. There is no good news without an Incarnation, and yet an Incarnation is inexplicable. Without a Savior who is truly human there never can be any brotherhood for me. And without a Savior who is truly God there can never be any certainty of triumph. And yet when I try to comprehend that union, of Godhead and of manhood in one person, I am involved in deep and dazzling darkness. If it were only a matter of curious inquiry, then should I toss it from me in contempt. But the divinity of Christ is not a theory. It is the final verdict of the Christian heart. Men did not reach the truth that Christ is God because they brooded upon it in the silence; they reached the truth that Jesus Christ is God, because in Christ they found themselves redeemed. Just when every human arm was powerless, they found in Christ a power that could save. Just when every human helper failed, they found in Jesus a sufficient helper. Until at last, out of experienced fact, there rose the glowing conviction on the church that Christ was very God and very man. Nothing but that conviction would suffice to interpret the wonder of Christian experience. It has come with certainty to twice ten million souls, and will continue to do so to the end. And yet that truth, so vital to the faith, that Jesus Christ is human and divine, is something no intelligence can fathom. All theology has tried to grasp it, and all theology has tried in vain. Every heretic has but sought to make it logical, and to translate it into the terms of current thought. And all the time the church of the living God, magnificently and transcendently illogical, has guarded in her creed those contradictions through which we live, and in which we are strong. It is of the essence of God to be omniscient, yet Jesus of Nazareth was not omniscient. It is of the being of God to be omnipresent, yet Jesus certainly was not omnipresent. And if you tell me, in the language of St. Paul, that Christ emptied Himself when He became a man, I ask you—do you fathom that kenosis? Remember that the church has never thought to fathom it. Her creed is far more negative than positive. Her creed is a protest against poor consistencies. It is meant to register and not to reconcile. And when we seek to penetrate that mystery, of God incarnate in the Christ of Nazareth, it is well to remember that the seraphs' wings are as the wings of the universal church. With twain of them she has gone forth to serve, voyaging to every continent and island. With twain of them she has covered up her feet, soiled and bleeding with her ceaseless ministry. And with twain of them she has ever veiled her eyes, and cried continually Holy, Holy, Holy, certain only of the tremendous fact that the Word was made flesh and dwelt among us.

It is well, too, to be reminded of the seraphim when our thoughts lead us to the death of Jesus. There is something in that death which we shall never fathom, though we brood upon it till the end of time. When another Sabbath morning comes, many of us shall gather at the Communion Table. There we shall eat the bread and drink the wine in the sweet and simple ritual of our faith. And a voice shall rehearse to us the old, old story, and read the institution of the feast, and tell us that in the bread and wine we do show the Lord's death until He come. Yet that cross, which knits us all together and is our ground of pardon and acceptance—how infinitely mysterious it is! Call it a substitution if you will, and I shall agree with you it is a substitution. Call it an atonement if you will, and I shall agree with you that it was that. And yet when you have used these lofty words, and taken all the light which they can give, is there not something left that is still dark? That Christ has died for me, and that I live in Him, is surer for me than any law of nature. But how He died for me and how I live in Him, baffles my clearest hours to understand. And men explain it to me in deep treatises, and I thank God for all explaining treatises, and yet, when all is said, I feel I live by something that has never been explained. I am a little tired of theories of atonement. I have tried so many theories of atonement. I have tried Anselm,[2] and the saint of Row, and Dr. Dale,[3] and Dr. Gore,[4] and fifty of them. And from them all, and all their lofty argument, so penetrating and so reverent and so noble, I just come back to this in hours of need—*Simply to Thy cross I cling*. How Christ has saved me because He died for me, is something I never expect to understand. That He has saved me because He died for me, is something I no more doubt than that I live. And perhaps we were just meant to leave it there, until we know even as we are known, when the day breaks and the shadows flee away. What I want to impress upon you younger men is that we live by what we cannot fathom. It is not the things we can explain that help us; it is generally the things we *can't* explain. And so it is often the first mark of wisdom not to reject what seems incomprehensible, but to bow the head between the mystic wings, and cry with the seraphim, Holy, Holy, Holy.

Once again I join this glorious company when I am troubled about foreknowledge and free will. That is a question which is very old, and yet is always new. Every age has its peculiar problems, which spring from the conditions of that age. I believe that God gives every generation some problem which it is set to solve. But underneath these problems which emerge are other problems which abide, and one of these is the problem of free will. You remember how Milton makes it the discourse of the angels who had been cast from Paradise.[5] That was in the dark backward and abysm of time, before the Spirit had brooded upon chaos. Yet not a week has passed since someone came to me, in a great agony about a tragic accident, to ask if I thought that God had ordained that. If God be infinite in power and wisdom, then must His will be at the back of everything. And if I am a man, responsible to Him, then do I know in my heart I must be free. Yet how I can be free, and God omnipotent, and how I can choose when the Almighty orders, is something which no philosopher can tell me. When a man is determined to rule his life by logic, then must he choose between these two alternatives. He may reject his freedom, and may become a fatalist, in passionate loyalty to a foreordering God. Or else in passionate loy-

---

2. Anselm (c. 1033–1109), English archbishop of Canterbury and theologian.

3. Robert William Dale (1829–1895), English Congregational minister and writer.

4. Charles Gore (1853–1932), Anglican bishop and Oxford scholar.

5. In *Paradise Lost* by John Milton (1608–1674).

alty to freedom, he may reject a foreordaining God, and cease to believe in the divine decrees. The one alternative leads on to slavery, and the other alternative leads on to atheism. Yet man was never meant to be a slave, and spite of antagonisms, man must have his God. And it is then that mysticism comes, and calls us to launch into the silent deep, and bids us cover our eyes as do the seraphim in the light that is too fierce for human gaze. For man does not live by reconciling mysteries; he lives by mysteries he cannot reconcile. He lives by things too vast for human thought, as he lives by thoughts that lie too deep for tears. He lives by the fullness of the life of God, which we but apprehend in scattered rays now, but in whose glory we shall all be bathed when the time of the singing of the birds is come. Yes: now we see in part, and know in part, and we cannot piece the parts into a whole. And we seem to catch innumerable footfalls, and we cannot hear the beating of one heart. But some day we shall live within that heart, and find that all life's opposites are one, and apprehend in an eternal harmony that for which we were apprehended of Christ Jesus.

The wind bloweth where it listeth, and thou hearest the sound thereof, but canst not tell whence it cometh, and whither it goeth: so is every one that is born of the Spirit (John 3:8).

22

The Tidings of the Breeze

This is one of the most profound sayings that ever fell upon a listening ear, and yet it bears to us every mark of being occasional and unpremeditated. The time was night—the place some quiet cottage—the theme the regeneration of the Spirit. And then it may be, right across the talk, there came the sighing of the night wind around the cottage. And Jesus, whose ear was ever quick to catch and use the parables of nature, said, "Hark, Nicodemus, don't you hear it? The wind bloweth where it listeth." It is Christ's parable, infinitely beautiful, of the life not of the flesh but of the spirit. It is Christ's picture of certain large realities in the experience of the regenerate. And the question which I wish to ask, on this Sunday commemorative of the day of Pentecost, is what features of the breeze does our Lord seize upon as illustrative of the spiritual life?

The first feature which our Lord selects is liberty—the wind bloweth where it listeth. In every literature and for every man the wind is the emblem of glad and glorious liberty. You may tell its direction, whether east or west; you may devise instruments to measure its velocity; you may watch its path across the field of corn, or where the giants of the forest bow before it; but spite of all minutest observation, and all the imprisoning energies of science, the breeze still is gloriously free. You can raise no barriers that will block its progress. You can forge no chains that will confine it. You cannot divert it as it crosses the ocean, or bid it halt in its hurrying for an hour. Tonight, as long centuries ago, when it set the tent of Abraham aquivering, the wind bloweth *where it listeth.*

Now there are two elements of this liberty which science has made very plain to us, and the first is that *it is not a lawless liberty.* I do not say that we understand its laws yet as we understand the laws of light, for instance. There is much that is obscure and very baffling in the origin and traveling of the wind. Yet for every zephyr of the summer evening, and for every storm that whistles down the glen, there are adequate causes known to the Creator, and gradually becoming known to us. The wind bloweth where it listeth, but it is never a lawless or capricious liberty. It is not the child of any sudden fury, irresponsible, arbitrary, uncontrolled. It is a liberty based upon a reign of law—enjoyed in harmony with the whole scheme of nature—obedient to the great Creator's purpose, no less than the seraphim around the throne.

But not only is it a liberty of law; *it is also a liberty of service.* There are few services more rich and wonderful than the service of the freedom of the wind. We never talk of the wind working, it is true; we talk of the wind playing in the forest. But sometimes, when our children are at play, they are working for manhood better than they know. And so when the wind, rejoicing in its freedom, is so happy that we say it *plays*, it is working magnificently all the time. It is ripening the seeds within a million flowers; it is filling the ears of corn across the field. It is building the cones on every Scotch fir tree; it is preparing for another harvest home. It is carrying a thousand ships across the sea, and cleansing away the vapors of impurity, and coming to many a slum in the great cities as the angel of purity and health.

My brother, the wind bloweth where it listeth, and so is everyone that is born of the Spirit. Stand fast in the liberty wherewith Christ has made you free: where the Spirit of the Lord is, there is liberty. And it is not freedom from the Law of God—it is not freedom to follow every passion—it is not freedom to do just as we please when hands are beckoning and voices calling. It is the freedom of an indwelling spirit poured into our hearts by Jesus Christ, so that we are no longer in bondage to the outward, but moved by a principle of life within. And it, too, issues in unequaled service, for there is no service in the world like that which Christ inspires. It is the service of the son who loves and not the service of the slave who fears. And it thinks no toil too great to be attempted—and none so trifling that it may be despised—just as the wind that carries the great argosy[1] carries also the pollen of the willow.

The next feature which our Lord chooses is its utterance—the wind bloweth, and thou hearest the sound thereof. And as He spoke He said "Hark" to Nicodemus, and they heard it sighing down the village street. Listening, they heard the night bird calling as it winged its way in the darkness to the hills. Listening, they heard in yonder tavern the roistering laughter of the village prodigals. And then there came a pause, and riot ceased, and the dogs out in the street were at their offal, and Christ said "Hark," and Nicodemus hearkened, and round the cottage they heard the sound thereof. It was a peculiar and distinctive music. There was no mistaking it for any other—no mistaking it for any sound of riot, nor for the crying of any fevered child. And Christ—I fancy with that smile of His which must so often have lit up His words—said, "So is every one that is born of the Spirit."

Again there are two elements in this utterance which it is well that we should bear in mind. And the first is that *the music of the wind is the music of movement and obstruction.* It is because the wind is moving that we hear it, but the music is not struck out by movement only. It becomes audible to us in all its voices only when there is resistance in its path. As the breeze passes over the summer meadow there is not a whisper to indicate its presence. We would never know that the wind was blowing there, save for the tossing of a million daisies. But when it beats on the cheek of him who breasts the hill—when it hurls itself against the cottage-gable—when it leaps angrily upon the armies of the forest, and they lift up their branches to defy it—*then* do we hear the music of the wind. So the spiritual life has its peculiar utterance, because it moves, and moving is obstructed. If there were no obstructions, no obstacles, no difficulties, it might glide so silently that we should never hear it. It is in meeting these, and overcoming them, in the wonderful power of an indwelling Savior, that men, marveling, hear the sound thereof.

And then, as every one of us has known, *it is a music of infinite*

1. a large merchant ship

variety—from the faintest melody as of some distant harp, to the magnificence as of some mighty organ. Now it is like the melancholy sighing of a human heart from which all hope has fled. Now it is like the murmuring of waters amid the rocks and under the thick heather. And now it is like the thrilling song of battle that warriors sing when the lust of fight is on them, and they have found foemen worthy of their steel. So is everyone that is born of the Spirit—the life in Christ has got a thousand voices. It is no harsh monotone, constantly repeated, unvarying, unmusical, unending. It is infinitely varied as the wind is varied, with a thousand cadences as of the olian harp—from the loud note of the trumpet in the morning to the scarce audible whisper of the dying. Do not say that when a man is Christ's, he must show it in this way or in that way. Euroclydon[2] is very different from zephyr, yet both of them are the breathing of the wind. So every life that is inspired of heaven has its distinctive spiritual utterance, for there are diversities of gifts but the same Spirit.

The next feature which our Savior seizes on is the unknown and mysterious origin of the wind. The wind bloweth where it listeth, and thou canst not tell whence it cometh. "Hark, Nicodemus, do you hear it—crying and calling in the village street? Come now, you are a master in Israel, answer me this: Where has it traveled from?" And then when Nicodemus deprecated, as who would say, "Lord, how could *I* tell that?" Christ in His infinitely winsome way said, "So is everyone that is born of the Spirit." Now of course, to a certain limited extent, we always *can* tell which way the wind has come. We have our vanes to indicate its course, and a straw will show which way the breeze is blowing. If from the west, it has traveled from the sea; if from the north, it has reached us from the hills. If it be balmy, it tells of warmer lands; and if it be icy, it speaks to us of snow. And yet, when all is known that can be known, what a range and reach there is that we know nothing of! The wind bloweth where it listeth, and thou canst not tell whence it cometh. Where did it come from, that breath of heavenly wind that fanned your cheek as you came to church tonight? What glens—what moors—what villages—what cities has it traveled through, and passed, in coming hither? Sooner or later men find the source of rivers, though they be hidden and shrouded as that of ancient

2. The east-northeast wind of the south central Mediterranean, mentioned by Luke in Acts 27:14.

Nile. But the wind, that river of the upper air—thou canst not tell, says Jesus, whence it cometh.

Now if there is one thing clear and constant it is that of spiritual renewal *that* is true. There was never a man yet who was born of God who did not feel that it ran into the mysteries. Of course to a certain extent, as with the wind, we can trace back the course of spiritual renewal. Perhaps we can point to a sermon or a prayer, or a quiet talk with somebody we trusted; perhaps we can point to a striking and signal providence, or to a terrible illness when we fought with death, or to an open grave when the dull earth that thudded seemed to be falling on the heart. So is everyone that is born of the Spirit. We can trace out the history a little way. We can say it was this or that which changed us to the depths, in the unerring providence of God. But when we have said all that, and said it gratefully, then overpowers us the wonder of it all, and saved by grace when we deserved the darkness, we can but whisper, "*We know not whence it cometh.*" Who can tell—or who shall ever tell—what was behind that hour of decision? What prayers of a mother, when we were little children, and she stole in at night and prayed when we were sleeping? And that is many years ago, dear friend, and you have lived a sorry life since then, God knows; but tonight, "Arise, shine, for thy light is come"—yes, come, and thou knowest not whence it cometh. Respond to the infinite love of Christ tonight, and His Holy Spirit will come down and fill you. And you will go out, wondering and awed, and crying, "I have got it, and know not whence it came." But some day, when the veil is lifted, you shall know, and you shall find behind it all a Savior's sacrifice, and a mother's prayers, and a minister's entreaty, and a love of God that chose you in eternity.

Then the last feature which our Savior seizes on is its unknown and unreckonable goal. The wind bloweth where it listeth, and thou canst not tell whither it goeth. "Come, Nicodemus, thou who teachest others—thou hearest it—where is it going tonight?" "Lord, I cannot tell where it is going"—and so is everyone that is born of the Spirit. Over the city, and then whither away? An hour hence, and where shall the breeze be? Will it fill some sail—ruffle yon mountain lake—travel to cities where the speech is strange? You know not, brother; and I am here to tell you that if you open your heart to the Spirit of God tonight, no man can tell what power and use and blessing *you* shall travel on to from this hour. There are men and women in this church this evening, and I know quite well whither they are going. They are going to useless lives and unregarded graves, with not one tear of genuine regret for them. But let a man respond to Christ tonight, and receive the outpouring of the Holy Spirit—and you know not whither you shall go. You shall go to a life that is a joyous thing. You shall go to a life that is a conquering thing. You shall go to a power and usefulness and honor that will amaze yourself, knowing what you are. And then at last, kept by the power of God, and plucked as a brand by Christ out of the burning, you shall go to be with Him, which is far better.

In all points tempted like as we are, yet without sin (Heb. 4:15).

23

The Sinlessness of Christ

It might seem at first as if the sinlessness of Jesus were a matter far away from human need. It is as if we discussed the color of the stars, or the density of water in the depth of ocean. Why should we trouble ourselves, it may be asked, over an abstract question such as this? Were it not better, in a reverent faith, to leave these dark mysteries alone? Enough for me (a man might say) is that Jesus of the gospel story who was the friend of publicans and sinners and who went about doing good. The one fatal objection to that attitude is that to a thoughtful mind it never can be permanent. Steadily, whatever point we start from, we are forced into the presence of this problem. And especially is that true of all of us who believe in a gospel of redemption, and who cannot conceive of a message of good news which has not redemption at its heart. The keystone of our faith is this, that Jesus the Lord suffered for our sins. But if Christ was sinful, as you and I are sinful, then not for our sins, but for His own, He died. So all the efficacy of that atoning death, with all the preaching of Christ crucified, rests ultimately on the sinlessness of Jesus. It is not, then, an unimportant theme. It is one of the most important of all themes. It lifts the cross out of the realm of tragedy into the clear air of willing sacrifice. Only if Jesus Christ was sinless can we be certain of what is all-important—that in a free action of redeeming love He died for our sins according to the Scriptures.

Now when you study *the New Testament writings*—I mean the writings outside the four gospels, one thing that becomes plain is this, that they all record the sinlessness of Jesus. However the writers differ in their outlook—and each of them has his peculiar outlook—however they may diverge from one another in their conception of the work of Jesus, yet there is one point on which they all agree, and that is in conceiving Christ as sinless. John had lain upon the Master's bosom, and he writes, "In Him there was no sin." Peter had known Him in the closest intimacy, and he writes, "He died, the righteous for the unrighteous." Paul writes, "He who knew no sin was made sin for us." And the writer of Hebrews, in our text tonight, says, "He was tempted in all points like as we are, yet without sin." These are but a few texts out of many which indicate a perfect unanimity. Each writer may use the fact in his own way, but all of them insist upon the fact. And what we have to ask tonight is this, How was that profound impression generated, so that not one writer of the New Testament doubts for a moment the sinlessness of Christ?

Let me say in passing that it helps us to conceive how powerful this impression really was, when we recall *the nature of the earliest heresies*. When men today have doubts about the Lord, it is the divinity that is the point of difficulty. You and I may doubt if He was God, but we never for an instant doubt that He was man. Yet the singular thing is that in the earliest heresies the point of difficulty was the opposite. Men did not doubt if Jesus was divine then, but they doubted if He was really human. Now it seems to me that no mere moral grandeur will ever quite explain these earliest heresies. One is not less a man, but more a man, if he is morally and spiritually wonderful. That strange belief, uttered in early heresies, that Christ was not human as you and I are human, can only rest on the profound impression that He stood apart from all in being sinless. The nearer, then, to the historic Christ, the more intense the belief that He was sinless. The closer that men stand to Him, the more profound does the impression grow. And so I say what we must do tonight is to go back to the record of the gospel story, and try if we can discover thence how that impression was created.

In the first place I should like to make clear to you that it was certainly not created by insistence. Christ never insisted on His sinlessness—never took pains to prove that He was sinless. There are some things on which our Lord insisted with a self-assertion that is most magnificent. I am the truth, He said—I am the life. No man comes to the Father but by Me. Yet though no one who ever taught mankind has made such stupendous claims as Jesus Christ, you never find Him saying, "I am sinless." On the contrary one might almost say that He deliberately veiled that fact. So did He live in fellowship with outcasts that they called Him the friend of publicans and sinners. And once when a lawyer, with the gloss of compliment, came to Him and said, "Good Master," Christ checked him instantly—"Why callest thou me good? there is none good but one, that is, God." Clearly then, for reasons we can guess at, Christ did not passionately insist upon His sinlessness. However the impression was created, it certainly never was created so.

How then was the impression generated? Well, the first answer we should all give is this. We should say that *these men who companied with Jesus did not recollect one deed of sin.* When the years of ministry were closed, they would recall it all in tender memory. They would summon to the sessions of sweet thought the days they had spent together in the villages. And as they did so and as they talked together of the time when it was bliss to be alive, silently it would be borne in upon them that they had never seen one trace of sin in Jesus. They had been with Him in His temptations, and they had seen Him in the widest range of circumstances. They had known Him in hunger and in weariness; they had watched Him in rapture and in agony. Yet now, as they looked back upon it all, in the penetrative light of memory, they could not recollect one single incident which suggested to them the thought that Christ had sinned. Thus was it at first that the deep impression was created. It was a judgment based upon the memory of the wonderful years that they had spent with Jesus. Could they have recalled one single instance in which the conduct of Jesus had been flawed, then neither in Peter nor in John would we have found the sinlessness of Christ.

Now all that is absolutely true, yet it is far from being all the truth. It is quite impossible to build a Christian doctrine on any negative basis such as that. Granted that they had never known Christ sinning, is that any adequate proof that He was sinless? Had they been watching Him, with eyes unwearied, from the moment of His birth on to the cross? On the contrary; they had only known Him for three brief years out of the three-and-thirty, and of these three years there was many a day when they were never in His company at all. What of the long years of village childhood? What of the crucial time of ripening manhood? What of these still and happy days in Bethany when Martha and Mary were the only company? There was no Peter to be observant there, nor was there any John to watch and to remember; there was only the love of women so adoring that the universal voice has called it blind. Had any of the disciples detected sin in Jesus, we would never have had the faith that He was sinless. But to call Him sinless because they saw no sin is something that no reasonable man can do. For immediately, doing it, there rise before him all these unchronicled and unrecorded years, when Christ was hidden from the eyes of watchers, in shadows that were enwrapping as the grave.

The true foundation of the doctrine lies deeper than any absence of the act. It was not thus, at least not thus alone, that the profound impression was created. What impressed men in Jesus Christ was not the absence of any act of sin. *What impressed men in Jesus Christ profoundly was the absence of any* consciousness *of sin.* It was that never once He made confession. It was that never once He betrayed penitence. It was that never once upon His lips was there whisper of remorse or of regret. The nearer that a man lives to God the more intensely active is his conscience. He becomes sensitive to shades of guilt that are imperceptible to common men. Yet Christ, who lived in a fellowship with God that is admittedly unique and uncommunicable, never betrays so much as by a word the faintest trace of consciousness of sin. As Simon Peter grew in spirituality, he cried, "Depart from me, O Lord, for I am a sinful man." As Paul advanced in the deep things of heaven he came to know he was the chief of sinners. But Jesus, who through all His earthly years was walking in perfect union with His Father, never once whispered, "Father, I have sinned." We see Him in those high and holy seasons when He was looking back upon His past. We overhear Him in His hours of prayer; we see Him in the agonies of death. Yet in such seasons when purest and holiest souls feel above everything their need of mercy, the pure and holy soul of Jesus Christ was absolutely unconscious of that need. We have had very many shining saints in Christendom, and they have differed vastly from each other. But there is one point in which they are all kin, whatever their century or their communion. And it is this, that as they have wrestled heavenward, and grown in grace and fellowship with God, out of the depths has come the fervent cry, "God be merciful to me a sinner." It is not your worldly man who utters that. It is not your nominal and easy Christian. As life in God becomes more real and deep, steadily the sense of sin is deepened. And the one thing you never will explain in the experience of Jesus Christ, is that with a life in God unparalleled, He never had any consciousness of sin. And He was always talking about sin, remember. It was a theme which was ever on His lips. He poured the vials of His withering anger upon the man who thought that he was righteous. Looking abroad upon the world of men He saw no hope for them except in penitence—"I will arise and go unto my father, and say unto him, Father, I have sinned." Now it was that fact, as I understand the gospels, which created the profound impression of Christ's sinlessness. It was that He had eyes to see sin everywhere—yet had no eyes to see it in Himself. It was that other men, when they are called to die, cry out into the dark, "Father, forgive me"; but that the Master, when He came to die, said, "Father, forgive them"—not, forgive Me. There is not a trace in Christ of any healed scar. There is not a trace of regret or of remorse. In all the history of the Redeemer there is no word of penitence nor any sign of shame. And all this, with a heart so sensitive—with a life so flooded and absorbed with God—can only mean that Jesus Christ was sinless.

I have spoken of the prayers of Jesus. Let me as I pass on say one thing more about them. I want you to note another feature of them that is exceedingly suggestive and significant. No one can study the prayers of Jesus Christ without discovering what they owe to the Old Testament. Christ fed His piety, and nourished it, on the sublime words of psalmist and of prophet. And yet although His soul was steeped in prophecy, and though the language of it rose to His lips in prayer, there is one point at which He stops, saying, as it were, "Thus far and no further." It was with the Scripture that He met the tempter. It was with the Scripture that He assailed His adversaries. It was of the Scripture that His heart was full as He hung in His last hours upon the cross. Yet never once, though claiming as His own that wonderful heritage of faith and prayer—*never once does He personally use the cry of prophet or psalmist for forgiveness*. Isaiah had cried, "Woe is me, for I am a man of unclean lips." David had cried, out of a broken heart, "Against Thee, Thee only, have I sinned." Yet Christ, who was so steeped in these old writings that their language rose to His lips as if by instinct, never uses—never repeats—these penitential and broken-hearted prayers. Now all that we ever find in Holy Scripture is the transcript of our deepest life. We only can use its language with sincerity when it has some link with our experience. All that answers to us as if it were our own, comes to our lips when we draw near to God; all else, though it speak as with the tongue of angels, can never rise to heaven in our prayers. Why is it then that Jesus Christ is silent, with such a treasury ever at His hand? Why does He use the psalmist's adoration, yet never in one word the psalmist's penitence? The only answer of which I can think is that in all the experience of Jesus there was nothing which answered to that heavenward cry in which psalmist and prophet prayed for pardon. Had He felt in Himself the slightest need, He would have used the penitential language. For there is nothing like it in the world, it is so poignant and sincere. Yet Christ, who used all else, never used that—never took up a single word of it, though from a child in the sweet home of Nazareth He had been fed on the word of Holy Scripture.

There is one other aspect of the matter that I can hardly avoid saying a word upon. It is that, if Christ be sinless, then what becomes of His temptations? Now let me say, and say with all my heart, that I hold the temptations of Jesus to have been intensely real. He is no brother to me unless in all reality He was tempted as the Son of man. And the point is, how could He be tempted so—truly intensely and terribly tempted—if He was indeed a sinless Savior? I shall not profess to give a perfect answer. I am not here to give little answers to great questions. But I am here to suggest to you such thoughts as I may have brooded on in quiet hours. And I think that there are two considerations which throw no little light upon the difficulty, and these two I would put thus.

The first is that *the most bitter temptations are not always dependent upon sin.* They spring from the conflict, not between right and wrong, but from the conflict between right and right. If a man, for instance, is tempted to be drunken, then of course within his heart there must be evil. And if all temptations were of that complexion, then Christ our Savior could never have been tempted. But I submit that in this life of ours there are other temptations more bitter than that, which if a man has experienced and resisted, he has sounded all the depths of moral trial. Here, for instance, is a student who has come up from a humble village home. And he is brilliant, and is carrying all before him, and the way is opening for a fine career. And then some day there comes to him the news that his father is smitten with some dread paralysis, and that the little village business will be ruined unless the son comes home, and comes at once. On the one hand is his duty to his mother, and to the little children at his mother's feet. On the other hand is his duty to himself, and to the gifts of intellect which God has given him. And what I say is, that in these rival voices, calling each of them as with the voice of heaven, there are all the elements of a moral conflict beside which that of the drunkard is a sham. For you have not exhausted moral conflict when you have told of the conflict between good and evil. Subtler than that, and sometimes far more terrible, is the conflict between good and good—the duty that we owe ourselves, faced by the duty that we owe a brother; the duty that we owe a wife and children faced by the duty that we owe to heaven. What I mean is that if all human progress were merely a progress from bad to good, then in Christ, who was entirely good, there could have been no progress through antagonism. But if within the circle of the good many of our sorest battles must be fought, then I see not why a sinless Savior might not be tempted as we are. Nay, if sinless, may it not be the case that He felt temptation more terribly than we? For there are calls that are deadened for everyone of us just because our hearts are dulled through sin. Had we been less dulled, with what intense appeal certain claims might have come home to us, and so would the temptation have been awful.

And the last thought that I would leave with you is that the sinlessness of Christ was not a gift. *The sinlessness of Christ was not a gift to Him, rather I should call it an attainment.* "Why callest thou *Me* good?" He said; "there is none good but one, that is, God." Christ never claimed and never had on earth an absolute and unconditioned goodness. His was the goodness that was always perfect, because through every condition it was tested, and never failed, even in hours of agony, in a perfect and filial response. The God who dwells in heaven cannot be tempted. He lives in absolute and unconditioned goodness. He dwells in heaven, where no temptation is, above the smoke and stir of this dim spot. But Christ was human to the very depths, and knew all the play of emotion and of impulse, and felt every influence that breathed upon Him, crying to Peter, "Get thee behind Me, Satan." From moment to moment He had to choose His course. From moment to moment He had to trust His Father. From moment to moment He had to resist, even though it was a mother who appealed. And we call Him sinless not as God is sinless, who cannot be tempted nor touched in the high heaven, but as one who never failed and never faltered in the fulfillment of His

Father's will. To you and me the heavenly Father speaks as He spoke to the well-beloved Son. And you and I hearing Him, misinterpret Him, and at the end of the day are sorry and ashamed. Christ caught the faintest syllable of heaven. Christ interpreted it all without a flaw. Christ bowed to it joyfully and without a murmur, even when the will of God was Calvary. That is the sinlessness of Jesus Christ—not an unethical gift, but an achievement. It was wrought out from stage to stage in perfect obedience to the heavenly Father. And so do I think there falls an added glory on the deep mystery of Jesus' sinlessness, when we remember that right to the very end He was tempted in all points like as we are.

And I have heard of thee, that thou canst
. . . dissolve doubts (Dan. 5:16).

24

The Dissolution of Doubt

George Müller of Bristol,[1] that eminent philanthropist, who did such a mighty work for orphan children, was once asked by an admiring friend if he had ever doubted. "Yes, once," was his reply, "I doubted for five minutes." In all his years of strenuous activity, with their unceasing strain upon his faith, only once could he remember doubting, and in five minutes his doubt had disappeared. Probably, like Sir Thomas Browne of Norwich,[2] he conquered his doubts upon his knees. There is a singular virtue in the bended knee for driving out into the night these darker visitants. But I wonder if there is anyone here tonight who has reached the intelligence of mature manhood, and who could say he has only doubted for five minutes. It would be nearer the experience of some of us to say that we once believed for five minutes. We had five minutes once when the heavens were opened, and Jesus was standing on the right hand of God. But doubt—it is so inwrought into our fiber, it is so interfused with the very air we breathe, that some of us seem to do little else than doubt. Sometimes we doubt

1. George Müller (1805–1898), orphanage founder and leader of the Christian Brethren movement.
2. Sir Thomas Browne (1605–1682), English physician and writer.

the efficacy of prayer, and sometimes the fact that Jesus Christ is risen. Sometimes in a silent universe we doubt the pitying love of the Almighty. And I want to ask tonight how is that born, and what does it mean, and how may we get rid of it—for no man can be content to be a doubter.

Sometimes doubt is born of argument, and of the clash of living mind on mind. The spark flashes when the flint is struck, and the flash illuminates the darkness. It may be a word spoken by a friend; it may be a point of view given in a college lecture; it may be a learned argument for orthodoxy which has effects that never were intended; so, often suddenly and sometimes gradually, in ways we can trace and from hours we can recall, the dark unhappiness of doubt is born. Of course for this there must be preparation, and life is strangely rich in preparation. Life not only prepares us to believe; it also often prepares to disbelieve. Sickness may do it with its attendant gloom, or moral battles fought and lost in secret, or something base flashing upon us in the life of someone of whom we thought the world. Then in that hour comes the argument—comes the suggestion—comes the random word. And it fits in with all that we have suffered, and gives a kind of logic to despair. So by the touch of the outward on the inward—by the voice that answers to unuttered voices—often at definite moments doubt is born.

Deeper than that, *doubt may be created by the spirit of the age in which we live*. For every age has its peculiar spirit and men must breathe it whether they will or no. That is the great argument of Mr. Lecky in his interesting volumes on the *Rise of Rationalism*. He shows how beliefs are altered not by argument, but by the silent spread of a new spirit. And when that spirit is the spirit of questioning, as it is in every sphere of life today, it takes no formal proofs to suggest doubt. There is little actual denial; now there is a mighty deal of actual uncertainty. The word *infidelity* has an old-fashioned sound; there are no infidels now, only agnostics. And it is this questioning, inquiring, eager spirit, which hangs like an atmosphere over our generation, which makes it so hard for many to believe—so easy for multitudes to doubt. Long before we have heard any argument, we are predisposed to doubt by our environment. There is a subtle, impalpable, pervasive spirit which is at work within us, and beneath our consciousness. And it is that, although we know it not—that heritage in which we all are brothers, that makes it so easy to say with doubting Thomas, Except I see, I will not believe.

But our doubts have not only an intellectual basis; *our doubts have also got a moral basis.* We doubt not only because of what we know: we sometimes doubt because of what we are. I am far from saying that all doubt runs down to, and has its roots in, disobedience. To say that were to be uncharitable to many an earnest struggler in the dark. But I do say there are some here tonight, as there are in every company of men and women, who would be freed from their worst doubts immediately if they would only cease to live as they are living. If the lenses of a telescope are false, it will never rightly show the arc of heaven. If the glass in the window is irregular, it will distort the meadow and the hill. And if the heart be sinful and be wrong with God, and be clinging to what is immoral and unclean, then all the facts in the universe of truth will show themselves in a distorted way. There is a doubt which is the child of earnestness, and there is a doubt which is the child of sin. It has its roots not in speculative difficulty; it has its roots in moral disobedience. And the moment a man gives up that disobedience, and hates it, and cleaves to what is good, in that moment for him the sun has risen, and the time of the singing of the birds has come.

Now of course there is another side to doubt. There is what Tennyson called the sunnier side. *Its very existence is a kind of silent witness to the lofty way in which our Maker treats us.* Were we His slaves He would say to us, *Do this*, and without any choice we would obey. Were we His creatures, like the beast or bird, He would say, *Believe this*, and we must needs believe it. But we are of more value to Him than many sparrows, for we are made in His image and fashioned in His likeness, and so does He stoop from heaven in His great mercy, and say to us, *Come, let us reason together.* In other words, were we less great, any such thing as doubt would be impossible. We should obey as behemoth obeys, or as the swallow in its appointed season. And if life for us is nobler than for behemoth, and far more glorious than for any swallow, it means that we stand toward God in such a freedom that doubt always must be possible. Let no man think, then, that just because he doubts he is therefore displeasing to our heavenly Father. Our Father knows far better than we do the perils and the pains of every privilege. And so He is compassionate and merciful, and infinitely patient in His discipline, and the smoking flax He will not quench.

It is also one of the sunnier sides of doubt that *it so often testifies to spiritual earnestness.* He who is quite indifferent never doubts: it might be better for him if he did. Do you remember how Cowper puts it?

> He who never doubted of his state,
> He may, perhaps, perhaps he may, too late.[3]

I dare say that in an ordinary week I put in the mailbox several score of letters. And putting them there I never add a thought to them, being quite confident that they will be delivered. But now and again among these scores of letters there is one that is very important and decisive, and about that letter I begin to doubt. What if it should never be delivered? What if the manuscript in it should be lost? What if the bank notes which it contains should never reach their destination? Such doubts will come to everyone of us, and, coming, they do not mean that we are faithless, but they mean that here is a thing which really matters to us, and about which we are genuinely concerned. So is it with the great transactions of religion. When it means nothing to us we never think of doubting. When it is as indifferent to us as a picture postcard, it never occurs to us to worry over it. But when in contradistinction to all that faith lives for us—God speaks—Christ shows His wounds—then in such an hour our doubts are born. That is why the busiest time of doubt is the time of opening womanhood and manhood. It is the time when our fathers' and our mothers' God has to become our God, or to be nothing. It is the time when the memories of childhood are not any longer enough to ride the whirlwind—when life and love and passion and repentance call for a Savior who shall be our own. Such a season comes to every man, to some far more intensely than to others. And everything has to be lost that it be found again, and everything has to die that it may live. And what I say is that a time like that almost inevitably is a time of doubt, and I call that the sunnier side of doubt. In such a time let a man be true, and the days will pass and all come right again. Let him cling to the truth he knows, however fragmentary, and the fragments will round into the perfect circle. And by and by the waters will be still, and the grass green beside the waters' margin, and every lily of the field will speak of God, who has clothed it in its raiment of delight.

But if doubt has got its sunnier side, we know also that it has its darker side. The man who doubts is never on the hills; his path is in the valley of the shadow. He is not glad as the little child is glad, for

3. William Cowper (1731–1800), English poet.

he cannot trust as little children do. And life loses its zest and its enthusiasm, for the air is chill and the dank mist is everywhere. But all that could be borne with a brave heart, and buried in the deeps with other sorrows, if it were not for one other effect of doubt. Do you remember the great words of Shakespeare?

> Our doubts are traitors,
> And make us lose the good we oft might win
> By fearing to attempt.

Or do you remember, in the *Idylls of the King*, how Lancelot goes out to seek the Holy Grail, and how he comes to a certain portal that was guarded by lions? As he advances, says Tennyson,

> With sudden-flaring manes
> Those two great beasts rose upright like a man,
> Each gript a shoulder, and I stood between;
> And, when I would have smitten them, heard a voice,
> "Doubt not, go forward; if thou doubt, the beasts
> Will tear thee piecemeal."

My brother, that is the darker side of doubt. *It is the check it gives to noble action.* It is the power it has, so subtle and so deadly, to paralyze the hand that holds the sword. And in a world like this, where each is given his place not for the sake of dreaming but of doing, that is why doubting is such a fatal habit. All work that is to tell and to abide springs from and is inspired by conviction. It is not cleverness, it is conviction that kindles up into effectual deed. And that is why, when you have a doubting age, though it be most wonderfully clever, you miss the ring of the heroic note and the achievement of the heroic deed. They tell us we have no great men today, and then they blame that on democracy. Men blame democracy that we have no great names now, in literature or in art or in the state. But the real reason is not the new democracy; the real reason is that subtle doubt, which we draw in with every breath we breathe in this questioning and so critical day. It is that which is the enemy of greatness. It is that which checks and hampers high achievement. The man who hesitates, we say, is lost, and he who has learned to doubt is always hesitating. For greatness has a certain simplicity about it, and a high trustfulness as of a child, and walks before God, although the heavens be dark, with the glad confidence that all is well.

So now in closing I turn to ask this question, What has Christ to say about our doubts? I shall suggest to you three lines of thought which you can elaborate from the gospels for yourselves.

In the first place, strange though it may seem, *there were times when Jesus deliberately deepened doubt*. Before He healed the wound made by the arrow, deliberately He drove the arrow deeper. Just as Jesus, the conqueror of death, began His conquest by making death more terrible—just as He darkened it into a gloom unfathomable before He shed on it the light of resurrection—so sometimes you will find the Lord, whose passion was to kindle men to faith, beginning that by stirring men to doubt. Sometimes He would quote the prophets so that men felt they had never understood them. Sometimes he would so cover his Messiahship as to make even the disciples doubt Him. Sometimes He would so reach the heart that the whole universe began to reel, and men who thought their feet were on a rock felt that they were moving on the sand. You will often find that ministry in Jesus. If He is very gracious, He can be very stern. If He is going to lead men to the heights, He sometimes begins by leading to the depths. And so I say that time and again, as you follow in the footsteps of the Master, you find Him first not quickening to faith, but to the humbling discipline of doubt. Now do you see the meaning of that discipline? I want you to bear it in mind, my doubting brother. I want you to believe, when doubts assail you, that it may not be the devil who is busy. It may be Christ, the same today as yesterday, unsettling everything for you in love, that by and by you may have such standing ground as the world cannot give and cannot take away.

In the next place you will observe that *Christ was always gentle with the doubter.* Christ could be very terrible with men, but He was never terrible with doubting men. I read in Scripture of the wrath of the Lamb, and the wrath of the Lamb was something very awful. And I open the gospel and I find it there, flashing now on this man, now on that. But never do I find the wrath of the Lamb, which kindling burns and burning scorches, directed against the doubting heart. Nicodemus doubted, and with him Christ was beautifully and infinitely patient. John the Baptist doubted, and to him Christ gave such praise as man had never got. Thomas doubted, and cried aloud his doubts, saying, I will not believe except I see—and Jesus showed him where the spear had pierced, and the woundprints in His hands and side. Once more, do you see the meaning of that gentleness? It tells you how Jesus thinks of you tonight. It tells you, my doubting comrade, that you are not faced by an angry Savior. It tells you that even now He understands you, and does not mean to leave you nor forsake you, but is going to bring you, sooner than you think, into the garden where the roses grow.

And then, lastly, you will observe that *Christ turned the doubter to immediate action.* For truth was not something to be inquired about to Jesus; truth for Jesus was something to be lived. Seek ye first the kingdom of God, and all these things shall be added unto you. If any man will do His will, he shall know of the doctrine whether it be of God. That is to say, the road that Christ elects to the dissolving of all honest doubt, is the road that has its beginning in obedience. For every man, however dark his heaven, still knows what is right and still knows what is wrong. And every man, though he lose the angel voices, has still the voice of conscience in his breast. And what Christ says is that if you follow that, and do what is right though there be none to cheer you, slowly the stars will shine for you again, and you will be brought into a larger room. Then shall we know, says the grand old prophet, if we follow on to know the Lord. And if you do that, and take up the next duty, and play the man, and scorn what is debasing, then sooner than you think you will win back again what you have loved long since and lost awhile.

It is not good that the man should be alone
(Gen. 2:18).
I was left alone, and saw this great vision
(Dan. 10:8).

25

Society and Solitude

In the early ages of the church—ages that teemed with fantastic speculation—there was a sect of mystics who spoke much of angels, and gave them a place that dominated everything. By them the gulf was bridged between God and man; by them creation and the law were mediated; and all these angels in their unceasing agencies were regarded not as single but in pairs. Now that was a dream of oriental mystics, but I think we can see the facts that gave it birth. For human life, when you begin to brood on it, is it not strangely paired in its experiences? I have always understood such men as Swedenborg, who found in marriage the key to every mystery, when I remember how in human life God has set one thing over against the other. We do not live through an unbroken day; we live through the pairing of the night and day. We do not live through an unbroken peace, but through the marriage of battle and of peace. And so no human life is perfected if it be passed entirely in society; it needs for its perfecting, as Swedenborg[1] would say, the marriage

1. Emanuel Swendenborg (1688–1772), Swedish philosopher and Neoplatonist.

of society and solitude. A life that has never known the sweets of solitude has always something lacking in its music. There is silence needed as well as human speech for the waking of all that is within us. Yet on the other hand no fate could be more dreadful than that of the sailor marooned on the Pacific, never to hear again another's voice—never to touch again another's hand. It is not good for man to be alone, yet when I was alone I saw the vision. God has so made us that for our fullest life we need society and solitude. And it is on that I want to dwell this evening, showing you the respective gains of these estates, and remembering that whom God has joined together man must not put asunder.

In the first place, then, I would say this, that in society we find our duty, while in solitude we find our dream.

Now I am not going to discuss with you what duty is, for I am not here as a lecturer on ethics. But there is one thing about duty I want you to observe—a thing I think that often is forgotten. There is really no such thing as abstract duty except in the pages of the poet. Wordsworth may write his noble ode to duty, and there are few nobler odes in any language. But the duty of which Wordsworth sings, and sings with a passion which he rarely equaled, is the duty of poetry and not of life. Duty is what I owe to persons, of whom I am one, and all the world the rest. Duty is born in the fact that we are social, and linked together in a thousand kinships. The deepest thing in life is not *I must*; the deepest thing in life is social instinct, out of whose womb is born, in God's development, the overwhelming compulsion of the *ought*. If you are a student, your duty as a student takes into its compass other people. It is not an abstract and exclusive thing; it is a social and inclusive thing. It touches your father who has battled for you, and your mother who is longing to be proud of you; it touches all the unknown men and women whose doctor or whose minister you shall be. The duty of a wife involves her husband; that of a father the welfare of his children. The duty of a citizen involves the other citizens of his commonwealth. And that is what I mean when I point out to you that it is in society we find our duty, waking to it just because hands are clasped, and other lives are in union with our own.

Indeed, so eminently is this the truth that the thought of duty just grows as does society. The more intricate a man's relationships, the greater the possibilities of duty. We are taught that in primeval times the only organization was the tribe. Historically, the unit of the tribe came before the unit of the family. And we know that in the dim and distant ages the thought of duty was very rudimentary, and rose but a little above the savage thought of being loyal for purposes of safety. Then the race progressed, and life grew more involved, and relationships became ever more elaborate. And the home was formed, and the state came into being, and the church declared the glory of communion. And all the time, right through the ages, you find the thought of duty growing ampler, until it has risen to that range and compass which it has in the Christian life today. In society we find our duty, and as society is enriched our duty grows. Every new tie that a man forms brings with it duties unsuspected once. Not in the shrinking from our human kinships, but in the taking them up with loyal hearts, are we gradually taught what duty means.

But human life is more than duty, if it be framed on the pattern of God. It must have room for dream as well as duty; for "then I beheld," as well as "Now I must." In the prophet's picture of the age of gold, do you remember one arresting feature? The young men were to see visions, and the old men were to dream dreams. That is to say, in the life that is made perfect there must be vision as truly as obedience, and God, I take it, has appointed solitude just that we may find our vision there. Are there not moments when we look backward, and see the past as in the light of heaven? Are there not hours when we look forward, and darkness scatters and the sun has risen? And very generally these hours of vision—these great illuminative unifying hours—are hours when the human spirit is alone. That was why Jesus said to the disciples, Come ye into a desert place, and rest awhile. They had been doing their duty in heroic fashion, and now they needed their vision recreated. And that is why He says to you and me, Come ye apart into a desert place, which, when we reach it and find the waters flowing, is not so sour and desert as it seemed. Sometimes the season which God uses is the silent hour of the sleepless night. Sometimes it is those days of happy quiet that wait upon the bed of convalescence. Sometimes it is those seasons of retirement, when we leave the call and clamor of the city, to light on the sleep that is among the lonely hills and the silence that is in the starry sky. It is not good for man to be alone. Nothing is good that negatives our duty. It is not good for man to be alone, since what we are depends on what we ought. But when I was alone I saw the vision, and we like Daniel still have need of solitude; for if in society we find our duty, it is in solitude we find our dream.

In the second place, I would have you note that in society we find our wealth while in solitude we find our poverty.

Of course I am not speaking of material wealth nor of the riches that lie in outward gains. We have been taught by One who ought to know that life does not consist in its abundance. For wealth does not lie in any costly luxuries, nor in any adornment of marble or of gold, nor in expensive pleasures, nor rare and curious delicacies, which are the craving and the curse of many. But it lies in a life of true and humble service, and in self-conquest and in faith and in humility, and in the last and crowning victory of love. It is such things, and such things only, that are worthy of the name of wealth. It is the growing conquest of the devil, and the driving of him, beaten, every day. It is the influence which flows from character—the strengthening of trust and of affections—the life so lived, that though we know it not, men may thank God for us and may take courage.

Now I have but to indicate that thought for you to see how true my second point is. If a man's life consists in things like these, then in society we find our wealth. In that noble story, *The Cloister and the Hearth,* do you remember the experience of Gerard? He went apart and broke his human ties in a false sense of what he owed to God. And then the novelist, in his own fine way, shows us what a sorry business it all was, and how Gerard only lived again when he came back to his family and his home. *There* was his wealth, where God had placed him, and where was the happy laughter of his children. There he became a man again, and went out to minister in his plague-stricken parish. And so for you and me the wealth of life is found where men are and where women are, where will is sharpened by the other will, and human life is interlocked with life. It is through service that our lives are rich, and there is no service without some society. It is in sacrifice that life is rich, and sacrifice is sacrifice for others. It is in human love that life is rich, and so are there never riches for the hermit, for only where there are hearts to answer ours can the music of love steal upon the ear.

But if in society we find our wealth, is it not in solitude we find our poverty? God has appointed solitude for man, that he might learn how in His sight he is poor. I do not hesitate to ring out the burning words of the old prophet. I know, and I want you to know, that "all our righteousnesses are as filthy rags." And if it be true that in the sight of heaven we are poor and naked and in need of everything, then I say God has appointed solitude that we might find in it our poverty. For often, amid the voices of the world, the voice of accusing conscience is inaudible, and often amid the applause of men we lose the true sense of what we are, and often we are so busied in society, and so immersed in multifarious tasks, that we know not how it fares within in the hidden kingdom of the soul. It is then that God appoints us times of solitude. He says to us again, Come ye apart. He wakes us in the hours of the night. He lays us down upon a bed of sickness. And then, with all the clamor hushed, and the world and all its voices at a distance, do men begin to cry out of the depths, God be merciful to me a sinner. Then do we see, as in a vision, how little spiritual progress we have made. Then do we see all that we might have done to make others happier who love us. Then do we see, stripped of every coloring, the poorness and the meanness of our lives—and all our righteousnesses are as filthy rags. When the knights of the round table were in company, there was a mystical glory on the company. But when they separated each on his own quest, then was there weakness and the end of glory. And when we separate out of our kindly companies that shelter us from heaven and ourselves, then do we too learn that we are poor. It is not good for man to be alone. It would be fatal if it were always thus. Life is a rich thing, and God has meant it so, and therefore has He set the solitary in families. But after all we are poor and helpless sinners, needing the wedding garment and all else, and—when I was alone I saw the vision.

Then, in the third and last place, note that in society we find ourselves, while in solitude we find our God.

One of the strongest instincts of the heart is its instinct for self-realization. There is no longing more radical within us than the longing to live out what we are. You have it in the activities of children, when they romp and when they disobey. You have it in every poem, and in every picture, and in every work that human hands have wrought. You have it in every stirring of rebellion, such as we are watching now in central Europe, whose peoples, burdened with misrule, are thrilling with the enthusiasm to be free. Self-repression is not a Christian end; it is the means to a more glorious end. It is a gateway into that life abundant for which the human heart is always craving. God has so made us that we must lose ourselves, but not as though that were the desired perfection. We are to lose ourselves that we may find ourselves, and be what in the sight of heaven we are.

Well now, it is a simple truth that we so find ourselves only in society. Only by sharing in the common life does the single life blossom as the rose. Just as the glowing embers on the hearth flicker out and are quenched if they be scattered, yet drawn together into a common center burn up into a lively flame; so human lives, could they be isolated, would lose all warmth and radiance and would perish, for they too need communion for vitality. If a child were left upon a desert island, it is conceivable it might not die. Feeding on berries and on shellfish, it might conceivably keep itself alive. But do you see, as it grew up to manhood what a poor and empty thing its life would be, only a little different from the beasts. Every power that you and I possess would be latent in that lonely mortal. All that is best and brightest in humanity might be in rudiment within his being. Yet lacking the interaction with fellowmen, and the play of mind on mind and heart on heart, what a maimed—what a lost life that would be! We really live only in others' lives. We have no true being except in others' being. We do not really *live* if we be selfish, closing the doors upon intruding feet. We live in burdens larger than our own, and tasks that involve the destiny of others, and joys and sorrows that like the rain of heaven fall on the evil and the good. No man lives to himself, says Scripture. When we live to ourselves we are not living. We live in human bonds, and life's relationships, and the sweet ties that hold us to each other. And that is what I mean, and what all teachers mean, when, thinking of our self-realization, we say that it is in society we find ourselves.

Now far be it from me even to suggest that in that common life there is no God. Where two or three are gathered together, there always God is in the midst. All I say is, that if in this life of ours it is in society we find ourselves, often, yes, very often, it is in solitude we find our God. For God is not in the tempest nor the whirlwind. He speaks to His children yet in the small voice. He comes to them when other sounds are hushed, and the soul is solitary and apart. He meets them in the secret hour of worship, and when the door is locked and when the knee is bent, and when the soul awaking to its sin feels itself in the wide world—alone. Not in Egypt did God meet with Moses, but in the spaces of the silent desert. Not with his company did God meet with Jacob, but where was the running of the lonely brook. And even Jesus, when the crowds were thronging and His heart was big with compassion for them all, yet left them, and went away to solitude, that in solitude He might have fellowship with God. It is not good for man to be alone. Alone, we could never reach to be ourselves. It takes home and market, it takes church and state, to fashion us into our true proportions. Yet are there visions of the eternal love, without which we can scarce live and cannot die; and—when I was alone I saw the vision

Behold, I stand at the door, and knock
(Rev. 3:20).

26

He Knocks

We are all familiar with the picture by a well-known artist which portrays Christ standing at the door.[1] It is one of the few pictures on a text of Scripture which have caught the imagination of the people. We see the door hanging on rusty hinges, and covered with the trailing growth of years. And we see Christ, clad in His kingly robes, out in the dew and darkness of the night. And in the one hand He bears a lighted lamp whose rays are penetrating through the chinks and crevices, and with the other He is knocking at the door. You know the title the artist gave that picture. He did not call it "Christ knocking at the door." He called it—and there is spiritual genius in the title—he called it, "I am the light of the world." For him the wonder of it all was this, that the light which is life and blessedness and victory should be so near the door of every heart.

And after all, when you come to think of it, that is the most wonderful thing about this text. It is not the knocking at the closed door; it is the overwhelming thought of Him who knocks. Were it some emperor, whose word is law to millions, it would be suffi-

1. "The Light of the World" (1854) by William Holman Hunt (1827–1910), British painter.

ciently awful and impressive. Were it some angel, as he who came to Abraham, it would be a very memorable visitant. But when a man goes apart into some silent place, and thinks that knocking at his heart is Christ, I tell you it thrills him to the very depths. Not Jesus, who walked amid the fields of Galilee. He is no longer walking amid the fields of Galilee. He is no longer rejected and despised, homeless, with no shelter for His head. He is the risen Christ, exalted to the heavens, invested with all the authority of glory, and yet behold He stands at the door and knocks. At the door of your heart, my brother and my sister. At the door of your heart this very Sabbath evening. You know what passions and what sins are knocking there, clamorous, urgent, eager to get in. And amid them all—that horrid, clamorous rabble—Christ is standing, the living, glorious Christ, and in infinite mercy He is knocking too.

And that just means, stripped of its metaphor, that Christ is not far away from any man. Wherever on earth there is a beating heart, there tonight there is a yearning Savior. The best is never far away from men. That is one of the joys of this strange life. God has not hidden what is true and beautiful in inaccessible and distant places. Sunshine and summer and the little children, and duty and chivalry and faith and love, are nearer than breathing and closer than hands and feet. The highest and holiest are never inaccessible. The beautiful and the best are always here. Here, in the great and smoky city, where we are toiling and sorrowing and rejoicing. And so I beg of you, who know all that, and through the lattice of whose life sweet love is looking, not to think it as a thing incredible that Christ should be very near to you tonight. My brother and sister, He is not far away. He has not gone on a journey to the Orient. He is not hidden in the light of heaven beyond the shining of the farthest star. Life is mysterious, and God is wonderful, and the infinite is round about us everywhere, and Christ is not far away from any man. But, Lord, I am a bad man—Behold I stand at the door and knock. But, Lord, You know that secret sin of mine, and what a wretched, hollow life I have been living. Yes, my brother, He understands all that, and for all that He shed His blood for you, and now He is standing knocking at your door. Your door—your life—your everlasting being. He wants to save it into life and victory. You know quite well that, unless something happens, life is going to be a sorry thing for you. Sir, there is someone standing at thy door who is able and waiting to make that something happen, as He has done for millions who have trusted Him—as He has done for him who speaks to you tonight.

And do you ask me in what way Christ knocks? I answer, in a hundred different ways. He has a knock that is very imperious sometimes, and sometimes one that is infinitely gentle. He knocks in all the mercies you enjoy, in health and strength and happiness and home. He knocks in the tender memories of childhood, of a father's character and of a mother's love. He knocks in the thought of all that has been done for you, and of the love that has girdled you from infancy, and of the mercy that has never yet forsaken you from the hour of your birth until today. Sometimes He knocks in the strange sense of loneliness that steals upon the heart on busiest days. Sometimes He knocks in all that deep unrest that craves it knows not what, and never finds it. Sometimes He knocks in bitter disappointments, and in bitter regrets over the might have been, and in love baffled till the heart is breaking. He is knocking when a man has sinned, and hates his sin, and loathes himself as vile. He is knocking in the despairing sense that our vices and habits are mightier than we. He is knocking in every business loss, in the hopeless tangle we have made of things, in the sickness that lays us prostrate for a season. He is knocking in the gift of little children, in the worries and trials and gladnesses of home. He is knocking in every parting from our loved ones, when they leave us for a distant land. He is knocking when two lives are joined together. He is knocking when two lives are separated—in the last parting when the grave is dug, and the heart is empty and the coffin full. Lo! I am with you always, even to the end of the world; always at the door and always knocking. Sometimes gently, as with an infant's hand, and sometimes mightily and terrible and loudly. And that is our hope—that Christ is not far away, but that He is here in infinite grace to save. For when He ceases knocking we are lost.

Indeed, I have often thought in quiet moments that that is the truest interpretation of all life. When I think of all that life has meant for me, it seems like someone knocking all the time. You remember that famous moment in Macbeth when the murderers hear the knocking at the door. And you recall how De Quincey[2] in his so subtle essay has shown us the dramatic significance of that—how into a room reeking of blood and murder, self-absorbed, oblivious of environment, the knocking came, and with it in a flash the thought of the great world that lay beyond. Shakespeare did not summon any calling voices. He was too consummate a master to do

---

2. Thomas De Quincey (1785–1859), English author and literary critic.

that. Your inferior dramatist who knew not life would have given you shouting and the trampling of men's feet. But Shakespeare gives a knocking at the door—some hand, unknown, knocking, that is all, and the murderers, who had forgotten everything, awaken to realize the world again. My brother and sister, if we were left alone we should be always in danger of forgetting everything—we should forget, if left alone, that God hates sin, that death is coming, and that heaven is real. And so, as I look back over my life, it seems to me there has never been a providence but has been meant by God to be interpreted like that knocking at the door in Shakespeare. In every triumph someone has been knocking; in every failure someone has been knocking—in every hour of pain and call of duty and baffled effort and yearning for the beautiful. Until at last there grows upon a man the sense that life is deep and rich and wonderful; a little chamber red with blood and sin, but round it a spiritual, unseen environment. Infinite love is pressing in upon us; infinite grace that can save unto the uttermost; infinite power that can redeem the weakest, and cleanse him and set him on his feet. And to all that, out of the selfishness which is our birthmark and our heritage, we are awakened by the knocking of the Christ.

To come back to that picture of which I spoke in starting, I remember somewhere reading a story about it. Whether it was in the life of Holman Hunt or elsewhere, I cannot charge my memory to say. But the story was that when the picture was finished a friend came into the studio to inspect it. And he looked at it, and admired its exquisite grace, and saw at once its spiritual significance. And then he turned to the artist and he said to him, "It is very beautiful, but there is one mistake." "A mistake?" said the artist, astonished—"What mistake? Is there anything wrong with the dress or with the hand?" "No, no," said the visitor; "It isn't that. The mistake is not in the dress; it's in the door. Look you—you have painted a door here, and it is very beautifully painted, but you have forgotten to put any handle to the door." And the story told how Holman Hunt explained to his visitor that that was no mistake. Had there been any handle on the outside, he told him, Christ would have turned it, and would have entered in. But this was a door that had no handle there—a door that could only be opened from the *inside*. If any man will open to Me, I will come in to him and sup with him.

And that just means, stripped of its imagery, that to the knocking of Jesus Christ we must respond. We must open our hearts to the living, present Christ, and say, "Come in, thou blessed of the Lord."

No man has a profounder faith than I have in the absolute sovereignty of Almighty God. I should not be a Scotsman if I disbelieved it, and I should be untrue to all that God has shown me. There is not a man here in this church tonight who has been saved by grace and brought into Christ Jesus, who does not know from the bottom of his soul that God will have mercy on whom He will have mercy. Far away beyond our human will there is the eternal and electing will of heaven. If there be one thing clear to a man as life rolls on, it is that before his choosing, God has chosen him. And yet so intricate are earth and heaven, and so respectful of His children's liberty is God, that till a man lift up his voice and cries "I will," Jesus Christ will never cross the door. That is just where so many are making a mistake. They are always waiting for something irresistible. They are waiting for the moment when some power divine will shatter the door, and enter in, in spite of them. My brother, I want to tell you tonight quite plainly—that you may go out into the street and think upon it—I want to tell you that hour will never come. If any man will open the door—it is the one condition of all blessing. You must respond. You must open wide your being. You must say to the living Lord and Christ "Come in." And the wonder of the Christian gospel is just this, that all you have striven and struggled for and failed in, becomes a thrilling power and possibility the moment with all your heart you have done that. That was the message that rang through a dying world and made it hope again and live again. I want you to remember that the Christian gospel is the most wonderful thing that every reached humanity. It is no scheme of social reform. We could have that and more without a Christ. It is peace with God and victory for you. The sunshine is a very marvelous creation, but it will never open any shutters for you. You must open them—a very simple thing—and all the mystery of the light will flood the room. And so with Christ—more glorious than sunshine—Christ the living, reigning, mighty Lord—if any man will open, I will come in. My brother and sister, you need Him very badly, and you will need Him more and more every year you live. Things are not going well with you; you know it. You are making a poor business of it all. Now write to me tonight when you get home—and you need not sign your name if you don't want to—and tell me that on this eighteenth day of May you have opened the door to the Lord Jesus Christ.

A time to rend, and a time to sew
(Eccl. 3:7).

27

Rending and Sewing

These words occur in a discourse upon timeliness, couched in the vivid language of the Oriental. They teach us that quite invaluable lesson that for everything under heaven there is a time. Men have often noted the timeliness of Jesus as one of the striking features of His life. At that time Jesus answered and said, and the time is always exquisitely chosen. He knew, for He had learned it from His Father, that for everything under heaven there is a time, and that in its own time everything is beautiful. The right word may be wrong at the wrong hour. The fitting action must have its fitting moment. God has made everything beautiful in its time, and out of its time the fairest may be ugly. There is a time to weep and a time to laugh; a time to rend and a time to sew; there is a time to be born and a time to die. The words, then, of our text tonight are these—there is a time to rend and a time to sew. I have chosen them because they seem to me to give vivid expression to a law of progress. And on that law I should like to dwell a little, keeping close to the imagery of our passage, and trying to illustrate it in various spheres.

There is a time to rend and a time to sew: *think first, then, of the world that lies around us*. It has been rent by the hand of the Creator into all its infinite variety of beauty. There is one great word that runs like a refrain through the opening chapters of the book of Genesis. It is the word *divide*—"and God divided" is like the chorus of the creation story. He rent the luminous ether into stars; He rent the veil of night and waked the dawn; He rent the land into the snowy peaks and into the valleys where the rivers flow. There is a proverb that says "divide and conquer," and we may say that God divided and conquered. He divided night from day, and sun from moon, and conquered chaos and gave a world of beauty. But the singular thing about that world of beauty is that no man thinks of it as a divided thing—it is knit up again into a perfect whole. Forever there is a perfect harmony between the thousand voices of the world; and night and day, and frost and sun and rain, are toiling together in a common ministry, and deep is always calling to deep, and night is ever answering to day, and the whole universe is as one glorious temple where dwells the Spirit of the Lord. There was a time to rend in the Creator's plan, and then in that plan there was a time to sew. There was a time to separate into a thousand parts, and then a time to knit these parts again. There was a time to break the mass of chaos, and then a time so to unite these breakings, that if there is one thing which is clear today it is what we call the unity of nature.

The same truth is evident again in God's method of bringing blessing to mankind. That there is a time to rend and a time to sew is but another spelling of election. Have you ever thought of what election is? Well, I shall tell you what election is. It is not the fiat of an almighty despot; it is the way of heaven for blessing men. It is the separating of the individual; it is the choosing and calling of the one, that from the one, so called and separated, a blessing might be extended to mankind. There was a time to rend when Abraham was chosen, and torn away from his kindred and his home. There was a time to rend when Israel was chosen, and separated from all the nations of the earth. And then, being so rent and separated, and driven as it were apart into a solitude, who does not see that in the ways of God after that rending there came a time to sew? In thee, and in thy seed, said God to Abraham, shall all the families of the earth be blessed. And out of Israel—separated Israel—there came the light that lights every man. So is there rending for a reuniting, a breaking asunder for a richer unity, a call to a single soul, "Come thou apart," and then the message, "Go into all the world."

Coming now a little nearer home, *does not that law meet us in our daily life*? There is a time to rend there, and a time to sew, and it is through that rending and sewing that we are enriched. When Jacob said farewell, and left his home, that was the rending of many a fond tie. And his mother kissed him, and his father wept for him, for they might never see their son again. And yet had Jacob never crossed the threshold, and never been torn from the tenderness of home, you and I would not have sung together, "O God of Bethel, by whose hand." He had to be separated that he might find himself, in a life reknit in worthier relationship. He had to be rent from father and from mother that he might rise to the fellowship of God. And so it may be that you and I tonight, as we look backward upon our years of journeying, may see that for us too as for the patriarch there has been a time to rend and one to sew. Among all the memorable hours of a man's life, there is none more memorable than that of leaving home. It is then that he understands what home has been, and how tender was the love that shielded him. And he leaves it, however bright his hopes, with a certain nameless sinking of the heart, for there is no happiness like that of home, and no love like a mother's love. But there is a time to rend—God wills it thus. Duty is calling, and he cannot stay. And he goes out into the world, and he is lonely, and his lodging at evening is a dreary place. And then the years go by, and other interests gather, and by the blessing of God new ties are formed, and when love comes and hearts are knit together, he finds that with God there is a time to sew. Other hearts have begun to beat with his. Other voices answer to his own. There is the cry of babyhood upon the mother's bosom, and the patter of little feet upon the floor. So is home left to be reformed again, and the life is emptied that it may be refilled, and through such rending and sewing are we rich.

The same law is also very evident in the progress of the spiritual life. Most men come to their own in spiritual things through a time of rending and of sewing. Of course it is not always so, for God fulfills Himself in many ways. There are men whose path is as the shining light that shines more and more unto the perfect day. There are men whose heaven has never known a cloud, and for whom the music has never died away, and who have grown as the lily in the summer meadow. Such lives are often exquisitely beautiful, and sweet with the serenity of heaven. But for most men it is not thus, I take it, that the faith of maturity is reached. It is reached through many a doubt and many a questioning, through much rejecting and reconstituting, through seasons when in all the arch of heaven there was not the shining of one star. For often in opening manhood comes a period when the faith of childhood can no longer satisfy; a time when there is no healing and no help in the simple pieties of early days; yet let a man cling to what is right in the days when the foundations tremble, and his feet shall yet be set in a large room. There is a time to rend, and sometimes it arrives in the first tragic experience of sorrow. There is a time to rend, and sometimes it arrives in the first listening to college lectures. And all the faith that like a seamless garment had been woven for us in the home of childhood, seems to be torn into a thousand shreds. My brother, if that be your experience, remember it is nothing to be proud of. There are many who have never known it, whose latchet you are unworthy to unloose. But also remember that, if it come to you, you are never to rest in it as something final; God rends that He may sew again. They say that life is never quite so sweet as in the hours after a lovers' quarrel. There is a depth then of mutual tenderness that was being lost in the unruffled days. And so when a man has quarreled with his faith, and in the goodness of God has found his faith again, there is a gladness in it that is only comparable to the new light in the eyes that answer ours. For now has our father's God become our God—now have we something that is our very own—it may be less, and yet it may be more, than the loose acceptance of unthinking days. For now, whatever mysteries there be, we at least are certain of this one thing: that neither height nor depth, nor life nor death, can separate us from the love of God which is in Christ.

May I say in passing how wonderfully this is illustrated in the drama of the book of Job? The whole experience of Job may be summed up in this, that God has a time to rend and one to sew. There was a man called Job, and he was an upright man, and walked reverently and humbly with his Maker. He had been happy—he had been very prosperous—and he had never questioned his ancestral faith. And then in the mysterious ordering of God, who does according to the counsel of His will, there came for Job a time to rend. And his cattle were all rent away from him, and then his children were all rent away from him, and his home was ruined, and his very body became a loathsome and unsightly thing. Until at last his old and easy faith that had so comforted and cheered him once, was rent and tattered into a thousand shreds. Then was Job brought into despair, and he cried out in rebellion against God. And it was all so hopeless and so dark that his wife bade him curse God and die. And the wonderful thing in that most wonderful book is how that faithful and heroic soul fights his way out of the pit of hell into the sunshine of the broad heavens again. "I have heard of Thee by the hearing of the ear," he cries, "but now mine eye seeth Thee." The old traditional faith had once been his; now he had a real and living faith. And so by rending and reknitting did the patriarch come to his kingdom in the end, finding the peace that the world cannot give, and at its darkest cannot take away.

Then once again we find this law at work in the long history of the church of Christ, and nowhere perhaps more manifestly so than in the history of the church of Christ in Scotland. Men may talk of schism as they will, and of all the evils that follow in its train. But to me it is certain, if anything is certain, that God in Scotland has had His times to rend. And one was the period of the Reformation, and another was when the Erskines[1] left the church, and a third was the great year of the Disruption.[2] All that was deepest in the religious life cried in such seasons, "There is a time to rend." Conscience cried it, and spiritual liberty, and the imperiled rights of the Redeemer. And yet if God has had His times to rend, in the story of the church we love so well, do not forget He has His times to sew. I have heard men speak of being anchored to the disruption, as if we ever could be anchored to disruptions. Every secession, every disruption, is but a movement to a richer unity. We have been rent that we may be reknit—driven apart that we may be one again. And these are the true children of the past who see in the rending of the past the hand of God, yet are ever praying and ever looking for a reknit and reunited future.

And there is one difference between rending and sewing that it is well that we ever bear in mind. I mean that rending is momentary work, and sewing is long and tedious work. The one is swift and sudden and impressive, and on a large scale may strangely thrill the heart; the other is a weary, tedious business. There is nothing spectacular about the seamstress as with weary eyes she bends over her seam. There is nothing remarkable about the mother as she sews the little garments of her children. And so when the bride of Christ which is the church is led in providence to her sewing task, there may be little to thrill the heart in that. Sewing is a work that calls for patience. It is a mother's ministry of love. There is many a little

1. Ebenezer Erskine (1680–1754), founder of the Secession Church in Scotland.
2. In 1843 when 474 ministers withdrew from the Church of Scotland to form the Free Church of Scotland.

sacrifice that she will make to get the sewing done for school tomorrow. And so the church, with a love that hopes all things, and with a patience that is not easily baffled, will take herself to the service of reunion. It is far easier to rend than to reknit; far easier to separate than to unite again. For the one is swift and has the charm of daring, and the other is long and tedious and difficult. Yet both are in the ordering of Him who has said to us, "I came to send a sword," and yet will never rest until at length He has gathered the scattered sheep into one flock.

In closing, and in a word or two, *I want to take this thought on to the grave.* Sooner or later in every family circle there comes the sad and bitter time to rend. I was walking the other afternoon in one of our mighty cities of the dead. And the day was still, and everything was calm, save for the subdued roar of our great city. And as I listened to it, and thought of all the life there, and then turned to the graves beside my feet, I heard as it were a voice from every grave crying to me, "There is a time to rend." And I cried back again in the faith of Jesus Christ, "If there is a time to rend, there is a time to sew." I cannot believe that lives which have been one are to be separated forever and forever. In ways we know not, in unions that are spiritual, in perfect and interpenetrating fellowship, ties that are broken shall be reknit again in the full fruition of the love of God. That is the deepest craving of the heart, and "if it were not so I would have told you." There is a time to rend when the new grave is full, and a time to sew on resurrection morning. So through rending and sewing comes the universe, and spiritual victory, and a victorious church, and so shall there come our perfect life of fellowship, when the day breaks and the shadows flee away.

How much then is a man better than a sheep? (Matt. 12:12).

28

Christ's Teaching on Man

Not very far away from where we sit there are gleaming the lights of our great city hospitals. We can see with the mind's eye the quiet wards, and the nurses moving in their gracious ministry. There the poorest citizens are treated with all the appliances that riches can command. There are they tended by night and day, with a skill that is as wise as it is kind. And if we ask ourselves, as thoughtful men, to what it is that we owe such institutions, the answer is not very far to seek. It is not enough to say we owe them to the generous support of a compassionate public. We want to find the source of that compassion, which is peculiar to the Christian era. And we find it, without any question, in the new conception of what man is, which we owe to our Lord and Savior Jesus Christ.

Indeed if one were asked the most distinctive feature of those ages which we call the Christian era, I do not think we should much err in answering that it was just that altered thought of man. We divide the history of the world into two parts, the one before Christ and the other after Christ. That in itself is an unequaled tribute to the centrality of the Redeemer. Well, among all the differences of these two eras, I say that none perhaps is so remarkable as the difference which is known to every student in the accepted estimate of man. It has breathed a new spirit into literature. It has created a passion for social service. It has built those splendid palaces of healing, where is the hand of science and the heart of mercy. All this, and a vast deal more than this, has been wrought by the new idea of man which Christendom owes to the Lord Jesus Christ. On that new thought of man, then, I desire to speak for a little while this evening, and I do it the more readily because today our thoughts are going out toward our hospitals.

There are one or two preliminary things I want to say, and the first of them is this, that *the doctrine of man, whatever it may be, is always the other side of the doctrine of God.* As is the thought of God in any faith, so is the thought of man in that same faith. The one controls and dominates the other, giving it its color and its content. Tell me the kind of God a people worships—tell me their thought of the Being in the heavens—and I shall tell you what they think of man in his value and his freedom and his destiny. Now we are not dealing with Christ's thought of God tonight, but we all know something of the wonder of it. We know how infinitely rich in personality is the Father of our Lord Jesus Christ. And I throw out the hint that knowing it, we shall expect to find in Jesus' view of man a grandeur, a freedom, and a depth that are without parallel in any teaching.

Again it is well that we should bear in mind that *Jesus laid down nothing about man's origin.* His view of man is a religious view; it is in no sense a scientific one. That man as such was a child of God, and that he owed his being to the Creator's hand is a truth which Christ never stays to prove—He assumes it, taking it for granted. But beyond that, practicing a silence which is as wonderful as any speech, He leaves the utmost freedom for inquiry. His view of man is not bound up with any theory of man's physical origin. It can be held by the most advanced of scientists as fully as by the humblest peasant. The one man by whom it cannot be held is the man who makes a jest of human nature, and who, so scorning it, sets a stumbling block before the feet of one of these little ones. That Christ in His infinite humiliation may have shared in the current beliefs of His own day, is not only possible, but as it seems to me, adds to the wonder and depth of His abasement. But that He should have thought to lay on us these limitations which He assumed in mercy, must be something wholly and forever alien from the spirit and mind of Him who is the truth. Christ has involved us in no theory here. He has not barred the door on scientific progress. He has left it open to every earnest seeker to follow the truth wherever it may lead. A man may be convinced with all his heart in the unbroken evolution of humanity, and yet may worship at the feet of Jesus, crying with Peter, You are the Son of God.

And another thing it is well to remark is that Christ's view is based on observation. It was not the dreaming of a doctrinaire; it was fashioned in closest contact with humanity. I have read some learned books dealing with children, and been entirely humbled with their learning. But the strongest impression made on me by some of them was that the writer had never known a child. So are there certain theories of man that are entirely admirable and excellent, save for the one unfortunate detail that the man they analyze is nonexistent. There are people who are enamored of humanity. They will talk to you by the hour about humanity. Christ did not care one farthing for humanity; He cared with all His heart for men and women. And the great glory of His view is this, that it is not elaborated in any solitude, but is wrought out in daily loving contact with actual sinning men and sinning women. He did not come to them with any creed, determined to find that creed in every bosom. He came with a single eye, and with a heart of love, to find what was there, and only what was there. And so He saw in man such height and depth, such light and shadow, such infinite variety, as never had been seen on earth before. He knew that the eye might be so evil that the whole body might be full of darkness; and yet He knew there was a cry for home in the soul of the prodigal among the swine. He knew that out of the heart there spring adulteries, and all the lust that dwells so close to hate, and yet He knew that we who are so vile can give good gifts to our children. Now the real worth of any viewpoint depends on the range of facts that it interprets. If it be broad enough to embrace all contrarieties, the chances are it is the view of God. And the view of man that Jesus Christ has given us shall ever stand conspicuous in this, that it was wrought out, not in dreams of solitude, but in daily loving contact with His kind.

Coming now to the teaching in itself, the first thing to be said is this, that in His thought, as in His love, *Christ made the individual the unit*. He did not regard men as on the scale of fifty. He did not think of them as on the scale of ten. He thought of men, and lived for them, and died for them, upon the scale of one. Now to you and me, brethren, that is such a commonplace that we can scarcely conceive of any other reckoning. But one of the primary lessons of all history is that our commonplaces were once incredibilities. And though of course there never was a time in which men did not live their individual lives, yet it is no exaggeration to declare, as one has done, that Jesus Christ discovered the individual. To the ancient Jews, among whom Christ was born, in relation to God the nation was the unit. At an earlier period we have a time when it was the family who took the eye of heaven. But Christ as it were disrobed the individual, disengaged him out of all relationships, and revealed forever the truth that in himself man was the object of divine regard. There is joy in the presence of the angels of God over one sinner who repents. Take heed that you despise not one of these little ones; it is not God's will that *one* of them should perish. It was for one coin the woman swept the house; for one sheep the shepherd left the flock; for one son, and him a sorry prodigal, the father in the home was brokenhearted. If you go back into the ancient world I shall tell you the kind of feeling you discover. You discover men claiming divine protection because they were members of a tribe or family. And the wonderful thing in Jesus Christ is this, that from such relationships He disengaged the soul, and, never despising the family or the state, flashed all the light of heaven upon the one. That is what is meant when it is said that Christ discovered the individual. It does not mean that there ever was an age when the separate heart had not its separate sorrow. But it means that Jesus, out of all societies, disentangled the individual being, putting a crown of glory on its head, and the staff of the good shepherd in its hand. In what innumerable ways that has affected Christendom I have not time to dwell upon tonight. It has given a new note to literature. It has breathed a new spirit upon art. It has shown itself in the ward of the infirmary where there may be fifty patients under one surgeon, yet each of them, as an individual being, is tended with an individual care.

But there is something deeper still in Jesus' view, for Christ did not only discover the individual *He taught us also that that individual is of infinite value in the eyes of God.* There are some secrets for which men have toiled, and when they have found them they have been brokenhearted. What they discovered has proved itself so tragical that they have prayed to heaven to make them blind again. But Christ, discovering the individual, found in that secret such a wealth of glory that the name He chose for Himself was Son of Man. They say that a diamond which today is blazing upon the crown of a European monarch lay for weeks upon a stall in Rome, labeled "Rock crystal, one franc." And may we not reverently say that Jesus Christ, purchasing the rock crystal for His own, has found something more precious than a diamond. For it is not man as rich that Jesus thinks of. It is not man as learned or as powerful. The ancient world was quick to recognize the value of the learned or the powerful man. The differentia of Christ is this, that He stands up and faces that old world, and says that the thing of infinite worth to God is not man as powerful but man as man. Strip him of all the art of Greece. Take from him all the might of Rome. Call him a prodigal, and let him feed the swine; call him a sunken creature of the street. Yet even then, disrobed of every grace, sunken into the mire and trampled on, even then, says Christ, in God's eyes man is a being of a worth unspeakable. There is a great deal talked today about the mystery of personality. Men are giving their deepest thought to that, and already there are signs of a rich harvest. But the deepest mystery of personality, if you will only sit down and think about it, is just that at its shallowest and worst it would be of infinite value in the eyes of heaven. I tell you it is an overwhelming thought. It is enough to make one thrill to realize it—that the sorriest wretch whose every breath is vile, is precious because he is a man. And that is the great truth which Christ has taught us, and which is so inwrought into our scheme of life, that not only in the church but in the world today it has the accent of the commonplace.

Now I said at the beginning that the thought of man is always relative to the thought of God. And I said it because I was looking forward to the point of the argument we have now reached. You know—all of you know perfectly—what was Jesus' controlling thought of God. *From first to last our Savior thought of God under the deep and tender name of* Father. And you see at a glance, do you not, how this new doctrine of the infinite preciousness of every man springs from the thought of the fatherhood in heaven? Does a father wait to love his children till they have come to discretion or maturity? Does he wait until one son has risen to honor, and another has become a prosperous citizen? On the contrary, he never loves them more than in the happy and helpless days of childhood, when there is never a scrap of learning in the brain, and never a jingle of money in the purse. Nay, if among that little family there be one that is sickly or weakly or deformed—one with a twisted limb, or with a shrunken arm, or with an intelligence arrested strangely—is not that the very child the father loves with an ineffable and yearning tenderness, so that he often prays for it, and sometimes quietly weeps, in the long silent watches of the night? That is the mystery of human fatherhood, and Christ has taught us when we pray to say, Our Father. And we lift our eyes at the command of Jesus, and lo, there is a Father on the throne. And so do we learn that man as man, simply and solely because he is a child, is infinitely and forever precious in the eyes of Him with whom we have to do. For remember that the son is still a son, though he have wandered away to the far country. He may be a prodigal—he may be lost—but he has never ceased to be a child. And just because, through all his degradation, nothing can cancel that filial relationship, there is a welcome for him in the father's home, and a yearning in the father's heart.

May I say, too, that this thought of the worth of man is enormously strengthened by the Incarnation? Christ took on Him not the nature of angels, but He took on Him the seed of Abraham. If there is one truth to which all thinking leads me it is the preexistence of Christ Jesus. To me the Bible is an unmeaning riddle if Christ began to be when He was born. But if He came from heaven—the eternal Logos—to tabernacle with us for a little season, then in the circumstances of His coming I learn the infinite worth of man as man. One of the most curious books that was ever written has been lately translated by one of our professors here. It is the life of one Apollonius of Tyana,[1] who was for long regarded as a kind of rival Christ. For he too healed the sick as Jesus did, and he too raised the dead as Jesus did, and he too, as the people of Tyana had it, was the son not of a mortal but of God. Quite so: we understand all that at once, but there is one difference which is overwhelming. For Apollonius was the child of a vast wealth and the scion of a very noble family. But Jesus was the son of a poor mother, for whom there was no room in Bethlehem, and who, where the dumb beasts were in their stalls, brought her firstborn child into the world. That does not mean that God entering humanity was bringing down the mighty from their seats. But it *does* mean that the incarnate God was showing forth the worth of man as man. Not manhood in any might or splendor, but manhood at its lowliest and its least, was the tabernacle of the eternal Son.

Is it not true also that this thought of man sheds a great light on Jesus' thought of sin? It helps us to fathom that intense abhorrence with which our Savior contemplated sin. There were things that

1. A neopythagorean philosopher who died c. 98 and whose biography presents him as a pagan counterpart to Jesus.

Jesus took no notice of, and there were others He treated as supremely petty. But there was one thing which always stirred Him to the deeps, and that was the spectacle of sin. And He abhorred it in its guilt and power not merely because it was a grief to God, but because it wrought such irreparable havoc on a being who was so infinitely precious. If I spill the ink bottle on some cheap novel, that is a matter of very small concern. But if I spill it on some priceless manuscript, then the pity of that blot is great. And it is just because man is precious in Christ's eyes—more precious than any priceless manuscript—that He felt the infinite pity of it all, when He looked on the disfigurements of sin. Whenever you have low thoughts of personality, you have low conceptions of the power of evil. Whenever you have lofty views of man, sin stands out there positive and terrible. And if you want to understand Christ's thought of sin, and all the passion of His abhorrence of it, I say you must bear in mind that in His eyes the poorest wretch was of a worth unspeakable. He was always pitiful toward the sinner; He was always pitiless toward the sin. He hated it with all the hate of heaven, which is far more terrible than all the hate of hell. And He hated it because it spoiled the beauty, and marred the strength, and slew the joy and peace of the most wonderful and precious thing in the whole universe of God.

Then the third point I wish to note is this, that such a view involves man's immortality. The immortality of man in Jesus' eyes rests on the fact that he is the child of God. In one of the most exquisite of all his dialogues Plato handles the theme of immortality. And he discusses it and argues for it, and builds up lofty reasons for its certainty. But Jesus never discusses immortality—for Him it is a thing to be assumed—He cannot conceive of any other destiny for a being so infinitely dear to God. If man were a trifle in the eyes of heaven, then like a trifle he might cease to be. But if man is infinitely dear to God, then it is impossible that he should perish. Girt with a love so mighty in its tenderness, able to look up and say My Father, it was simply impossible for Christ to think that the coffin and the grave should be the end. If one of your little children lay dying, and looked up at you and smiled, and said *My Father*, would you not barter everything you had for the power to bring that child to life again? And God in heaven always has that power, and He is our Father with a father's heart, and we, even the sorriest of us all, have never ceased at our worst to be His children. It is that filial relationship, in Christ's eyes, which makes the thought of extinction quite impossible. To be what we are within the heart of God must mean and can only mean to be forever. For love is loth to lose what it holds dear, and wants it not for an hour but forever, and only says farewell when forced to do it, which forcing has no place in the divine.

Such then is the teaching of Jesus about man, and now in closing let me say this to you. All doctrine has an influence upon conduct, and we see this perfectly in our Redeemer. Holding such a view of man as that, He was always reverent and always courteous. If the meanest life was of an infinite value it was not likely that Christ would be contemptuous. *And so you find Him reverent and courteous, quite independent of any social station*, and you find Him kindly when other men were harsh, and hopeful sometimes when all the world despaired. And it all sprang from His undying faith in the infinite preciousness of man as man. He never could scorn the most degraded creature, when He thought of what that creature meant for God. So you and I who name the name of Christ must see to it as we take our journey, that we are looking out on men and women with somewhat of the look of our Redeemer. We are not called upon for any easy tolerance, as if moral distinctions were to be obliterated. We are *not* called upon to think of evil lightly as if it were only good in manufacture. But we *are* called upon to think that every man, however lost, is still the Father's child, and is so precious to the heart of God that He will never leave him nor forsake him. Remembering that, we also shall be reverent, and always pitiful, and always hopeful. Remembering that, we shall delight to serve and count it a glad thing that we are brothers.

Cleanse thou me from secret faults
(Ps. 19:12).

29

Secret Faults

On the Sabbath evening preceding the Communion there is an old Scottish custom which I like to honor. It is that of preparing ourselves for the Lord's Table by some quiet exercise of self-examination. When the Communion comes our thoughts shall be all of Christ—of His infinite love to us, and our infinite debt to Him. We shall look outward to an atoning sacrifice, on which we rest and through which we have peace. But tonight is the fitting occasion to look inward, and to examine ourselves, lest we eat and drink unworthily: and that is why I have chosen as our text this evening, "Cleanse thou me from secret faults."

Now you all understand, I hope, what is meant by secret faults. They are the faults that are secret from ourselves. They are the sins and failings in your life and mine of which we are unconscious. There are some faults we can keep secret from the world, and yet they are well known to those at home. The people we meet in the street may not suspect them, but the wife or the mother knows them all too well. And there are other sins which a man may do in business, so that his name smells rank amid honorable dealers, yet the shadow of them may never touch his home, nor the innocent faces of his adoring children. Such faults are secret beyond a certain circle. Love casts the mantle of her glorious silence round them. But it is not these of which the psalmist thinks when he cries, Cleanse Thou me from secret faults. He thinks of the faults which you and I have tonight—of the sins which in the sight of God we are committing—and yet we are ignorant of them, and have never been wakened to them, and are not conscious they are there at all.

Now that there are such faults in everyone of us may be demonstrated along many lines. Think, for instance, how certain it becomes when we remember what we see in others. Is there any one known to you, however good or beautiful, on whose faults or failings you could not put your finger? Is there any friend or lover or child or wife or minister whose weakness you have not long ago detected? They may not see it—it never obtrudes on them—they are quite unconscious that it is striking you. And so do our neighbors move among us daily, and we see a hundred faults which they are blind to. Do not think to exempt yourself, I beg of you, from this general censure of humanity. You are bone of their bone, flesh of their flesh, born with their weakness, tempted with their sin. The very fact that all of us can see the mote that is in a brother's eye is proof that there is somewhat in our own.

The certainty of such faults is proved again by our general ignorance of our own nature. There is not a man or woman in this church this evening whose life is not full of secret possibilities. Let the finger of love but touch a woman's heart, and you shall hardly know that woman by and by. Let motherhood come with all its infinite mystery, and she is enriched to the very heavens. Let a man be converted by the grace of God, as Paul was converted on the Damascus road, and life is expanded into undreamed-of fullness. We all surprise each other now and then, and now and then we all surprise ourselves; when love comes, or some great wave of feeling, or the sound of trumpet and the call to battle. And if we believe in secret possibilities, on the basis of which Christ wrought from first to last, must we not also believe in secret sins? The fact is we should believe it instantly, if it were not for the presence of self-love. Love thinks no evil of the loved one, even when the loved one is oneself. And so in our secret virtues we believe, and in the hidden possibilities within us, but from our secret faults we turn away. That common attitude is intellectual cowardice. It is a man's first duty to face all the facts. To flatter other men is bad enough, but to flatter one's own self is far more deadly. And therefore if you believe in hidden heights within you, I ask you also to believe in hidden depths, and to go out tonight and cry as David cried, "Cleanse thou me from secret faults."

Once again I should infer this truth from the deadening power of long-continued habit. There are sins which were not secret long ago, but habit and custom have made them secret now. I well remember when I went to Dundee from the dear seclusion of my manse in Thurso, how at first I found it hard to sleep at nights for the incessant noise of railway and of street. In Thurso, when night fell, the quiet was perfect. The countryside might have been wrapped in snow. There was no sound except the northern wind, and sometimes the mystical calling of the sea. And then in the city there was the midnight traffic, and the jar and jolt and shrieking of the railway, and one lay awake repeating, "Sleep no more, Dundee has murdered sleep."[1] All that lasted for a week or two, and then the clamorous voices became silent. And they died away, and were no longer audible, and never disturbed the beatitude of rest. Still was the wagon straining on the causeway, and still the engine laboring through the dark, but habit had made one oblivious of it all. For good or for evil, in this life of ours, habit is always busy doing that. Things that would wake us once, and make us start affrighted, are robbed of their power to disturb our slumber. And so the sins that long ago were open, and shocked us, and made us blush to think of them, may have become with passing years our secret sins. You would have been very unhappy once, when day was over, if you had flung yourself down upon a prayerless bed. And yet it may be that you do it now with never a thought that you are grieving God. You would have been miserable once, and full of guilty shame, had you been cruel, dishonest, or impure. And yet it may be that tonight you sin these sins without any inward unhappiness at all. My brother and sister, that is Satan's triumph—to take our open sins and make them secret, to take the faults that shamed us long ago, and make us habituated and accustomed to them. When a man has ceased to be shamed and shocked by sin, when he does habitually what once he loathed and hated, let him beware for his immortal soul, for final impenitency crouches at the door. Cleanse Thou me, O Lord, from secret faults. They were not secret once, in happy childhood. Then they distressed me, and sent me out in misery, but they do not distress me for a moment now. So from the pressure of habit and of custom, touching us all into a certain hardness, may we be sure that

1. A play on Macbeth's words, "Sleep no more! Macbeth doth murder sleep."

we need the psalmist's prayer as we look forward to another sacrament.

And may I say in passing that among all our sins there are perhaps none more perilous than our secret sins. And they are perilous just because in them we have the preparation for our open falls. Our great sins are seldom momentary overthrows. They seldom reach us like bolts out of the blue. These dark and tragic falls that we all know are not isolated and independent things. They reach us by the hidden ways of darkness, and out of the silent and interior life, so that on every hour of wreckage and disaster there is the pressure of our secret faults. For every noble act you ever did, there was a conscious and an unconscious preparation. You were getting ready for it not only when you strove: you were getting ready when you never dreamed of it. By every virtue you clung to in the dark—by every beautiful thought you ever cherished—by the self-denials of each common morning—you have been getting ready for your nobler hours. That is the road by which we reach our victories, and that is the road by which we reach our tragedies. Our sudden overthrows, when character is forfeited, are never quite so sudden as we think. Through secret faults—through covetings unchecked—through lusts unbridled when they were still imaginings does a man go out to his hours when peace is lost, and the shame of the vanquished is written on his brow. Professor Drummond,[2] in his *Tropical Africa*, tells of the secret ravages of the white ants. He tells of their enormous powers of destruction, and how insidiously and secretly they work. He tells how a man may be sitting in his hut, and may think it as strong as on the day he built it, when suddenly he may waken to discover that there is nothing around him but a shell. Silently the white ants have been at work, eating out the heart of every beam: no one has seen them—no one has heard them toiling—no one has had any warning of their presence. And then in a moment comes the revelation, when the very pillars of the house do tremble, and the revelation is but secret ravage. Cleanse Thou me from secret faults—keep back Thy servant from presumptuous sins. Answer that first prayer, our blessed Savior, and in it we shall have our answer to the second. For all those open shames of word and deed that we cannot remember tonight without self-loathing are but the lurid flowering of that nightshade whose roots are in the secret of the heart.

In closing, I am eager to suggest to you that our secret sins have

---

2. Henry Drummond (1851–1897), Scottish clergyman and African explorer.

one peculiar office. Above all other sins which we commit, they lead us to feel our utter need of Christ. Let me make that plain by a simple illustration. If some beautiful garden that you love is only disfigured by a weed or two, it is quite within your power to pluck those weeds out, though they may be rank as docken or poisonous as hemlock. But if the soil be foul—filled through and through with seeds—tangled with rootstocks of pestilential things—then cleansing is quite another matter. My brother and sister, when you come to think of it, that is like the garden of your heart. If all that needs to be plucked is a few habits, then do it in God's name, for you have power to do it. But when you awake to the appalling certainty that down in the heart there is a world of sin, in that hour you feel you need a Savior. Not what we know, but what we do not know, is the deepest cry of the human soul to Christ—that world unfathomed beneath the sight of consciousness, out of which spring adulteries and murders. You cannot reach that world which lies unseen, away deep down in your mysterious being, and yet unless it is reached and cleansed by somebody you know there can never be victory for you. It is just there that Jesus Christ draws near. He is able to save even to the uttermost. He is able and willing this very summer evening to work a radical cleansing within you.

But I say unto you . . . (Matt. 11:22).

30

The Decisiveness of Christ

There is one element in the character of Jesus which is well worthy of our consideration. It is the element which, in default of a better word, one might describe as His *decisiveness*. In other men, even the greatest, you catch continually the note of hesitancy. Even in the most dogmatic person you have the occasional sense of possible mistake. But in the Jesus given us in the gospels there is not the faintest trace of such a hesitancy. There is an absolute and instantaneous certainty in the face of every problem and perplexity. In other lives, if such certainty be found, it is found generally in exalted hours. It is found in those rare and elevated moments when the mists are scattered somehow, and we know. But with Jesus this decisiveness was normal. He had not to wait for any glorious hours. It never seems to have left Him for an instant as He moved among the villages of Galilee. From the first recorded utterance of His boyhood, "Wist ye not that I must be about My Father's business?" on to the last glad triumph on the cross, when He exulted in the thought that it was finished, there is not visible one shadow of perplexity, nor any halting as of uncertain feet, nor any clouding, even for a moment, of the serene decisiveness of Christ.

This is all the more notable when we remember how infinitely gracious Jesus was. The mystery of His decisiveness is deepened greatly when we associate it with the beauty of His character. When men have a habit of laying down the law, they may convince us but they rarely charm us. Your citizen who is always in the right may generally reckon on being held a nuisance. And the unique thing about our Lord is this, that He was always laying down the law, yet men found Him infinitely gracious. He was dogmatic and yet they clung to Him. He was intolerant yet infinitely winsome. He was always judging without the slightest hesitancy, and yet men never felt He was censorious. There was in our Lord a constant self-assertion that is quite unparalleled in human history, yet I do not think that any lip was curled when He said He was meek and lowly in heart. It is such antinomies in Jesus' character that have made men call Him utterly inexplicable. No one would ever have dreamed of such a character, had not such a character actually existed. To be full of grace has been the lot of some, and to be full of truth the lot of others, but to be full of grace and truth is the unique prerogative of Christ.

We catch that note of decisiveness in many spheres, and first in regard to the long past of Israel. There is nothing more striking in the gospel record than the attitude of our Savior to that past. What thoughts He cherished about the past of Greece we neither know nor are we meant to know. Nor shall we ever know what thoughts He cherished about the magnificent grandeur which was Rome. But how He viewed the glorious past of Israel, with its song of psalmist and oracle of prophet, all that is written so that he who runs may read. For Christ that story of Israel was divine. It was the revelation of His God. One jot or tittle of the law was not to pass till everything had been fulfilled. And yet though He reverenced it with a far deeper reverence than any scribe who sat in Moses' seat, He judged it with unfaltering decision. He utters His judgments on these old enactments with the perfect freedom of a full authority. *This* He accepts as something always valid; *that* He rejects as something only temporary. He moves among these glories of the past not as a subject who has no right to question, but as a king who has the power to abrogate, as certainly as He has the power to endorse. Moses said unto you so and so, but I say unto you so and so. He has the fullest authority to ratify, and He has the fullest authority to cancel. And all this from a Galilean villager who had never had any learning from the schools, and who had been cradled in His village home in intensest devotion to the past. Had Jesus been a reckless demagogue, we could more easily have understood that attitude.

There are demagogues who do not care one scrap for all that is highest and holiest in antiquity. But Jesus cared intensely for antiquity, for He saw in it the handiwork of God, and yet He judged it, and praised it, and condemned it, with a decision from which was no appeal.

The same striking feature of decisiveness is seen again in regard to His own person. Christ never seems to have doubted for an hour that He was supremely and ineffably great. I have through my life been a reader of biographies, which I take to be the most fruitful of all reading. Well, in all the great lives that I ever read, there is one thing evident and universal. It is that every life has had its faltering hours, when vision has failed and inspiration vanished, when a man's confidence in his power and genius has silently and unaccountably deserted him. You find it in every life of men of action. You find it in every life of men of thought. You find it conspicuously and remarkably in the biography of every saint. Yet Christ, who was a man of thought and action, as surely as He was the ideal of sainthood, was never visited by any hour like that. Other men rise into the thought of greatness; Christ was possessed with it from the beginning. Other men win it, and in dejection lose it; Christ never lost it in any hour of agony. Rejected by His own people and betrayed, Pilate said to Him, Art Thou a king? And Jesus replied, Thou sayest I am a king. There is something very wonderful in that, and I would give much that you should feel the wonder of it. That is a consciousness not merely notable; that is a consciousness which is unique. And when you have difficulties about the Virgin Birth, and about miracles, and the Resurrection, I beg you to turn your thoughts to facts like these if you wish to feel the mystery of Christ. No one doubted that He was meek and lowly. Everyone saw that He would not strive nor cry. There was a loving gentleness about this man of Nazareth which drew the burdened and the broken to Him. And yet this loving, gentle, lowly man said, I am the way—I am the truth—I am the life; and, Before Abraham was, I am.

That unfaltering sense of His preeminence is sometimes witnessed by our Lord's comparisons, and there are two such comparisons so vivid that it is worthwhile to recall them for a moment. To the Jews of our Lord's time there was one name in history that stood out glorious above all other names, and there was one building that meant more to them than any other building in the world.

The name so preeminent was that of Solomon, and the building so solitary was the temple. These two summed up, for every pious Jew, all that was highest and holiest in the past—

all that was most magnificent in empire, all wealth of argosies from distant shores, all near protection of a covenant God who had His place of rest between the cherubim. No king had ever been so great as Solomon; no building ever so holy as the temple. To it the heart of every exile turned, and for it even the exile would have died. And now comes Jesus and, to men and women burning with passionate convictions such as these, quietly says, I am greater than Solomon, and, a greater than the temple is here. Had He been a stranger with an alien upbringing that would have been easier to understand. But He was no stranger with an alien upbringing; He was the son of Mary, and the child of Nazareth. He had been fed upon the Jewish Scriptures; He had been kindled as a boy with Jewish memories, and yet with a quiet, unfaltering decision He placed Himself supreme above them all.

The same decisiveness is very marked again in our Lord's handling of the character of others. There is a ring of finality in all His judgments which is very arresting and impressive. Every age has its own problems which it must wrestle with and seek to answer. But there is one problem common to all ages, and that is the problem of a human life. And men are always trying to solve that problem, and are always baffled in their attempts to solve it, there is such intertwining of evil and of good in the most commonplace and ordinary mortal. If all that was noble in a human character stood out apart and separate from the base, how easy it would be to judge a brother, and to classify him, and assign him to his deserts. And it is just because in actual human life there is no such cleavage between light and darkness that men are so baffled in their attempts to judge. Sometimes all that is fairest in a character is perilously akin to what is foulest; sometimes all that is basest in a character is irradiated by gleams of very heaven, until at last in the common lives around us we meet so much that is awesome and inscrutable that we feel how impossible it is to judge. There are people who have a wonderful intuition into character. They seem to detect, as by a kind of instinct, the innermost nature of the folk they meet. Yet even they can never be quite sure that they have solved the secret of a character, for something always may emerge tomorrow that contradicts the impression of today. It is not the great only who are misunderstood; every one of us is misunderstood. We baffle each other, and perplex each other, and are insoluble enigmas to our dearest. We are a little better than the most loving think, and a little worse than the nastiest imagine; and if one thing is certain in this mortal life, it is that no one has ever seen us as we are.

Now it is just here, I say with the fullest confidence, that Jesus of Nazareth stands unique. There is not one trace that He was ever baffled by the haunting problem of human personality. Born in a remote and quiet village, He went abroad into the world of men. There, with an utter freedom from convention, He mingled in every circle of society. And if one thing is certain in that unfettered intercourse, which brought Him into touch with rich and poor, it is that His every judgment was decisive. One hour He was disputing with the Pharisees; the next He was in the company of Mary. Now it was a rich young ruler who was at His feet, and now it was a woman who had been a sinner. And always, without one trace of hesitancy, you have the Savior praising or condemning with an authority from which is no appeal. One man He commands to follow Him; another He bids go to his home again. One man He overwhelms with woe unutterable; over another He pronounces pardon. And all this He is doing every day, and in the course of His ordinary ministry, and with people whom He has never seen before, till suddenly they are forced into His presence. There is something very wonderful in that; there is something quite unparalleled in that. And if you have doubts about the Resurrection, let me say, I want you to give your thoughts to facts like these. Do not brood upon your resurrection difficulties; brood upon these great facts in Jesus' life, till it comes home to you, as it has come to many of us, that this is none other than the Son of God.

Then lastly, this decisiveness of Christ comes to its climax as regards the future. You find no shadow of doubt upon His heart as He looks forward to the coming ages. There are men who have started out with glowing hopes, and then their hopes have gradually died. For sorrow has come, and very bitter enmity, and they have lost the vision of the morning. But on that night on which He was betrayed, when everything was dark and spoke of treachery, Christ was certain that He would be remembered. He had no hesitancy about the past, handling its content with a swift decisiveness. He had no hesitancy with any human soul that rose up out of the crowd and stood before Him. And equally certain with these facts is this, that He knew no hesitancy about the future, nor about the absolute power that He would wield when the small and great were gathered before God. You remember what Danton[1] at the French Revolution cried out with all the passion of his heart. He cried out—and he meant it from the depths—"Let my name be blighted, but let France be free." And that is a cry that has echoed down the ages from the lips of every patriot and prophet, with the one exception of the Lord Jesus Christ. Others have been content to die, if only the cause for which they fought should triumph. Others have been content to be forgotten, if only their message should inspire mankind. But Christ was never content to be forgotten, and never dreamed that He would be forgotten, but in the very center of all coming ages knew that He would bless and would condemn. While we must be on our guard against interpreting literally the poetic and pictorial language of the Master, there can be no question that Christ anticipated a day of judgment when the secret of every life would be revealed. And the amazing thing is that in that day of judgment it is His presence that is to search the character, and His estimate that is to turn the scale of heavenly blessedness or awful loss. Whenever Christ speaks about a day of judgment, it is He Himself who is the central figure. It is He who separates the sheep and goats. It is He who says, Depart, I never knew you. And that magnificence of royal authority, which is interwoven with the whole gospel story, is the climax of the decisiveness of Christ. Did you ever think how different it was from the outlook of the old Jewish prophets? They had their vision of a coming day, but in that day you never light on them. Then Christ took up that old prophetic vision, and glorified it, and touched it with eternity, and in the center of it all He puts one figure, and that one central figure is Himself. My brother and sister, either that is blasphemy, or it is something different from humanity. Either it is wild, defiant atheism, or else in the sweep of it it is divine. And as reasonable beings you have to ask yourselves, knowing the tenor of the life of Jesus, which of the two conclusions is more likely. For myself it is such facts that are determinative. They lead me in Christ to the very feet of God. Though it were proved to me that Jesus never rose, Jesus would still be more than man for me. Down in the depths of His moral and spiritual being I light on things I cannot understand, unless that solitary lowly figure was different from us children of mortality.

---

1. George Jacques Danton (1759–1794), French revolutionary executed by Robespierre.